Magic, Science and Religion
and Other Essays

Religious Traditions of the World

Titles available from Waveland Press

Magic, Science and Religion

AND OTHER ESSAYS BY

Bronislaw Malinowski

WITH AN INTRODUCTION BY ROBERT REDFIELD

WAVELAND

PRESS, INC.

Long Grove, Illinois

For information about this book, contact:
Waveland Press, Inc.
4180 IL Route 83, Suite 101
Long Grove, IL 60047-9580
(847) 634-0081
info@waveland.com
www.waveland.com

This collection was originally published in 1948.
Reissued 1992 by Waveland Press, Inc.

ISBN 0-88133-657-2

Printed in the United States of America

17   16   15   14   13   12   11

Bronislaw Malinowski, one of the founders of modern anthropology, was born in Cracow, Poland, in 1884. Trained at the London School of Economics, he is known for his functional theory of anthropology and his exemplary fieldwork pioneering the technique of participant observation. He was Professor of Anthropology at the University of London from 1927 until his death in 1942. His major works include *Crime and Customs in Savage Society* (1926), *Sex and Repression in Savage Society* (1927), *The Sexual Life of Savages* (1929), and *Coral Gardens and Their Magic* (1935). His ethnography *Argonauts of the Western Pacific* (1922), based on fieldwork in the Trobriand Islands during World War I, remains classic.

The essay "Baloma; the Spirits of the Dead" was first published in 1916; "Magic, Science and Religion" in 1925; and "Myth in Primitive Psychology" in 1926. This collection was originally published in 1948.

Acknowledgments

To The Society for Promoting Christian Knowledge for permission to use "Magic, Science and Religion."

To John Hawkins & Associates, Inc. for permission to use "Myth in Primitive Psychology," copyright © 1948 by Bronislaw Malinowski.

To The Journal of the Royal Anthropological Institute of Great Britain and Ireland, for permission to use "Baloma; the Spirits of the Dead in the Trobriand Islands," originally issued in Volume 35, of the Journal, 1916.

Table of Contents

Introduction

No writer of our times has done more than Bronislaw Malinowski to bring together in single comprehension the warm reality of human living and the cool abstractions of science. His pages have become an almost indispensable link between the knowing of exotic and remote people as we know our own neighbors and brothers, and conceptual and theoretical knowledge about mankind. The novelist of talent brings particular men and women to our direct acquaintance, but he does not convert this swift and intimate understanding into the formal generalizations of science. On the other hand, many scientific students of society state such general formulations, but without providing that direct acquaintance with real people—that sense of being there as the work is done or the spell performed—which makes the abstract generalization truly meaningful and convincing. Malinowski's gift was double: it consisted both in the genius given usually to artists and in the scientist's power to see and to declare the universal in the particular. Malinowski's reader is provided with a set of concepts as to religion, magic, science, rite and myth in the course of forming vivid impressions and understandings of the Trobrianders into whose life he is so charmingly drawn.

"I shall invite my readers,"—so writes Malinowski—"to step outside the closed study of the theorist into the open air of the Anthropological field . . ." The "Anthropological field" is almost always the Trobriand Islands. Following Malinowski, we are soon "paddling on the lagoon, watching the natives under the blazing sun at their garden work, following them through the patches of jungle; and . . . on the winding beaches and reefs, we shall learn about their life." The life we learn about is both Trobriand life and the life of common humanity. The criticism so often leveled at Malinowski that he generalized from a single case loses much of its force if the assumption may be admitted that there are a common human nature and a universal culture pattern. No writer ever better justified the assumption. We may learn much of all societies from a single society, of all men from a few men, if unusual insight is combined with patient and prolonged study of what other students have written about other societies.

Malinowski looks at the people, then looks back at the books, and then looks again at the people. He does not, as some have done, look at the people, if at all, to find there what the books have told him he should find. The eclecticism of Malinowski's theory is compelled by the fact that the human reality to which he always returns cannot be fully represented by any single theoretical emphasis. Consider how, in the illuminating essay "Magic, Science and Religion" he takes account of the various views of religion which Tylor, Frazer, Marett, and Durkheim have respectively given, and how religion emerges in those pages more multidimensional than in any single account of any one of these other anthropologists. Religion is not only people explaining and projecting their dreams; it is not only a sort of spiritual electric—mana—; it is not solely to be recognized in social communion—no, religion and magic are ways men must have, being men, to make the world acceptable, manageable, and right. And we see the truth of the many-sided view in the windings and twistings of rite and myth, work and worship, in this now well-known island world in New Guinea.

Perhaps it is because he is always so faithful to the reality of the one well-considered, intimately known instance that his method falls short of the requirements of the scientist's formal rule book. If comparisons are made between the Trobriand Islanders and other groups, they are mostly implicit. The materials from the Trobriand Islands, while immensely abundant and rich, are nowhere exposed to us to be fully appraised or to be counted. The notebooks are not opened to us to order and to choose. There is no proof, in any formal sense.

Clyde Kluckhohn[1] has characterized the method as that of "The well-documented anecdote set firmly in a ramified context." This is well said. In the following papers we shall see how often a formulation about society, an insight into human behavior, is established by the vivid recollection of some simple experience in these islands. The description of the natives fishing on the lagoon makes the whole essay on language; the episode about the Trobrianders walking single-file who are interested but not terrorized by hearing a ghost in a yam garden, and several other such stories, make the basis for the discussion of the spirits of the dead and their manifold significance. We are convinced, not by formal proof, but by following Malinowski in his demonstration of the meaning and function of belief and rite in a society, which, while alien to us, we are nevertheless made to feel is ourselves in another form.

Anthropological science, he is in effect telling us, is also an art. It is the art of seeing perceptively a human and social situation. It is the art of taking a warm interest in the particular while seeking in it the universal.

For equally he is telling us that the art of ethnographic insight, fully to perform its task, must become science. In the last pages of the paper on the *Spirits of the Dead* he

[1] Clyde Kluckhohn, "Bronislaw Malinowski, 1884–1942," Jour. Amer. Folklore, Vol. 56, Jul-Sep, 1943, No. 221, pp. 214.

dismisses as false "the cult of 'pure fact'." "There is a form of interpretation of facts without which no scientific observation can possibly be carried on—I mean the interpretation which sees in the endless diversity of facts general laws—which classifies and orders phenomena, and puts them into mutual relationship."

Malinowski's later and more elaborate attempts to order the facts into theoretical systems, notably the two books published after his death, have exposed him to criticism for weakness in the system. But in the papers collected in this volume the theory is simple: it consists chiefly of clarifying distinctions as to some of the principal recurrent and universal kinds of human social behavior, and of stimulating analysis of the ways in which each of these fills the needs of man and maintains the society.

With respect to at least one pair of closely related subjects—religion and myth—the papers that are here reprinted contain Malinowski's clearest and best considered formulations. No one of his full-length books deals centrally with the topic of religion. (The Riddell Lecture on "The Foundations of Faith and Morals" was published as a pamphlet in 1936). Three of the papers in the present volume deal with or touch on that topic. The first paper discusses the resemblances and differences of "Religion, Magic, and Science" with more lucid clarification than does any other of Malinowski's writings—or does any other writing, perhaps. His gifted pen brings home to understanding many matters that are often unclear. "Science," he writes, "is founded on the conviction that experience, effort and reason are valid—magic on the belief that hope cannot fail nor desire deceive." The sentences comparing and contrasting religion and magic are as good.

The little book on *Myth in Primitive Psychology*, long unavailable, will be welcomed in this collection by those who know it and have found in it the first and still the best work cutting through the thicket of difficulties placed in the way of understanding myth and legend and folk tale by many who wrote of these things from a textual knowledge of them only. Malinowski's essay makes myth and tale parts of the meaning and function of the life of the people who tell them.

The essay on *The Spirits of the Dead in the Trobriand Islands* represents Malinowski's writings for more technically interested readers. It is provided with more native texts and other source materials than are the other papers here included. The paper also illustrates the way in which a theme—here the spirits of the dead—takes Malinowski into many aspects of native life besides religion and magic. The reader interested in the problem of primitive understanding of paternity will want to compare what Malinowski writes here on that subject with the later and considerably amended statement which he made in his work *The Sexual Life of Savages*. And the little essay on anthropological field method that concludes the paper is of value to every anthropologist.

ROBERT REDFIELD

The University of Chicago

Magic, Science and Religion
and Other Essays

Magic, Science and Religion

There are no peoples however primitive without religion and magic. Nor are there, it must be added at once, any savage races lacking either in the scientific attitude or in science, though this lack has been frequently attributed to them. In every primitive community, studied by trustworthy and competent observers, there have been found two clearly distinguishable domains, the Sacred and the Profane; in other words, the domain of Magic and Religion and that of Science.

On the one hand there are the traditional acts and observances, regarded by the natives as sacred, carried out with reverence and awe, hedged around with prohibitions and special rules of behavior. Such acts and observances are always associated with beliefs in supernatural forces, especially those of magic, or with ideas about beings, spirits, ghosts, dead ancestors, or gods. On the other hand, a moment's reflection is sufficient to show that no art or craft however primitive could have been invented or maintained, no organized form of hunting, fishing, tilling, or search for food could be carried out without the careful observation of natural process and a firm belief in its regularity, without the power of reasoning and without confidence in the power of reason; that is, without the rudiments of science.

The credit of having laid the foundations of an anthropological study of religion belongs to Edward B. Tylor. In his well-known theory he maintains that the essence of primitive religion is animism, the belief in spiritual beings, and he shows how this belief has originated in a mistaken but consistent interpretation of dreams, visions, hallucinations, cataleptic states, and similar phenomena. Reflecting on these, the savage philosopher or theologian was led to distinguish the human soul from the body. Now the soul obviously continues to lead an existence after death, for it appears in dreams, haunts the survivors in memories and in visions and apparently influences human destinies. Thus originated the belief in ghosts and the spirits of the dead, in immortality and in a nether world. But man in general, and primitive man in particular, has a tendency to imagine the outer world in his own image. And since animals, plants, and objects move, act, behave, help man or hinder him, they must also be endowed with souls or spirits. Thus animism, the philosophy and the religion of primitive man, has been built up from observations and by inferences, mistaken but comprehensible in a crude and untutored mind.

Tylor's view of primitive religion, important as it was, was based on too narrow a range of facts, and it made early man too contemplative and rational. Recent field work, done by specialists, shows us the savage interested rather in his fishing and gardens, in tribal events and festivities than brooding over dreams and visions, or explaining "doubles" and cataleptic fits, and it reveals also a great many aspects of early religion which cannot be possibly placed in Tylor's scheme of animism.

The extended and deepened outlook of modern anthropology finds its most adequate expression in the learned and inspiring writings of Sir James Frazer. In these he has set forth the three main problems of primitive religion with which present-day anthropology is busy: magic and its relation to religion and science; totemism and the sociological aspect of early faith; the cults of fertility and vegetation. It will be best to discuss these subjects in turn.

Frazer's *Golden Bough,* the great codex of primitive magic, shows clearly that animism is not the only, nor even the dominating belief in primitive culture. Early man seeks above all to control the course of nature for practical ends, and he does it directly, by rite and spell, compelling wind and weather, animals and crops to obey his will. Only much later, finding the limitations of his magical might, does he in fear or hope, in supplication or defiance, appeal to higher beings; that is, to demons, ancestor-spirits or gods. It is in this distinction between direct control on the one hand and propitiation of superior powers on the other that Sir James Frazer sees the difference between religion and magic. Magic, based on man's confidence that he can dominate nature directly, if only he knows the laws which govern it magically, is in this akin to science. Religion, the confession of human impotence in certain matters, lifts man above the magical level, and later on maintains its independence side by side with science, to which magic has to succumb.

This theory of magic and religion has been the starting point of most modern studies of the twin subjects. Professor Preuss in Germany, Dr. Marett in England, and MM. Hubert and Mauss in France have independently set forth certain views, partly in criticism of Frazer, partly following up the lines of his inquiry. These writers point out that similar as they appear, science and magic differ yet radically. Science is born of experience, magic made by tradition. Science is guided by reason and corrected by observation, magic, impervious to both, lives in an atmosphere of mysticism. Science is open to all, a common good of the whole community, magic is occult, taught through mysterious initiations, handed on in a hereditary or at least in very exclusive filiation. While science is based on the conception of natural forces, magic springs from the idea of a certain mystic, impersonal power, which is believed in by most primitive peoples. This power, called *mana* by some Melanesians, *arungquiltha* by certain Australian tribes, *wakan, orenda, manitu* by various American Indians, and nameless elsewhere, is stated to be a well-nigh universal idea found wherever magic flourishes. According to the writers just mentioned we can find among the most primitive peoples and throughout the lower savagery a belief in a supernatural, impersonal force, moving all those agencies which are relevant to the savage and causing all the really important events in the domain of the sacred. Thus *mana*, not animism, is the essence of "pre-animistic religion," and it is also the essence of magic, which is thus radically different from science.

There remains the question, however, what is *mana*, this impersonal force of magic supposed to dominate all forms of early belief? Is it a fundamental idea, an innate category of the primitive mind, or can it be explained by still simpler and more fundamental elements of human psychology or of the reality in which primitive man lives? The most original and important contribution to these problems is given by the late Professor Durkheim, and it touches the other subject, opened up by Sir James Frazer: that of totemism and of the sociological aspect of religion.

Totemism, to quote Frazer's classical definition, "is an intimate relation which is supposed to exist between a group of kindred people on the one side and a species of natural or artificial objects on the other side, which objects are called the totems of the human group." Totemism thus has two sides: it is a mode of social grouping and a religious system of beliefs and practices. As religion, it expresses primitive man's interest in his surroundings, the desire to claim an affinity and to control the most important objects: above all, animal or vegetable species, more rarely useful inanimate objects, very seldom man-made things. As a rule species of animals and plants used for staple food or at any rate edible or useful or ornamental animals are held in a special form of "totemic reverence" and are tabooed to the members of the clan which is associated with the species and which sometimes performs rites and ceremonies for its multiplication. The social aspect of totemism consists in the subdivision of the tribe into minor units, called in anthropology *clans, gentes, sibs,* or *phratries.*

In totemism we see therefore not the result of early man's speculations about mysterious phenomena, but a blend of a utilitarian anxiety about the most necessary objects of his surroundings, with some preoccupation in those which strike his imagination and attract his attention, such as beautiful birds, reptiles and dangerous animals. With our knowledge of what could be called the totemic attitude of mind, primitive religion is seen to be nearer to reality and to the immediate practical life interests of the savage, than it appeared in its "animistic" aspect emphasized by Tylor and the earlier anthropologists.

By its apparently strange association with a problematic form of social division, I mean the clan system; totemism has taught anthropology yet another lesson: it has revealed the importance of the sociological aspect in all the early forms of cult. The savage depends upon the group with whom he is in direct contact both for practical co-operation and mental solidarity to a far larger extent than does civilized man. Since—as can be seen in totemism, magic, and many other practices—early cult and ritual are closely associated with practical concerns as well as with mental needs, there must exist an intimate connection between social organization and religious belief. This was understood already by that pioneer of religious anthropology, Robertson Smith, whose principle that primitive religion "was essentially an affair of the community rather than of individuals" has become a *Leitmotiv* of modern research. According to Professor Durkheim, who has put these views most forcibly, "the religious" is identical with "the social." For "in a general way . . . a society has all that is necessary to arouse the sensation of the Divine in minds, merely by the power that it has over them; for to its members it is what a God is to its worshippers."[1] Professor Durkheim

[1] *The Elementary Forms of the Religious Life,* p. 206.

arrives at this conclusion by the study of totemism, which he believes to be the most primitive form of religion. In this the "totemic principle" which is identical with *mana* and with "the God of the clan . . . can be nothing else than the clan itself." [2]

These strange and somewhat obscure conclusions will be criticized later, and it will be shown in what consists the grain of truth they undoubtedly contain and how fruitful it can be. It has borne fruit, in fact, in influencing some of the most important writing of mixed classical scholarship and anthropology, to mention only the works of Miss Jane Harrison and Mr. Cornford.

The third great subject introduced into the Science of Religion by Sir James Frazer is that of the cults of vegetation and fertility. In *The Golden Bough,* starting from the awful and mysterious ritual of the wood divinities at Nemi, we are led through an amazing variety of magical and religious cults, devised by man to stimulate and control the fertilizing work of skies and earth and of sun and rain, and we are left with the impression that early religion is teeming with the forces of savage life, with its young beauty and crudity, with its exuberance and strength so violent that it leads now and again to suicidal acts of self-immolation. The study of *The Golden Bough* shows us that for primitive man death has meaning mainly as a step to resurrection, decay as a stage of rebirth, the plenty of autumn and the decline of winter as preludes to the revival of spring. Inspired by these passages of *The Golden Bough* a number of writers have developed, often with greater precision and with a fuller analysis than by Frazer himself, what could be called the *vitalistic* view of religion. Thus Mr. Crawley in his *Tree of Life,* M. van Gennep in his *Rites de Passage,* and Miss Jane Harrison in several works, have given evidence that faith and cult spring from the crises of human existence, "the great events of life, birth, adolescence, marriage, death . . . it is about these events

[2] *Ibid.*

that religion largely focuses."[3] The tension of instinctive need, strong emotional experiences, lead in some way or other to cult and belief. "Art and Religion alike spring from unsatisfied desire."[4] How much truth there is in this somewhat vague statement and how much exaggeration we shall be able to assess later on.

There are two important contributions to the theory of primitive religion which I mention here only, for they have somehow remained outside the main current of anthropological interest. They treat of the primitive idea of one God and of the place of morals in primitive religion respectively. It is remarkable that they have been and still are neglected, for are not these two questions first and foremost in the mind of anyone who studies religion, however crude and rudimentary it may be? Perhaps the explanation is in the preconceived idea that "origins" must be very crude and simple and different from the "developed forms," or else in the notion that the "savage" or "primitive" is really savage and primitive!

The late Andrew Lang indicated the existence among some Australian natives of the belief in a tribal All-Father, and the Rev. Pater Wilhelm Schmidt has adduced much evidence proving that this belief is universal among all the peoples of the simplest cultures and that it cannot be discarded as an irrelevant fragment of mythology, still less as an echo of missionary teaching. It looks, according to Pater Schmidt, very much like an indication of a simple and pure form of early monotheism.

The problem of morals as an early religious function was also left on one side, until it received an exhaustive treatment, not only in the writings of Pater Schmidt but also and notably in two works of outstanding importance: the *Origin and Development of Moral Ideas* of Professor E. Westermarck, and *Morals in Evolution* of Professor L. T. Hobhouse.

[3] J. Harrison, *Themis*, p. 42.

[4] J. Harrison, op. cit. p. 44.

It is not easy to summarize concisely the trend of anthropological studies in our subject. On the whole it has been towards an increasingly elastic and comprehensive view of religion. Tylor had still to refute the fallacy that there are primitive peoples without religion. Today we are somewhat perplexed by the discovery that to a savage all is religion, that he perpetually lives in a world of mysticism and ritualism. If religion is co-extensive with "life" and with "death" into the bargain, if it arises from all "collective" acts and from all "crises in the individual's existence," if it comprises all savage "theory" and covers all his "practical concerns"—we are led to ask, not without dismay: What remains outside it, what is the world of the "profane" in primitive life? Here is a first problem into which modern anthropology, by the number of contradictory views, has thrown some confusion, as can be seen even from the above short sketch. We shall be able to contribute towards its solution in the next section.

Primitive religion, as fashioned by modern anthropology, has been made to harbor all sorts of heterogeneous things. At first reserved in animism for the solemn figures of ancestral spirits, ghosts and souls, besides a few fetishes, it had gradually to admit the thin, fluid, ubiquitous *mana*; then, like Noah's Ark, it was with the introduction of totemism loaded with beasts, not in pairs but in shoals and species, joined by plants, objects, and even manufactured articles; then came human activities and concerns and the gigantic ghost of the Collective Soul, Society Divinized. Can there be any order or system put into this medley of apparently unrelated objects and principles? This question will occupy us in the third section.

One achievement of modern anthropology we shall not question: the recognition that magic and religion are not merely a doctrine or a philosophy, not merely an intellectual body of opinion, but a special mode of behavior, a pragmatic attitude built up of reason, feeling, and will alike. It is a mode of action as well as a system of belief, and a sociological phenomenon as well as a personal experience. But with all this, the exact relation between the social and the individual contributions to religion is not clear, as we have seen from the exaggerations committed on either side. Nor is it clear what are the respective shares of emotion and reason. All these questions will have to be dealt with by future anthropology, and it will be possible only to suggest solutions and indicate lines of argument in this short essay.

II. RATIONAL MASTERY BY MAN OF HIS SURROUNDINGS

The problem of primitive knowledge has been singularly neglected by anthropology. Studies on savage psychology were exclusively confined to early religion, magic and mythology. Only recently the work of several English, German, and French writers, notably the daring and brilliant speculations of Professor Lévy-Bruhl, gave an impetus to the student's interest in what the savage does in his more sober moods. The results were startling indeed: Professor Lévy-Bruhl tells us, to put it in a nutshell, that primitive man has no sober moods at all, that he is hopelessly and completely immersed in a mystical frame of mind. Incapable of dispassionate and consistent observation, devoid of the power of abstraction, hampered by "a decided aversion towards reasoning," he is unable to draw any benefit from experience, to construct or comprehend even the most elementary laws of nature. "For minds thus orientated there is no fact purely physical." Nor can there exist for them any clear idea of substance and attribute, cause and effect, identity and contradiction. Their outlook is that of confused superstition, "prelogical," made of mystic "participations" and "exclusions." I have here summarized a body of opinion, of which the brilliant French sociologist is the most decided and competent spokesman, but which numbers besides, many anthropologists and philosophers of renown.

But there are also dissenting voices. When a scholar and

anthropologist of the measure of Professor J. L. Myres entitles an article in *Notes and Queries* "Natural Science," and when we read there that the savage's "knowledge based on observation is distinct and accurate," we must surely pause before accepting primitive man's irrationality as a dogma. Another highly competent writer, Dr. A. A. Goldenweiser, speaking about primitive "discoveries, inventions and improvements"—which could hardly be attributed to any pre-empirical or prelogical mind—affirms that "it would be unwise to ascribe to the primitive mechanic merely a passive part in the origination of inventions. Many a happy thought must have crossed his mind, nor was he wholly unfamiliar with the thrill that comes from an idea effective in action." Here we see the savage endowed with an attitude of mind wholly akin to that of a modern man of science!

To bridge over the wide gap between the two extreme opinions current on the subject of primitive man's reason, it will be best to resolve the problem into two questions.

First, has the savage any rational outlook, any rational mastery of his surroundings, or is he, as M. Lévy-Bruhl and his school maintain, entirely "mystical"? The answer will be that every primitive community is in possession of a considerable store of knowledge, based on experience and fashioned by reason.

The second question then opens: Can this primitive knowledge be regarded as a rudimentary form of science or is it, on the contrary, radically different, a crude empiry, a body of practical and technical abilities, rules of thumb and rules of art having no theoretical value? This second question, epistemological rather than belonging to the study of man, will be barely touched upon at the end of this section and a tentative answer only will be given.

In dealing with the first question, we shall have to examine the "profane" side of life, the arts, crafts and economic pursuits, and we shall attempt to disentangle in it a type of behavior, clearly marked off from magic and religion, based on empirical knowledge and on the confidence in logic. We shall try to find whether the lines of such behavior are defined by traditional rules, known, perhaps even discussed sometimes, and tested. We shall have to inquire whether the sociological setting of the rational and empirical behavior differs from that of ritual and cult. Above all we shall ask, do the natives distinguish the two domains and keep them apart, or is the field of knowledge constantly swamped by superstition, ritualism, magic or religion?

Since in the matter under discussion there is an appalling lack of relevant and reliable observations, I shall have largely to draw upon my own material, mostly unpublished, collected during a few years' field work among the Melanesian and Papuo-Melanesian tribes of Eastern New Guinea and the surrounding archipelagoes. As the Melanesians are reputed, however, to be specially magic-ridden, they will furnish an acid test of the existence of empirical and rational knowledge among savages living in the age of polished stone.

These natives, and I am speaking mainly of the Melanesians who inhabit the coral atolls to the N.E. of the main island, the Trobriand Archipelago and the adjoining groups, are expert fishermen, industrious manufacturers and traders, but they rely mainly on gardening for their subsistence. With the most rudimentary implements, a pointed digging-stick and a small axe, they are able to raise crops sufficient to maintain a dense population and even yielding a surplus, which in olden days was allowed to rot unconsumed, and which at present is exported to feed plantation hands. The success in their agriculture depends—besides the excellent natural conditions with which they are favored— upon their extensive knowledge of the classes of the soil, of the various cultivated plants, of the mutual adaptation of these two factors, and, last not least, upon their knowledge of the importance of accurate and hard work. They have to select the soil and the seedlings, they have appropriately to fix the times for clearing and burning the scrub, for planting and weeding, for training the vines of the yam plants. In all this they are guided by a clear knowledge of weather and seasons, plants and pests, soil and tubers, and by a conviction that this knowledge is true and reliable, that it can be counted upon and must be scrupulously obeyed.

Yet mixed with all their activities there is to be found magic, a series of rites performed every year over the gardens in rigorous sequence and order. Since the leadership in garden work is in the hands of the magician, and since ritual and practical work are intimately associated, a superficial observer might be led to assume that the mystic and the rational behavior are mixed up, that their effects are not distinguished by the natives and not distinguishable in scientific analysis. Is this so really?

Magic is undoubtedly regarded by the natives as absolutely indispensable to the welfare of the gardens. What would happen without it no one can exactly tell, for no native garden has ever been made without its ritual, in spite of some thirty years of European rule and missionary influence and well over a century's contact with white traders. But certainly various kinds of disaster, blight, unseasonable droughts rains, bush-pigs and locusts, would destroy the unhallowed garden made without magic.

Does this mean, however, that the natives attribute all the good results to magic? Certainly not. If you were to suggest to a native that he should make his garden mainly by magic and scamp his work, he would simply smile on your simplicity. He knows as well as you do that there are natural conditions and causes, and by his observations he knows also that he is able to control these natural forces by mental and physical effort. His knowledge is limited, no doubt, but as far as it goes it is sound and proof against mysticism. If the fences are broken down, if the seed is destroyed or has been dried or washed away, he will have recourse not to magic, but to work, guided by knowledge and reason. His experience has taught him also, on the other hand, that in spite of all his forethought and beyond all his efforts there are agencies and forces which one year bestow unwonted and unearned benefits of fertility, making everything run smooth and well, rain and sun appear at the right moment, noxious insects remain in abeyance, the harvest yields a superabundant crop; and another year again the same agencies bring ill luck and bad chance, pursue him from beginning till end and thwart all his most strenuous efforts and his best-founded knowledge. To control these influences and these only he employs magic.

Thus there is a clear-cut division: there is first the well-known set of conditions, the natural course of growth, as well as the ordinary pests and dangers to be warded off by fencing and weeding. On the other hand there is the domain of the unaccountable and adverse influences, as well as the great unearned increment of fortunate coincidence. The first conditions are coped with by knowledge and work, the second by magic.

This line of division can also be traced in the social setting of work and ritual respectively. Though the garden magician is, as a rule, also the leader in practical activities, these two functions are kept strictly apart. Every magical ceremony has its distinctive name, its appropriate time and its place in the scheme of work, and it stands out of the ordinary course of activities completely. Some of them are ceremonial and have to be attended by the whole community, all are public in that it is known when they are going to happen and anyone can attend them. They are performed on selected plots within the gardens and on a special corner of this plot. Work is always tabooed on such occasions, sometimes only while the ceremony lasts, sometimes for a day or two. In his lay character the leader and magician directs the work, fixes the dates for starting, harangues and exhorts slack or careless gardeners. But the two roles never overlap or interfere: they are always clear, and any native will inform you without hesitation whether the man acts as magician or as leader in garden work.

What has been said about gardens can be paralleled from any one of the many other activities in which work and magic run side by side without ever mixing. Thus in canoe building empirical knowledge of material, of technology, and of certain principles of stability and hydrodynamics, function in company and close association with magic, each yet uncontaminated by the other.

For example, they understand perfectly well that the wider the span of the outrigger the greater the stability yet the smaller the resistance against strain. They can clearly explain why they have to give this span a certain traditional width, measured in fractions of the length of the dugout. They can also explain, in rudimentary but clearly mechanical terms, how they have to behave in a sudden gale, why the outrigger must be always on the weather side, why the one type of canoe can and the other cannot beat. They have, in fact, a whole system of principles of sailing, embodied in a complex and rich terminology, traditionally handed on and obeyed as rationally and consistently as is modern science by modern sailors. How could they sail otherwise under eminently dangerous conditions in their frail primitive craft?

But even with all their systematic knowledge, methodically applied, they are still at the mercy of powerful and incalculable tides, sudden gales during the monsoon season and unknown reefs. And here comes in their magic, performed over the canoe during its construction, carried out at the beginning and in the course of expeditions and resorted to in moments of real danger. If the modern seaman, entrenched in science and reason, provided with all sorts of safety appliances, sailing on steel-built steamers, if even he has a singular tendency to superstition—which does not rob him of his knowledge or reason, nor make him altogether prelogical—can we wonder that his savage colleague, under much more precarious conditions, holds fast to the safety and comfort of magic?

An interesting and crucial test is provided by fishing in the Trobriand Islands and its magic. While in the villages on the inner lagoon fishing is done in an easy and absolutely reliable manner by the method of poisoning, yielding abundant results without danger and uncertainty, there are on the shores of the open sea dangerous modes of fishing and also certain types in which the yield greatly varies according to whether shoals of fish appear beforehand or not. It is most significant that in the lagoon fishing, where man can rely completely upon his knowledge and skill, magic does not exist, while in the open-sea fishing, full of danger and uncertainty, there is extensive magical ritual to secure safety and good results.

Again, in warfare the natives know that strength, courage, and agility play a decisive part. Yet here also they practice magic to master the elements of chance and luck.

Nowhere is the duality of natural and supernatural causes divided by a line so thin and intricate, yet, if carefully followed up, so well marked, decisive, and instructive, as in the two most fateful forces of human destiny: health and death. Health to the Melanesians is a natural state of affairs and, unless tampered with, the human body will remain in perfect order. But the natives know perfectly well that there are natural means which can affect health and even destroy the body. Poisons, wounds, burns, falls, are known to cause disablement or death in a natural way. And this is not a matter of private opinion of this or that individual, but it is laid down in traditional lore and even in belief, for there are considered to be different ways to the nether world for those who died by sorcery and those who met "natural" death. Again, it is recognized that cold, heat, overstrain, too much sun, overeating, can all cause minor ailments, which are treated by natural remedies such as massage, steaming, warming at a fire and certain potions. Old age is known to lead to bodily decay and the explanation is given by the natives that very old people grow weak, their oesophagus closes up, and therefore they must die.

But besides these natural causes there is the enormous domain of sorcery and by far the most cases of illness and death are ascribed to this. The line of distinction between sorcery and the other causes is clear in theory and in most cases of practice, but it must be realized that it is subject to what could be called the personal perspective. That is,

the more closely a case has to do with the person who considers it, the less will it be "natural," the more "magical."
Thus a very old man, whose pending death will be considered natural by the other members of the community,
will be afraid only of sorcery and never think of his natural
fate. A fairly sick person will diagnose sorcery in his own
case, while all the others might speak of too much betel
nut or overeating or some other indulgence.

But who of us really believes that his own bodily infirmi-
ties and the approaching death is a purely natural occurrence, just an insignificant event in the infinite chain of
causes? To the most rational of civilized men health, disease,
the threat of death, float in a hazy emotional mist, which
seems to become denser and more impenetrable as the fateful forms approach. It is indeed astonishing that "savages"
can achieve such a sober, dispassionate outlook in these
matters as they actually do.

Thus in his relation to nature and destiny, whether he
tries to exploit the first or to dodge the second, primitive
man recognizes both the natural and the supernatural
forces and agencies, and he tries to use them both for his
benefit. Whenever he has been taught by experience that
effort guided by knowledge is of some avail, he never
spares the one or ignores the other. He knows that a plant
cannot grow by magic alone, or a canoe sail or float without being properly constructed and managed, or a fight be
won without skill and daring. He never relies on magic alone,
while, on the contrary, he sometimes dispenses with it completely, as in fire-making and in a number of crafts and
pursuits. But he clings to it, whenever he has to recognize
the impotence of his knowledge and of his rational technique.

I have given my reasons why in this argument I had to rely
principally on the material collected in the classical land of
magic, Melanesia. But the facts discussed are so fundamental, the conclusions drawn of such a general nature, that
it will be easy to check them on any modern detailed ethnographic record. Comparing agricultural work and magic,

the building of canoes, the art of healing by magic and by natural remedies, the ideas about the causes of death in other regions, the universal validity of what has been established here could easily be proved. Only, since no observations have methodically been made with reference to the problem of primitive knowledge, the data from other writers could be gleaned only piecemeal and their testimony though clear would be indirect.

I have chosen to face the question of primitive man's rational knowledge directly: watching him at his principal occupations, seeing him pass from work to magic and back again, entering into his mind, listening to his opinions. The whole problem might have been approached through the avenue of language, but this would have led us too far into questions of logic, semasiology, and theory of primitive languages. Words which serve to express general ideas such as *existence, substance,* and *attribute, cause* and *effect,* the *fundamental* and the *secondary;* words and expressions used in complicated pursuits like sailing, construction, measuring and checking; numerals and quantitative descriptions, correct and detailed classifications of natural phenomena, plants and animals—all this would lead us exactly to the same conclusion: that primitive man can observe and think, and that he possesses, embodied in his language, systems of methodical though rudimentary knowledge.

Similar conclusions could be drawn from an examination of those mental schemes and physical contrivances which could be described as diagrams or formulas. Methods of indicating the main points of the compass, arrangements of stars into constellations, co-ordination of these with the seasons, naming of moons in the year, of quarters in the moon—all these accomplishments are known to the simplest savages. Also they are all able to draw diagrammatic maps in the sand or dust, indicate arrangements by placing small stones, shells, or sticks on the ground, plan expeditions or raids on such rudimentary charts. By co-ordinating space and time they are able to arrange big tribal gatherings and to combine vast tribal movements over extensive areas.[1] The use of leaves, notched sticks, and similar aids to memory is well known and seems to be almost universal. All such "diagrams" are means of reducing a complex and unwieldy bit of reality to a simple and handy form. They give man a relatively easy mental control over it. As such are they not—in a very rudimentary form no doubt—fundamentally akin to developed scientific formulas and "models," which are also simple and handy paraphrases of a complex or abstract reality, giving the civilized physicist mental control over it?

This brings us to the second question: Can we regard primitive knowledge, which, as we found, is both empirical and rational, as a rudimentary stage of science, or is it not at all related to it? If by science be understood a body of rules and conceptions, based on experience and derived from it by logical inference, embodied in material achievements and in a fixed form of tradition and carried on by some sort of social organization—then there is no doubt that even the lowest savage communities have the beginnings of science, however rudimentary.

Most epistemologists would not, however, be satisfied with such a "minimum definition" of science, for it might apply to the rules of an art or craft as well. They would maintain that the rules of science must be laid down explicitly, open to control by experiment and critique by reason. They must not only be rules of practical behavior, but theoretical laws of knowledge. Even accepting this stricture, however, there is hardly any doubt that many of the principles of savage knowledge are scientific in this sense. The native shipwright knows not only practically of buoyancy, leverage, equilibrium, he has to obey these laws not only on water, but while making the canoe he must have the principles in his mind. He instructs his helpers in them. He gives them the traditional rules, and in a crude and simple manner, using his hands, pieces of wood, and a limited technical vocabulary, he explains some general laws

[1] Cf. the writer's *Argonauts of the Western Pacific*, chap. xvi.

of hydrodynamics and equilibrium. Science is not detached from the craft, that is certainly true, it is only a means to an end, it is crude, rudimentary, and inchoate, but with all that it is the matrix from which the higher developments must have sprung.

If we applied another criterion yet, that of the really scientific attitude, the disinterested search for knowledge and for the understanding of causes and reasons, the answer would certainly not be in a direct negative. There is, of course, no widespread thirst for knowledge in a savage community, new things such as European topics bore them frankly and their whole interest is largely encompassed by the traditional world of their culture. But within this there is both the antiquarian mind passionately interested in myths, stories, details of customs, pedigrees, and ancient happenings, and there is also to be found the naturalist, patient and painstaking in his observations, capable of generalization and of connecting long chains of events in the life of animals, and in the marine world or in the jungle. It is enough to realize how much European naturalists have often learned from their savage colleagues to appreciate this interest found in the native for nature. There is finally among the primitives, as every fieldworker well knows, the sociologist, the ideal informant, capable with marvelous accuracy and insight to give the *raison d'être*, the function, and the organization of many a simpler institution in his tribe.

Science, of course, does not exist in any uncivilized community as a driving power, criticizing, renewing, constructing. Science is never consciously made. But on this criterion, neither is there law, nor religion, nor government among savages.

The question, however, whether we should call it *science* or only *empirical and rational knowledge* is not of primary importance in this context. We have tried to gain a clear idea as to whether the savage has only one domain of reality or two, and we found that he has his profane world of practical activities and rational outlook besides the sacred region of cult and belief. We have been able to map out the two domains and to give a more detailed description of the one. We must now pass to the second.

III. LIFE, DEATH, AND DESTINY IN EARLY FAITH AND CULT

We pass now to the domain of the *sacred*, to religious and magical creeds and rites. Our historical survey of theories has left us somewhat bewildered with the chaos of opinions and with the jumble of phenomena. While it was difficult not to admit into the enclosure of religion one after the other, spirits and ghosts, totems and social events, death and life, yet in the process religion seemed to become a thing more and more confused, both an all and a nothing. It certainly cannot be defined by its subject matter in a narrow sense, as "spirit worship," or as "ancestor cult," or as the "cult of nature." It includes animism, animatism, totemism, and fetishism, but it is not any one of them exclusively. The *ism* definition of religion in its origins must be given up, for religion does not cling to any one object or class of objects, though incidentally it can touch and hallow all. Nor, as we have seen, is religion identical with Society or the Social, nor can we remain satisfied by a vague hint that it clings to life only, for death opens perhaps the vastest view on to the other world. As an "appeal to higher powers," religion can only be distinguished from magic and not defined in general, but even this view will have to be slightly modified and supplemented.

The problem before us is, then, to try to put some order into the facts. This will allow us to determine somewhat more precisely the character of the domain of the *Sacred* and mark it off from that of the *Profane*. It will also give us an opportunity to state the relation between magic and religion.

1. THE CREATIVE ACTS OF RELIGION It will be best to face the facts first and, in order not to narrow down the scope of the survey, to take as our watchword the vaguest and most general of indices: "Life." As a matter of fact, even a slight acquaintance with ethnological literature is enough to convince anyone that in reality the physiological phases of human life, and, above all, its crises, such as conception, pregnancy, birth, puberty, marriage, and death, form the nuclei of numerous rites and beliefs. Thus beliefs about conception, such as that in reincarnation, spirit-entry, magical impregnation, exist in one form or another in almost every tribe, and they are often associated with rites and observances. During pregnancy the expectant mother has to keep certain taboos and undergo ceremonies, and her husband shares at times in both. At birth, before and after, there are various magical rites to prevent dangers and undo sorcery, ceremonies of purification, communal rejoicings and acts of presentation of the newborn to higher powers or to the community. Later on in life the boys and, much less frequently, the girls have to undergo the often protracted rites of initiation, as a rule shrouded in mystery and marred by cruel and obscene ordeals.

Without going any further, we can see that even the very beginnings of human life are surrounded by an inextricably mixed-up medley of beliefs and rites. They seem to be strongly attracted by any important event in life, to crystallize around it, surround it with a rigid crust of formalism and ritualism—but to what purpose? Since we cannot define cult and creed by their objects, perhaps it will be possible to perceive their function.

A closer scrutiny of the facts allows us to make from the outset a preliminary classification into two main groups. Compare a rite carried out to prevent death in childbed with another typical custom, a ceremony in celebration of a birth. The first rite is carried out as a means to an end, it has a definite practical purpose which is known to all who

practice it and can be easily elicited from any native informant. The post-natal ceremony, say a presentation of a newborn or a feast of rejoicing in the event, has no purpose:
it is not a means to an end but an end in itself. It expresses
the feelings of the mother, the father, the relatives, the
whole community, but there is no future event which this
ceremony foreshadows, which it is meant to bring about or
to prevent. This difference will serve us as a *prima facie*
distinction between magic and religion. While in the magical act the underlying idea and aim is always clear, straight-
forward, and definite, in the religious ceremony there is no
purpose directed toward a subsequent event. It is only possible for the sociologist to establish the function, the sociological *raison d'être* of the act. The native can always state
the end of the magical rite, but he will say of a religious
ceremony that it is done because such is the usage, or because it has been ordained, or he will narrate an explanatory
myth.

In order to grasp better the nature of primitive religious
ceremonies and their function, let us analyze the ceremonies
of initiation. They present right through the vast range of
their occurrence certain striking similarities. Thus the nov-
ices have to undergo a more or less protracted period of
seclusion and preparation. Then comes initiation proper,
in which the youth, passing through a series of ordeals, is
finally submitted to an act of bodily mutilation: at the
mildest, a slight incision or the knocking out of a tooth;
or, more severe, circumcision; or, really cruel and dangerous, an operation such as the subincision practiced in some
Australian tribes. The ordeal is usually associated with the
idea of the death and rebirth of the initiated one, which is
sometimes enacted in a mimetic performance. But besides
the ordeal, less conspicuous and dramatic, but in reality
more important, is the second main aspect of initiation:
the systematic instruction of the youth in sacred myth and
tradition, the gradual unveiling of tribal mysteries and the
exhibition of sacred objects.

The ordeal and the unveiling of tribal mysteries are usually believed to have been instituted by one or more legendary ancestors or culture heroes, or by a Superior Being of superhuman character. Sometimes he is said to swallow the youths, or to kill them, and then to restore them again as fully initiated men. His voice is imitated by the hum of the bull-roarer to inspire awe in the uninitiated women and children. Through these ideas initiation brings the novice into relationship with higher powers and personalities, such as the Guardian Spirits and Tutelary Divinities of the North American Indians, the Tribal All-Father of some Australian Aborigines, the Mythological Heroes of Melanesia and other parts of the world. This is the third fundamental element, besides ordeal and the teaching of tradition, in the rites of passing into manhood.

Now what is the sociological function of these customs, what part do they play in the maintenance and development of civilization? As we have seen, the youth is taught in them the sacred traditions under most impressive con ditions of preparation and ordeal and under the sanction of Supernatural Beings—the light of tribal revelation bursts upon him from out of the shadows of fear, privation, and bodily pain.

Let us realize that in primitive conditions tradition is of supreme value for the community and nothing matters as much as the conformity and conservatism of its members. Order and civilization can be maintained only by strict adhesion to the lore and knowledge received from previous generations. Any laxity in this weakens the cohesion of the group and imperils its cultural outfit to the point of threatening its very existence. Man has not yet devised the extremely complex apparatus of modern science which enables him nowadays to fix the results of experience into imperishable molds, to test it ever anew, gradually to shape it into more adequate forms and enrich it constantly by new additions. The primitive man's share of knowledge, his social fabric, his customs and beliefs, are the invaluable yield of devious experience of his forefathers, bought at an extravagant price and to be maintained at any cost. Thus, of all his qualities, truth to tradition is the most important, and a society which makes its tradition sacred has gained by it an inestimable advantage of power and permanence. Such beliefs and practices, therefore, which put a halo of sanctity round tradition and a supernatural stamp upon it, will have a "survival value" for the type of civilization in which they have been evolved.

We may, therefore, lay down the main function of initiation ceremonies: they are a ritual and dramatic expression of the supreme power and value of tradition in primitive societies; they also serve to impress this power and value upon the minds of each generation, and they are at the same time an extremely efficient means of transmitting tribal lore, of insuring continuity in tradition and of maintaining tribal cohesion.

We still have to ask: What is the relation between the purely physiological fact of bodily maturity which these ceremonies mark, and their social and religious aspect? We see at once that religion does something more, infinitely more, than the mere "sacralizing of a crisis of life." From a natural event it makes a social transition, to the fact of bodily maturity it adds the vast conception of entry into manhood with its duties, privileges, responsibilities, above all with its knowledge of tradition and the communion with sacred things and beings. There is thus a creative element in the rites of religious nature. The act establishes not only a social event in the life of the individual but also a spiritual metamorphosis, both associated with the biological event but transcending it in importance and significance.

Initiation is a typically religious act, and we can see clearly here how the ceremony and its purpose are one, how the end is realized in the very consummation of the act. At the same time we can see the function of such acts in society in that they create mental habits and social usages of inestimable value to the group and its civilization.

Another type of religious ceremony, the rite of marriage, is also an end in itself that it creates a supernaturally sanctioned bond, superadded to the primarily biological fact: the union of man and woman for lifelong partnership in affection, economic community, the procreation and rearing of children. This union, monogamous marriage, has always existed in human societies—so modern anthropology teaches in the face of the older fantastic hypotheses of "promiscuity" and "group marriage." By giving monogamous marriage an imprint of value and sanctity, religion offers another gift to human culture. And that brings us to the consideration of the two great human needs of propagation and nutrition.

2. PROVIDENCE IN PRIMITIVE LIFE Propagation and nutrition stand first and foremost among the vital concerns of man. Their relation to religious belief and practice has been often recognized and even overemphasized. Especially sex has been, from some older writers up to the psychoanalytic school, frequently regarded as the main source of religion. In fact, however, it plays an astonishingly insignificant part in religion, considering its force and insidiousness in human life in general. Besides love magic and the use of sex in certain magical performances—phenomena not belonging to the domain of religion—there remain to be mentioned here only acts of licence at harvest festivities or other public gatherings, the facts of temple prostitution and, at the level of barbarism and lower civilization, the worship of phallic divinities. Contrary to what one would expect, in savagery sexual cults play an insignificant role. It must also be remembered that acts of ceremonial licence are not mere indulgence, but that they express a reverent attitude towards the forces of generation and fertility in man and nature, forces on which the very existence of society and culture depends. Religion, the permanent source of moral control, which changes its incidence but remains eternally vigilant, has to turn its attention to these forces, at first drawing them merely into its sphere, later on submitting them to

repression, finally establishing the ideal of chastity and the sanctification of askesis.

When we pass to nutrition, the first thing to be noted is that eating is for primitive man an act surrounded by etiquette, special prescriptions and prohibitions, and a general emotional tension to a degree unknown to us. Besides the magic of food, designed to make it go a long way, or to prevent its scarcity in general—and we do not speak here at all of the innumerable forms of magic associated with the procuring of food—food has also a conspicuous role in ceremonies of a distinctly religious character. First-fruit offerings of a ritual nature, harvest ceremonies, big seasonal feasts in which crops are accumulated, displayed, and, in one way or another, sacralized, play an important part among agricultural people. Hunters, again, or fishers celebrate a big catch or the opening of the season of their pursuit by feasts and ceremonies at which food is ritually handled, the animals propitiated or worshipped. All such acts express the joy of the community, their sense of the great value of food, and religion through them consecrates the reverent attitude of man towards his daily bread.

To primitive man, never, even under the best conditions, quite free from the threat of starvation, abundance of food is a primary condition of normal life. It means the possibility of looking beyond the daily worries, of paying more attention to the remoter, spiritual aspects of civilization. If we thus consider that food is the main link between man and his surroundings, that by receiving it he feels the forces of destiny and providence, we can see the cultural, nay, biological importance of primitive religion in the sacralization of food. We can see in it the germs of what in higher types of religion will develop into the feeling of dependence upon Providence, of gratitude, and of confidence in it.

Sacrifice and communion, the two main forms in which food is ritually ministered, can now be held in a new light against the background of man's early attitude of religious reverence towards the providential abundance of food. That the idea of giving, the importance of the exchange of gifts in all phases of social contact, plays a great role in sacrifice seems—in spite of the unpopularity of this theory nowadays—unquestionable in view of the new knowledge of primitive economic psychology.[1] Since the giving of gifts is the normal accompaniment of all social intercourse among primitives, the spirits who visit the village or the demons who haunt some hallowed spot, or divinities when approached are given their due, their share sacrificed from the general plenty, as any other visitors or persons visited would be. But underlying this custom there is a still deeper religious element. Since food is to the savage the token of the beneficence of the world, since plenty gives him the first, the most elementary, inkling of Providence, by sharing in food sacrificially with his spirits or divinities the savage shares with them in the beneficial powers of his Providence already felt by him but not yet comprehended. Thus in primitive societies the roots of sacrificial offerings are to be found in the psychology of gift, which is to the communion in beneficent abundance.

The sacramental meal is only another expression of the same mental attitude, carried out in the most appropriate manner by the act by which life is retained and renewed—the act of eating. But this ritual seems to be extremely rare among lower savages, and the sacrament of communion, prevalent at a level of culture when the primitive psychology of eating is no more, has by then acquired a different symbolic and mystical meaning. Perhaps the only case of sacramental eating, well attested and known with some detail, is the so-called "totemic sacrament" of Central Australian tribes, and this seems to require a somewhat more special interpretation.

[1] *Cf.* the writer's *Argonauts of the Western Pacific*, 1923, and the article on "Primitive Economics" in the *Economic Journal*, 1921; as well as Professor Rich. Thurnwald's memoir on "Die Gestaltung der Wirtschaftsentwicklung aus ihren Anfangen heraus" in *Erinnerungsgabe fur Max Weber*, 1923.

implies, on the one hand, certain considerations and restraints—the most obvious being a prohibition to kill and to eat; on the other hand, it endows man with the supernatural faculty of contributing ritually to the abundance of the species, to its increase and vitality.

This ritual leads to acts of magical nature, by which plenty is brought about. Magic, as we shall see presently, tends in all its manifestations to become specialized, exclusive and departmental and hereditary within a family or clan. In totemism the magical multiplication of each species would naturally become the duty and privilege of a specialist, assisted by his family. The families in course of time become clans, each having its headman as the chief magician of its totem. Totemism in its most elementary forms, as found in Central Australia, is a system of magical co-operation, a number of practical cults, each with its own social basis but all having one common end: the supply of the tribe with abundance. Thus totemism in its sociological aspect can be explained by the principles of primitive magical sociology in general. The existence of totemic clans and their correlation with cult and belief is but an instance of departmental magic and of the tendency to inheritance of magical ritual by one family. This explanation, somewhat condensed as it is, attempts to show that, in its social organization, belief, and cult, totemism is not a freakish outgrowth, not a fortuitous result of some special accident or constellation, but the natural outcome of natural conditions.

Thus we find our questions answered: man's selective interest in a limited number of animals and plants and the way in which this interest is ritually expressed and socially conditioned appear as the natural result of primitive existence, of the savage's spontaneous attitudes towards natural objects and of his prevalent occupations. From the survival point of view, it is vital that man's interest in the practically indispensable species should never abate, that his belief in his capacity to control them should give him strength and endurance in his pursuits and stimulate his observation and knowledge of the habits and natures of animals and plants. Totemism appears thus as a blessing bestowed by religion on primitive man's efforts in dealing with his useful surroundings, upon his "struggle for existence." At the same time it develops his reverence for those animals and plants on which he depends, to which he feels in a way grateful, and yet the destruction of which is a necessity to him. And all this springs from the belief of man's affinity with those forces of nature upon which he mainly depends. Thus we find a moral value and a biological significance in totemism, in a system of beliefs, practices, and social arrangements which at first sight appears but a childish, irrevelant, and degrading fancy of the savage.

4. DEATH AND THE REINTEGRATION OF THE GROUP Of all sources of religion, the supreme and final crisis of life—death—is of the greatest importance. Death is the gateway to the other world in more than the literal sense. According to most theories of early religion, a great deal, if not all, of religious inspiration has been derived from it—and in this orthodox views are on the whole correct. Man has to live his life in the shadow of death, and he who clings to life and enjoys its fullness must dread the menace of its end. And he who is faced by death turns to the promise of life. Death and its denial—Immortality—have always formed, as they form today, the most poignant theme of man's forebodings. The extreme complexity of man's emotional reactions to life finds necessarily its counterpart in his attitude to death. Only what in life has been spread over a long space and manifested in a succession of experiences and events is here at its end condensed into one crisis which provokes a violent and complex outburst of religious manifestations.

Even among the most primitive peoples, the attitude towards death is infinitely more complex and, I may add, more akin to our own, than is usually assumed. It is often

stated by anthropologists that the dominant feeling of the
survivors is that of horror at the corpse and of fear of the
ghost. This twin attitude is even made by no less an authority than Wilhelm Wundt the very nucleus of all religious
belief and practice. Yet this assertion is only a half-truth,
which means no truth at all. The emotions are extremely
complex and even contradictory; the dominant elements,
love of the dead and loathing of the corpse, passionate
attachment to the personality still lingering about the body
and a shattering fear of the gruesome thing that has been
left over, these two elements seem to mingle and play into
each other. This is reflected in the spontaneous behavior
and in the ritual proceedings at death. In the tending of
the corpse, in the modes of its disposal, in the post-funerary
and commemorative ceremonies, the nearest relatives, the
mother mourning for her son, the widow for her husband,
the child for the parent, always show some horror and fear
mingled with pious love, but never do the negative elements
appear alone or even dominant.

The mortuary proceedings show a striking similarity
throughout the world. As death approaches, the nearest
relatives in any case, sometimes the whole community, forgather by the dying man, and dying, the most private act
which a man can perform, is transformed into a public,
tribal event. As a rule, a certain differentiation takes place
at once, some of the relatives watching near the corpse,
others making preparations for the pending end and its
consequences, others again performing perhaps some religious acts at a sacred spot. Thus in certain parts of
Melanesia the real kinsmen must keep at a distance and
only relatives by marriage perform the mortuary services,
while in some tribes of Australia the reverse order is observed.

As soon as death has occurred, the body is washed,
anointed and adorned, sometimes the bodily apertures are
filled, the arms and legs tied together. Then it is exposed
to the view of all, and the most important phase, the immediate mourning begins. Those who have witnessed death

and its sequel among savages and who can compare these events with their counterpart among other uncivilized peoples must be struck by the fundamental similarity of the proceedings. There is always a more or less conventionalized and dramatized outburst of grief and wailing in sorrow, which often passes among savages into bodily lacerations and the tearing of hair. This is always done in a public display and is associated with visible signs of mourning, such as black or white daubs on the body, shaven or disheveled hair, strange or torn garments.

The immediate mourning goes on round the corpse. This, far from being shunned or dreaded, is usually the center of pious attention. Often there are ritual forms of fondling or attestations of reverence. The body is sometimes kept on the knees of seated persons, stroked and embraced. At the same time these acts are usually considered both dangerous and repugnant, duties to be fulfilled at some cost to the performer. After a time the corpse has to be disposed of. Inhumation with an open or closed grave; exposure in caves or on platforms, in hollow trees or on the ground in some wild desert place; burning or setting adrift in canoes—these are the usual forms of disposal.

This brings us to perhaps the most important point, the two-fold contradictory tendency, on the one hand to preserve the body, to keep its form intact, or to retain parts of it; on the other hand the desire to be done with it, to put it out of the way, to annihilate it completely. Mummification and burning are the two extreme expressions of this two-fold tendency. It is impossible to regard mummification or burning or any intermediate form as determined by mere accident of belief, as a historical feature of some culture or other which has gained its universality by the mechanism of spread and contact only. For in these customs is clearly expressed the fundamental attitude of mind of the surviving relative, friend or lover, the longing for all that remains of the dead person and the disgust and fear of the dreadful transformation wrought by death.

One extreme and interesting variety in which this double-edged attitude is expressed in a gruesome manner is sarco-cannibalism, a custom of partaking in piety of the flesh of the dead person. It is done with extreme repugnance and dread and usually followed by a violent vomiting fit. At the same time it is felt to be a supreme act of reverence, love, and devotion. In fact it is considered such a sacred duty that among the Melanesians of New Guinea, where I have studied and witnessed it, it is still performed in secret, although severely penalized by the white Government. The smearing of the body with the fat of the dead, prevalent in Australia and Papuasia is, perhaps, but a variety of this custom.

In all such rites, there is a desire to maintain the tie and the parallel tendency to break the bond. Thus the funerary rites are considered as unclean and soiling, the contact with the corpse as defiling and dangerous, and the performers have to wash, cleanse their body, remove all traces of contact, and perform ritual lustrations. Yet the mortuary ritual compels man to overcome the repugnance, to conquer his fears, to make piety and attachment triumphant, and with it the belief in a future life, in the survival of the spirit.

And here we touch on one of the most important functions of religious cult. In the foregoing analysis I have laid stress on the direct emotional forces created by contact with death and with the corpse, for they primarily and most powerfully determine the behavior of the survivors. But connected with these emotions and born out of them, there is the idea of the spirit, the belief in the new life into which the departed has entered. And here we return to the problem of animism with which we began our survey of primitive religious facts. What is the substance of a spirit, and what is the psychological origin of this belief?

The savage is intensely afraid of death, probably as the result of some deep-seated instincts common to man and animals. He does not want to realize it as an end, he cannot face the idea of complete cessation, of annihilation. The idea of spirit and of spiritual existence is near at hand, furnished by such experiences as are discovered and described by Tylor. Grasping at it, man reaches the comforting belief in spiritual continuity and in the life after death. Yet this belief does not remain unchallenged in the complex, double-edged play of hope and fear which sets in always in the face of death. To the comforting voice of hope, to the intense desire of immortality, to the difficulty, in one's own case, almost the impossibility, of facing annihilation there are opposed powerful and terrible forebodings. The testimony of the senses, the gruesome decomposition of the corpse, the visible disappearance of the personality—certain apparently instinctive suggestions of fear and horror seem to threaten man at all stages of culture with some idea of annihilation, with some hidden fears and forebodings. And here into this play of emotional forces, into this supreme dilemma of life and final death, religion steps in, selecting the positive creed, the comforting view, the culturally valuable belief in immortality, in the spirit independent of the body, and in the continuance of life after death. In the various ceremonies at death, in commemoration and communion with the departed, and worship of ancestral ghosts, religion gives body and form to the saving beliefs.

Thus the belief in immortality is the result of a deep emotional revelation, standardized by religion, rather than a primitive philosophic doctrine. Man's conviction of continued life is one of the supreme gifts of religion, which judges and selects the better of the two alternatives suggested by self-preservation—the hope of continued life and the fear of annihilation. The belief in spirits is the result of the belief in immortality. The substance of which the spirits are made is the full-blooded passion and desire for life, rather than the shadowy stuff which haunts his dreams and illusions. Religion saves man from a surrender to death and destruction, and in doing this it merely makes use of the observations of dreams, shadows, and visions. The real nucleus of animism lies in the deepest emotional fact of human nature, the desire for life.

Thus the rites of mourning, the ritual behavior immediately after death, can be taken as pattern of the religious
act, while the belief in immortality, in the continuity of
life and in the nether world, can be taken as the prototype
of an act of faith. Here, as in the religious ceremonies previously described, we find self-contained acts, the aim of
which is achieved in their very performance. The ritual
despair, the obsequies, the acts of mourning, express the
emotion of the bereaved and the loss of the whole group.
They endorse and they duplicate the natural feelings of
the survivors; they create a social event out of a natural
fact. Yet, though in the acts of mourning, in the mimic
despair of wailing, in the treatment of the corpse and in
its disposal, nothing ulterior is achieved, these acts fulfill
an important function and possess a considerable value for
primitive culture.

What is this function? The initiation ceremonies we have
found fulfill theirs in sacralizing tradition; the food cults,
sacrament and sacrifice bring man into communion with
providence, with the beneficent forces of plenty; totemism
standardizes man's practical, useful attitude of selective
interest towards his surroundings. If the view here taken of
the biological function of religion is true, some such similar
role must also be played by the whole mortuary ritual.

The death of a man or woman in a primitive group, consisting of a limited number of individuals, is an event of no
mean importance. The nearest relatives and friends are
disturbed to the depth of their emotional life. A small community bereft of a member, especially if he be important,
is severely mutilated. The whole event breaks the normal
course of life and shakes the moral foundations of society.
The strong tendency on which we have insisted in the above
description: to give way to fear and horror, to abandon the
corpse, to run away from the village, to destroy all the be-
longings of the dead one—all these impulses exist, and if
given way to would be extremely dangerous, disintegrating
the group, destroying the material foundations of primitive
culture. Death in a primitive society is, therefore, much

more than the removal of a member. By setting in motion one part of the deep forces of the instinct of self-preservation, it threatens the very cohesion and solidarity of the group, and upon this depends the organization of that society, its tradition, and finally the whole culture. For if primitive man yielded always to the disintegrating impulses of his reaction to death, the continuity of tradition and the existence of material civilization would be made impossible.

We have seen already how religion, by sacralizing and thus standardizing the other set of impulses, bestows on man the gift of mental integrity. Exactly the same function it fulfills also with regard to the whole group. The ceremonial of death which ties the survivors to the body and rivets them to the place of death, the beliefs in the existence of the spirit, in its beneficent influences or malevolent intentions, in the duties of a series of commemorative or sacrificial ceremonies—in all this religion counteracts the centrifugal forces of fear, dismay, demoralization, and provides the most powerful means of reintegration of the group's shaken solidarity and of the re-establishment of its morale.

In short, religion here assures the victory of tradition and culture over the mere negative response of thwarted instinct.

With the rites of death we have finished the survey of the main types of religious acts. We have followed the crises of life as the main guiding thread of our account, but as they presented themselves we also treated the side issues, such as totemism, the cults of food and of propagation, sacrifice and sacrament, the commemorative cults of ancestors and the cults of the spirits. To one type already mentioned we still have to return—I mean, the seasonal feasts and ceremonies of communal or tribal character—and to the discussion of this subject we proceed now.

IV. THE PUBLIC AND TRIBAL CHARACTER OF
PRIMITIVE CULTS

The festive and public character of the ceremonies of cult is a conspicuous feature of religion in general. Most sacred acts happen in a congregation; indeed, the solemn conclave of the faithful united in prayer, sacrifice, supplication, or thanksgiving is the very prototype of a religious ceremony. Religion needs the community as a whole so that its members may worship in common its sacred things and its divinities, and society needs religion for the maintenance of moral law and order.

In primitive societies the public character of worship, the give-and-take between religious faith and social organization, is at least as pronounced as in higher cultures. It is sufficient to glance over our previous inventory of religious phenomena to see that ceremonies at birth, rites of initiation, mortuary attentions to the dead, burial, the acts of mourning and commemoration, sacrifice and totemic ritual, are one and all public and collective, frequently affecting the tribe as a whole and absorbing all its energies for the time being. This public character, the gathering together of big numbers, is especially pronounced in the annual or periodical feasts held at times of plenty, at harvest or at the height of the hunting or fishing season. Such feasts allow the people to indulge in their gay mood, to enjoy the abundance of crops and quarry, to meet their friends and relatives, to muster the whole community in full force, and to do all this in a mood of happiness and harmony. At times during such festivals visits of the departed take place: the spirits of ancestors and dead relatives return and receive offerings and sacrificial libations, mingle with the survivors in the acts of cult and in the rejoicings of the feast. Or the dead, even if they do not actually revisit the survivors, are commemorated by them, usually in the form of ancestor cult. Again, such festivities being frequently held, embody the ritual of garnered crops and other cults of vegetation. But whatever the other issues of such festivities, there can be no doubt that religion demands the existence of seasonal, periodical feasts with a big concourse of people, with rejoicings and festive apparel, with an abundance of food, and with relaxation of rules and taboos. The members of the tribe come together, and they relax the usual restrictions, especially the barriers of conventional reserve in social and in sexual intercourse. The appetites are provided for, indeed pandered to, and there is a common participation in the pleasures, a display to everyone of all that is good, the sharing of it in a universal mood of generosity. To the interest in plenty of material goods there is joined the interest in the multitude of people, in the congregation, in the tribe as a body.

With these facts of periodical festive gathering a number of other distinctly social elements must be ranged: the tribal character of almost all religious ceremonies, the social universality of moral rules, the contagion of sin, the importance of sheer convention and tradition in primitive religion and morals, above all the identification of the whole tribe as a social unit with its religion; that is, the absence of any religious sectarianism, dissention, or heterodoxy in primitive creed.

1. SOCIETY AS THE SUBSTANCE OF GOD All these facts, especially the last one, show that religion is a tribal affair, and we are reminded of the famous dictum of Robertson Smith, that primitive religion is the concern of the community rather than of the individual. This exaggerated view contains a great deal of truth, but, in science, to recognize where the truth lies, on the one hand, and to unearth it and bring it fully to light, on the other, are by no means the same. Robertson Smith did not do much more in this matter, in fact, than set forth the important problem: why is it that primitive man performs his ceremonies in public?

be savage or civilized, will under such conditions feel altered, uplifted, endowed with higher forces. And there can be no doubt that from many of these solitary experiences where man feels the forebodings of death, the pangs of anxiety, the exaltation of bliss, there flows a great deal of religious inspiration. Though most ceremonies are carried out in public, much of religious revelation takes place in solitude.

On the other hand there are in primitive societies collective acts with as much effervescence and passion as any religious ceremony can possibly have, yet without the slightest religious coloring. Collective work in the gardens, as I have seen it in Melanesia, when men become carried away with emulation and zest for work, singing rhythmic songs, uttering shouts of joy and slogans of competitive challenge, is full of this "collective effervescence." But it is entirely profane, and society which "reveals itself" in this as in any other public performance assumes no divine grandeur or godlike appearance. A battle, a sailing regatta, one of the big tribal gatherings for trading purposes, an Australian lay-corrobboree, a village brawl, are all from the social as well as from the psychological point of view essentially examples of crowd effervescence. Yet no religion is generated on any of these occasions. Thus the *collective* and the *religious*, though impinging on each other, are by no means coextensive, and while a great deal of belief and religious inspiration must be traced back to solitary experiences of man, there is much concourse and effervescence which has no religious meaning or religious consequence.

If we extend yet further the definition of "society" and regard it as a permanent entity, continuous through tradition and culture, each generation brought up by its predecessor and molded into its likeness by the social heritage of civilization—can we not regard then Society as the prototype of Godhead? Even thus the facts of primitive life will remain rebellious to this theory. For tradition comprises the sum total of social norms and customs, rules of art and knowledge, injunctions, precepts, legends and myths, and part of this only is religious, while the rest is essentially profane. As we have seen in the second section of this essay, primitive man's empirical and rational knowledge of nature, which is the foundation of his arts and crafts, of his economic enterprises and of his constructive abilities, forms an autonomous domain of social tradition. Society as the keeper of lay tradition, of the profane, cannot be the religious principle or Divinity, for the place of this latter is within the domain of the sacred only. We have found, moreover, that one of the chief tasks of primitive religion, especially in the performance of initiation ceremonies and tribal mysteries, is to sacralize the religious part of tradition. It is clear, therefore, that religion cannot derive all its sanctity from that source which itself is made sacred by religion.

It is in fact only by a clever play on words and by a double-edged sophistication of the argument that "society" can be identified with the Divine and the Sacred. If, indeed, we set equal the *social* to the *moral* and widen this concept so that it covers all belief, all rules of conduct, all dictates of conscience; if, further, we personify the Moral Force and regard it as a Collective Soul, then the identification of Society with Godhead needs not much dialectical skill to be defended. But since the moral rules are only one part of the traditional heritage of man, since morality is not identical with the Power of Being from which it is believed to spring, since finally the metaphysical concept of "Collective Soul" is barren in anthropology, we have to reject the sociological theory of religion.

To sum up, the views of Durkheim and his school cannot be accepted. First of all, in primitive societies religion arises to a great extent from purely individual sources. Secondly, society as a crowd is by no means always given to the production of religious beliefs or even to religious states of mind, while collective effervescence is often of an entirely secular nature. Thirdly, tradition, the sum total of certain rules and cultural achievements, embraces, and in primitive societies keeps in a tight grip, both Profane and Sacred. Finally, the personification of society, the conception of a "Collective Soul," is without any foundation in fact, and is against the sound methods of social science.

2. THE MORAL EFFICIENCY OF SAVAGE BELIEFS   With all this, in order to do justice to Robertson Smith, Durkheim, and their school, we have to admit that they have brought out a number of relevant features of primitive religion. Above all, by the very exaggeration of the sociological aspect of primitive faith they have set forth a number of most important questions: Why are most religious acts in primitive societies performed collectively and in public? What is the part of society in the establishment of the rules of moral conduct? Why are not only morality but also belief, mythology, and all sacred tradition compulsory to all the members of a primitive tribe? In other words, why is there only one body of religious beliefs in each tribe, and why is no difference of opinion ever tolerated?

To give an answer to these questions we have to go back to our survey of religious phenomena, to recall some of our conclusions there arrived at, and especially to fix our attention upon the technique by which belief is expressed and morals established in primitive religion.

Let us start with the religious act par excellence, the ceremonial of death. Here the call to religion arises out of an individual crisis, the death which threatens man or woman. Never does an individual need the comfort of belief and ritual so much as in the sacrament of the viaticum, in the last comforts given to him at the final stage of his life's journey—acts which are well-nigh universal in all primitive religions. These acts are directed against the overwhelming fear, against the corroding doubt, from which the savage is no more free than the civilized man. These acts confirm his hope that there is a hereafter, that it is not worse than present life; indeed, better. All the ritual expresses that belief, that emotional attitude which the dying man requires, which is the greatest comfort he can have in his supreme conflict. And this affirmation has behind it weight of numbers and the pomp of solemn ritual. For in all savage societies, death, as we have seen, compels the whole community to forgather, to attend to the dying, and to carry out the duties towards him. These duties do not, of course, develop any emotional sympathy with the dying —this would lead merely to a disintegrating panic. On the contrary, the line of ritual conduct opposes and contradicts some of the strongest emotions to which the dying man might become a prey. The whole conduct of the group, in fact, expresses the hope of salvation and immortality; that is, it expresses only one among the conflicting emotions of the individual.

After death, though the main actor has made his exit, the tragedy is not at an end. There are the bereaved ones, and these, savage or civilized, suffer alike, and are thrown into a dangerous mental chaos. We have given an analysis of this already, and found that, torn between fear and picty, reverence and horror, love and disgust, they are in a state of mind which might lead to mental disintegration. Out of this, religion lifts the individual by what could be called spiritual co-operation in the sacred mortuary rites. We have seen that in these rites there is expressed the dogma of continuity after death, as well as the moral attitude towards the departed. The corpse, and with it the person of the dead one, is a potential object of horror as well as of tender love. Religion confirms the second part of this double attitude by making the dead body into an object of sacred duties. The bond of union between the recently dead and the survivors is maintained, a fact of immense importance for the continuity of culture and for the safe keeping of tradition. In all this we see that the whole community carries out the biddings of religious tradition, but that these are again enacted for the benefit of a few individuals only, the bereaved ones, that they arise from a personal conflict and are a solution of this conflict. It must also be remembered that what the survivor goes through on such an occasion prepares him for his own death. The belief in immortality, which he has lived through and practiced in the case of his mother or father, makes him realize more clearly his own future life.

In all this we have to make a clear distinction between the belief and the ethics of the ritual on the one hand, and on the other the means of enforcing them, the technique by which the individual is made to receive his religious comfort. The saving belief in spiritual continuity after death is already contained in the individual mind; it is not created by society. The sum total of innate tendencies, known usually as "the instinct of self-preservation," is at the root of this belief. The faith in immortality is, as we have seen, closely connected with the difficulty of facing one's own annihilation or that of a near and beloved person. This tendency makes the idea of the final disappearance of human personality odious, intolerable, socially destructive. Yet this idea and the fear of it always lurk in individual experience, and religion can remove it only by its negation in ritual.

Whether this is achieved by a Providence directly guiding human history, or by a process of natural selection in which a culture which evolves a belief and a ritual of immortality will survive and spread—this is a problem of theology or metaphysics. The anthropologist has done enough when he has shown the value of a certain phenomenon for social integrity and for the continuity of culture. In any case we see that what religion does in this matter is to select one out of the two alternatives suggested to man by his instinctive endowment.

This selection once made, however, society is indispensable for its enactment. The bereaved member of the group, himself overwhelmed by sorrow and fear, is incapable of relying on his own forces. He would be unable by his single effort to apply the dogma to his own case. Here the group steps in. The other members, untouched by the calamity, not torn mentally by the metaphysical dilemma, can respond to the crisis along the lines dictated by the religious order. Thus they bring consolation to the stricken one and lead him through the comforting experiences of religious ceremony. It is always easy to bear the misfortunes—of others, and the whole group, in which the majority are untouched by the pangs of fear and horror, can thus help the afflicted minority. Going through the religious ceremonies, the bereaved emerges changed by the revelation of immortality, communion with the beloved, the order of the next world. Religion commands in acts of cult, the group executes the command.

But, as we have seen, the comfort of ritual is not artificial, not manufactured for the occasion. It is but the result of the two conflicting tendencies which exist in man's innate emotional reaction to death: the religious attitude consists merely in the selection and ritual affirmation of one of these alternatives—the hope in a future life. And here the public concourse gives the emphasis, the powerful testimony to the belief. Public pomp and ceremony take effect through the contagiousness of faith, through the dignity of unanimous consent, the impressiveness of collective behavior. A multitude enacting as one an earnest and dignified ceremony invariably carries away even the disinterested observer, still more the affected participant.

But the distinction between social collaboration as the only technique necessary for the enactment of a belief on the one hand, and the creation of the belief or self-revelation of society on the other, must be emphatically pointed out. The community proclaims a number of definite truths and gives moral comfort to its members, but it does not give them the vague and empty assertion of its own divinity.

In another type of religious ritual, in the ceremonies of initiation, we found that the ritual establishes the existence of some power or personality from which tribal law is derived, and which is responsible for the moral rules imparted to the novice. To make the belief impressive, strong, and grandiose, there is the pomp of the ceremony and the hardships of preparation and ordeal. An unforgettable experience, unique in the life of the individual, is created, and by this he learns the doctrines of tribal tradition and the rules of its morality. The whole tribe is mobilized and all its authority set in motion to bear witness to the power and reality of the things revealed.

Here again, as at the death, we have to do with a crisis in the individual life, and a mental conflict associated with it. At puberty, the youth has to test his physical power, to cope with his sexual maturity, to take up his place in the tribe. This brings him promises, prerogatives, and temptations, and at the same time imposes burdens upon him. The right solution of the conflict lies in his compliance with tradition, in his submission to the sexual morality of his tribe and to the burdens of manhood, and that is accomplished in the ceremonies of initiation.

The public character of these ceremonies avails both to establish the greatness of the ultimate lawgiver and to achieve homogeneity and uniformity in the teaching of morals. Thus they become a form of condensed education of a religious character. As in all schooling, the principles imparted are merely selected, fixed, emphasized out of what there is in the individual endowment. Here again publicity is a matter of technique, while the contents of what is taught are not invented by society but exist in the individual.

In other cults again, such as harvest festivals, totemic gatherings, first-fruit offerings and ceremonial display of food, we find religion sacralizing abundance and security and establishing the attitude of reverence towards the beneficent forces without. Here again the publicity of the cult is necessary as the only technique suitable for the establishment of the value of food, accumulation and abundance. The display to all, the admiration of all, the rivalry between any two producers, are the means by which value is created. For every value, religious and economic, must possess universal currency. But here again we find only the selection and emphasis of one of the two possible individual reactions. Accumulated food can either be squandered or preserved. It can either be an incentive to immediate heedless consumption and light-hearted carelessness about the future, or else it can stimulate man to devising means of hoarding the treasure and of using it for culturally higher purposes. Religion sets its stamp on the culturally valuable attitude and enforces it by public enactment.

The public character of such feasts subserves another sociologically important function. The members of every group which forms a cultural unit must come in contact with each other from time to time, but besides its beneficent possibility of strengthening social ties, such contact is also fraught with the danger of friction. The danger is greater when people meet in times of stress, dearth, and hunger, when their appetite is unsatisfied and their sexual desires ready to flare up. A festive tribal gathering at times of plenty, when everyone is in a mood of harmony with nature and consequently with each other, takes on, therefore, the character of a meeting in a moral atmosphere. I mean an atmosphere of general harmony and benevolence. The occurrence of occasional licence at such gatherings and the relaxation of the rules of sex and of certain strictures of etiquette are probably due to the same course. All motives for quarrel and disagreement must be eliminated or else a big tribal gathering could not peacefully come to an end. The moral value of harmony and good will is thus shown to be higher than the mere negative taboos which curb the principal human instincts. There is no virtue higher than charity, and in primitive religions as well as in higher it covers a multitude of sins; nay, it outweighs them.

It is, perhaps, unnecessary to go in detail over all the other types of religious acts. Totemism, the religion of the clan, which affirms the common descent from or affinity with the totemic animal, and claims the clan's collective power to control its supply and impresses upon all the clan members a joint totemic taboo and a reverential attitude towards the totemic species, must obviously culminate in public ceremonies and have a distinctly social character. Ancestor cult, the aim of which is to unite into one band of worshippers the family, the sib or the tribe, must bring them together in public ceremonies by its very nature, or else it would fail to fulfill its function. Tutelary spirits of local groups, tribes, or cities; departmental gods; professional or local divinities must one and all—by their very definition—be worshipped by village, tribe, town, profession, or body politic.

In cults which stand on the borderline between magic and religion, such as the Intichuma ceremonies, public garden rites, ceremonies of fishing and hunting, the necessity of performance in public is obvious, for these ceremonies, clearly distinguishable from any practical activities which they inaugurate or accompany, are yet their counterpart. To the co-operation in practical enterprise there corresponds the ceremony in common. Only by uniting the group of workers in an act of worship do they fulfill their cultural function.

In fact, instead of going concretely into all the types of religious ceremony, we might have established our thesis by an abstract argument: since religion centers round vital acts, and since all these command public interest of joint co-operative groups, every religious ceremony must be public and carried out by groups. All crises of life, all important enterprises, arouse the public interest of primitive communities, and they have all their ceremonies, magical or religious. The same social body of men which unites for the enterprise or is brought together by the critical event performs also the ceremonial act. Such an abstract argument, however, correct though it be, would not have allowed us to get a real insight into the mechanism of public enactment of religious acts such as we have gained by our concrete description.

3. SOCIAL AND INDIVIDUAL CONTRIBUTIONS IN PRIMITIVE RELIGION   We are forced therefore to the conclusion that publicity is the indispensable technique of religious revelation in primitive communities, but that society is neither the author of religious truths, nor still less its self-revealed subject. The necessity of the public *mise en scène* of dogma

and collective enunciation of moral truths is due to several causes. Let us sum them up.

First of all, social co-operation is needed to surround the unveiling of things sacred and of supernatural beings with solemn grandeur. The community whole-heartedly engaged in performing the forms of the ritual creates the atmosphere of homogeneous belief. In this collective action, those who at the moment least need the comfort of belief, the affirmation of the truth, help along those who are in need of it. The evil, disintegrating forces of destiny are thus distributed by a system of mutual insurance in spiritual misfortune and stress. In bereavement, at the crisis of puberty, during impending danger and evil, at times when prosperity might be used well or badly—religion standardizes the right way of thinking and acting and society takes up the verdict and repeats it in unison.

In the second place, public performance of religious dogma is indispensable for the maintenance of morals in primitive communities. Every article of faith, as we have seen, wields a moral influence. Now morals, in order to be active at all, must be universal. The endurance of social ties, the mutuality of services and obligations, the possibility of co-operation, are based in any society on the fact that every member knows what is expected of him; that, in short, there is a universal standard of conduct. No rule of morals can work unless it is anticipated and unless it can be counted upon. In primitive societies, where law, as enforced by judgments and penalties, is almost completely absent, the automatic, self-acting moral rule is of the greatest importance for forming the very foundations of primitive organization and culture. This is possible only in a society where there is no private teaching of morals, no personal codes of conduct and honor, no ethical schools, no differences of moral opinion. The teaching of morals must be open, public, and universal.

Thirdly and finally, the transmission and the conservation of sacred tradition entails publicity, or at least collectiveness of performance. It is essential to every religion that its dogma should be considered and treated as absolutely inalterable and inviolable. The believer must be firmly convinced that what he is led to accept as truth is held in safekeeping, handed on exactly as it has been received, placed above any possibility of falsification or alteration. Every religion must have its tangible, reliable safeguards by which the authenticity of its tradition is guaranteed. In higher religions, we know the extreme importance of the authenticity of holy writings, the supreme concern about the purity of the text and the truth of interpretation. The native races have to rely on human memory. Yet, without books or inscriptions, without bodies of theologians, they are not less concerned about the purity of their texts, not less well safeguarded against alteration and misstatement. There is only one factor which can prevent the constant breaking of the sacred thread: the participation of a number of people in the safekeeping of tradition. The public enactment of myth among certain tribes, the official recitals of sacred stories on certain occasions, the embodiment of parts of belief in sacred ceremonies, the guardianship of parts of tradition given to special bodies of men: secret societies, totemic clans, highest-age grades—all these are means of safeguarding the doctrine of primitive religions. We see that wherever this doctrine is not quite public in the tribe there is a special type of social organization serving the purpose of its keeping.

These considerations explain also the orthodoxy of primitive religions, and excuse their intolerance. In a primitive community, not only the morals but also the dogmas have to be identical for all members. As long as savage creeds have been regarded as idle superstitions, as make-believe, as childish or diseased fancies, or at best crude philosophic speculations, it was difficult to understand why the savage clung to them so obstinately, so faithfully. But once we see that every canon of the savage's belief is a live force to him, that his doctrine is the very cement of social fabric—for all his morality is derived from it, all his social cohesion and his mental composure—it is easy to understand that he cannot afford to be tolerant. And it is clear also that once you begin to play ducks and drakes with his "superstitions," you destroy all his morality, without much chance of giving him another instead.

We see thus clearly the need for the prominently overt and collective nature of religious acts and for the universality of moral principles, and we also realize clearly why this is much more prominent in primitive religions than in civilized ones. Public participation and social interest in matters religious are thus explicable by clear, concrete, empirical reasons, and there is no room for an Entity, revealing itself in artful disguise to its worshippers, mystified and misled in the very act of revelation. The fact is that the social share in religious enactment is a condition necessary but not sufficient, and that without the analysis of the individual mind, we cannot take one step in the understanding of religion.

At the beginning of our survey of religious phenomena, in Section III, we have made a distinction between magic and religion; later on in the account, however, we left the magical rites completely on one side, and to this important domain of primitive life we have now to return.

V. THE ART OF MAGIC AND THE POWER OF FAITH

Magic—the very word seems to reveal a world of mysterious and unexpected possibilities! Even for those who do not share in that hankering after the occult, after the short cuts into "esoteric truth," this morbid interest, nowadays so freely ministered to by stale revivals of half-understood ancient creeds and cults, dished up under the names of "theosophy," "spiritism" or "spiritualism," and various pseudo-"sciences," -ologies and -isms—even for the clear scientific mind the subject of magic has a special attraction. Partly perhaps because we hope to find in it the quintessence of primitive man's longings and of his wisdom—and that, whatever it might be, is worth knowing. Partly because "magic" seems to stir up in everyone some hidden mental forces, some lingering hopes in the miraculous, some dormant beliefs in man's mysterious possibilities. Witness to this is the power which the words *magic, spell, charm, to bewitch,* and *to enchant,* possess in poetry, where the inner value of words, the emotional forces which they still release, survive longest and are revealed most clearly.

Yet when the sociologist approaches the study of magic, there where it still reigns supreme, where even now it can be found fully developed—that is, among the Stone Age savages of today—he finds to his disappointment an entirely sober, prosaic, even clumsy art, enacted for purely practical reasons, governed by crude and shallow beliefs, carried out in a simple and monotonous technique. This was already indicated in the definition of magic given above when in order to distinguish it from religion we described it as a body of purely practical acts, performed as a means to an end. Such also we have found it when we tried to disentangle it from knowledge and from practical arts, in which it is so strongly enmeshed, superficially so alike that it requires some effort to distinguish the essentially different mental attitude and the specifically ritual nature of its acts. Primitive magic—every field anthropologist knows it to his cost—is extremely monotonous and unexciting, strictly limited in its means of action, circumscribed in its beliefs, stunted in its fundamental assumptions. Follow one rite, study one spell, grasp the principles of magical belief, art and sociology in one case, and you will know not only all the acts of the tribe, but, adding a variant here and there, you will be able to settle as a magical practitioner in any part of the world yet fortunate enough to have faith in that desirable art.

1. THE RITE AND THE SPELL   Let us have a look at a typical act of magic, and choose one which is well-known and generally regarded as a standard performance—an act of black magic. Among the several types which we meet in

savagery, witchcraft by the act of pointing the magical dart is, perhaps, the most widespread of all. A pointed bone or a stick, an arrow or the spine of some animal, is ritually, in a mimic fashion, thrust, thrown, or pointed in the direction of the man to be killed by sorcery. We have innumerable recipes in the oriental and ancient books of magic, in ethnographic descriptions and tales of travelers, of how such a rite is performed. But the emotional setting, the gestures and expressions of the sorcerer during the performance, have been but seldom described. Yet these are of the greatest importance. If a spectator were suddenly transported to some part of Melanesia and could observe the sorcerer at work, not perhaps knowing exactly what he was looking at, he might think that he had either to do with a lunatic or else he would guess that here was a man acting under the sway of uncontrolled anger. For the sorcerer has, as an essential part of the ritual performance, not merely to point the bone dart at his victim, but with an intense expression of fury and hatred he has to thrust it in the air, turn and twist it as if to bore it in the wound, then pull it back with a sudden jerk. Thus not only is the act of violence, or stabbing, reproduced, but the passion of violence has to be enacted.

We see thus that the dramatic expression of emotion is the essence of this act, for what is it that is reproduced in it? Not its end, for the magician would in that case have to imitate the death of the victim, but the emotional state of the performer, a state which closely corresponds to the situation in which we find it and which has to be gone through mimetically.

I could adduce a number of similar rites from my own experience, and many more, of course, from other records. Thus, when in other types of black magic the sorcerer ritually injures or mutilates or destroys a figure or object symbolizing the victim, this rite is, above all, a clear expression of hatred and anger. Or when in love magic the performer has really or symbolically to grasp, stroke, fondle the beloved person or some object representing her, he reproduces the behavior of a heartsick lover who has lost his common sense and is overwhelmed by passion. In war magic, anger, the fury of attack, the emotions of combative passion, are frequently expressed in a more or less direct manner. In the magic of terror, in the exorcism directed against powers of darkness and evil, the magician behaves as if himself overcome by the emotion of fear, or at least violently struggling against it. Shouts, brandishing of weapons, the use of lighted torches, form often the substance of this rite. Or else in an act, recorded by myself, to ward off the evil powers of darkness, a man has ritually to tremble, to utter a spell slowly as if paralyzed by fear. And this fear gets hold also of the approaching sorcerer and wards him off.

All such acts, usually rationalized and explained by some principle of magic, are *prima facie* expressions of emotion. The substances and paraphernalia used in them have often the same significance. Daggers, sharp-pointed lacerating objects, evil-smelling or poisonous substances, used in black magic; scents, flowers, inebriating stimulants, in love magic; valuables, in economic magic—all these are associated primarily through emotions and not through ideas with the end of the respective magic.

Besides such rites, however, in which a dominant element serves to express an emotion, there are others in which the act does forecast its result, or, to use Sir James Frazer's expression, the rite imitates its end. Thus, in the black magic of the Melanesians recorded by myself, a characteristic ritual way of winding-up the spell is for the sorcerer to weaken the voice, utter a death rattle, and fall down in imitation of the rigor of death. It is, however, not necessary to adduce any other examples, for this aspect of magic and the allied one of contagious magic has been brilliantly described and exhaustively documented by Frazer. Sir James has also shown that there exists a special lore of magical substances based on affinities, relations, on ideas of similarity and contagion, developed with a magical pseudo-science.

But there are also ritual proceedings in which there is neither imitation nor forecasting nor the expression of any special idea or emotion. There are rites so simple that they can be described only as an immediate application of magical virtue, as when the performer stands up and, directly invoking the wind, causes it to rise. Or again, as when a man conveys the spell to some material substance which afterwards will be applied to the thing or person to be charmed. The material objects used in such ritual are also of a strictly appropriate character—substances best fitted to receive, retain, and transmit magical virtue, coverings designed to imprison and preserve it until it is applied to its object.

But what is the magical virtue which figures not only in the last-mentioned type of act but in every magical rite? For whether it be an act expressing certain emotions or a rite of imitation and foreshadowing or an act of simple casting, one feature they have always in common: the force of magic, its virtue, must always be conveyed to the charmed object. What is it? Briefly, it is always the power contained in the spell, for, and this is never sufficiently emphasized, the most important element in magic is the spell. The spell is that part of magic which is occult, handed over in magical filiation, known only to the practitioner. To the natives knowledge of magic means knowledge of spell, and in an analysis of any act of witchcraft it will always be found that the ritual centers round the utterance of the spell. The formula is always the core of the magical performance.

The study of the texts and formulas of primitive magic reveals that there are three typical elements associated with the belief in magical efficiency. There are, first, the phonetic effects, imitations of natural sounds, such as the whistling of the wind, the growling of thunder, the roar of the sea, the voices of various animals. These sounds symbolize certain phenomena and thus are believed to produce them magically. Or else they express certain emotional states associated with the desire which is to be realized by means of the magic.

The second element, very conspicuous in primitive spells, is the use of words which invoke, state, or command the desired aim. Thus the sorcerer will mention all the symptoms of the disease which he is inflicting, or in the lethal formula he will describe the end of his victim. In healing magic the wizard will give word pictures of perfect health and bodily strength. In economic magic the growing of plants, the approach of animals, the arrival of fish in shoals are depicted. Or again the magician uses words and sentences which express the emotion under the stress of which he works his magic, and the action which gives expression to this emotion. The sorcerer in tones of fury will have to repeat such verbs as "I break—I twist—I burn—I destroy," enumerating with each of them the various parts of the body and internal organs of his victim. In all this we see that the spells are built very much on the same pattern as the rites and the words selected for the same reasons as the substances of magic.

Thirdly there is an element in almost every spell to which there is no counterpart in ritual. I mean the mythological allusions, the references to ancestors and culture heroes from whom this magic has been received. And that brings us to perhaps the most important point in the subject, to the traditional setting of magic.

2. THE TRADITION OF MAGIC Tradition, which, as we have several times insisted, reigns supreme in primitive civilization, gathers in great abundance round magical ritual and cult. In the case of any important magic we invariably find the story accounting for its existence. Such a story tells when and where it entered the possession of man, how it became the property of a local group or of a family or clan. But such a story is not the story of its origins. Magic never "originated," it never has been made or invented. All magic simply "was" from the beginning an essential adjunct of

all such things and processes as vitally interest man and yet elude his normal rational efforts. The spell, the rite, and the thing which they govern are coeval.

Thus, in Central Australia, all magic existed and has been inherited from the *alcheringa* times, when it came about like everything else. In Melanesia all magic comes from a time when humanity lived underground and when magic was a natural knowledge of ancestral man. In higher societies magic is often derived from spirits and demons, but even these, as a rule, originally received and did not invent it. Thus the belief in the primeval natural existence of magic is universal. As its counterpart we find the conviction that only by an absolutely unmodified immaculate transmission does magic retain its efficiency. The slightest alteration from the original pattern would be fatal. There is, then, the idea that between the object and its magic there exists an essential nexus. Magic is the quality of the thing, or rather, of the relation between man and the thing, for though never man-made it is always made for man. In all tradition, in all mythology, magic is always found in the possession of man and through the knowledge of man or man-like being. It implies the performing magician quite as much as the thing to be charmed and the means of charming. It is part of the original endowment of primeval humanity, of the *mura-mura* or *alcheringa* of Australia, of the subterrestrial humanity of Melanesia, of the people of the magical Golden Age all the world over.

Magic is not only human in its embodiment, but also in its subject matter: it refers principally to human activities and states, hunting, gardening, fishing, trading, love-making, disease, and death. It is not directed so much to nature as to man's relation to nature and to the human activities which affect it. Moreover, the effects of magic are usually conceived not as a product of nature influenced by the charm, but as something specially magical, something which nature cannot produce, but only the power of magic. The graver forms of disease, love in its passionate phases, the desire for a ceremonial exchange and other similar manifestations in the human organism and mind, are the direct product of the spell and rite. Magic is thus not derived from an observation of nature or knowledge of its laws, it is a primeval possession of man to be known only through tradition and affirming man's autonomous power of creating desired ends.

Thus, the force of magic is not a universal force residing everywhere, flowing where it will or it is willed to. Magic is the one and only specific power, a force unique of its kind, residing exclusively in man, let loose only by his magical art, gushing out with his voice, conveyed by the casting forth of the rite.

It may be here mentioned that the human body, being the receptacle of magic and the channel of its flow, must be submitted to various conditions. Thus the magician has to keep all sorts of taboos, or else the spell might be injured, especially as in certain parts of the world, in Melanesia for instance, the spell resides in the magician's belly, which is the seat of memory as well as of food. When necessary it is summoned up to the larynx, which is the seat of intelligence, and thence sent forth by the voice, the main organ of the human mind. Thus, not only is magic an essentially human possession, but it is literally and actually enshrined in man and can be handed on only from man to man, according to very strict rules of magical filiation, initiation, and instruction. It is thus never conceived as a force of nature, residing in things, acting independently of man, to be found out and learned by him, by any of those proceedings by which he gains his ordinary knowledge of nature.

3. MANA AND THE VIRTUE OF MAGIC The obvious result of this is that all the theories which lay *mana* and similar conceptions at the basis of magic are pointing altogether in the wrong direction. For if the virtue of magic is exclusively localized in man, can be wielded by him only under very special conditions and in a traditionally prescribed manner,

it certainly is not a force such as the one described by Dr. Codrington: "This *mana* is not fixed in anything and can be conveyed in almost anything." *Mana* also "acts in all ways for good and evil . . . shows itself in physical force or in any kind of power and excellence which a man possesses." Now it is clear that this force as described by Codrington is almost the exact opposite of the magical virtue as found embodied in the mythology of savages, in their behavior, and in the structure of their magical formulas. For the real virtue of magic, as I know it from Melanesia, is fixed only in the spell and in its rite, and it cannot be "conveyed in" anything, but can be conveyed only by its strictly defined procedure. It never acts "in all ways," but only in ways specified by tradition. It never shows itself in physical force, while its effect upon the powers and excellences of man are strictly limited and defined.

And again, the similar conception found among the North American Indians cannot have anything to do with the specialized concrete virtue of magic. For of the *wakan* of the Dakota we read "all life is *wakan*. So also is everything which exhibits power, whether in action, as the winds and drifting clouds, or in passive endurance, as the boulder by the wayside. . . . It embraces all mystery, all secret power, all divinity." Of the *orenda,* a word taken from the Iroquois, we are told: "This potence is held to be the property of all things . . . the rocks, the waters, the tides, the plants and the trees, the animals and man, the wind and the storms, the clouds and the thunders and the lightnings . . . by the inchoate mentality of man, it is regarded as the efficient cause of all phenomena, all the activities of his environment."

After what has been established about the essence of magical power, it hardly needs emphasizing that there is little in common between the concepts of the *mana* type and the special virtue of magical spell and rite. We have seen that the keynote of all magical belief is the sharp distinction between the traditional force of magic on the one hand and the other forces and powers with which man and nature are endowed. The conceptions of the *wakan, orenda,* and *mana* class which include all sorts of forces and powers, besides that of magic, are simply an example of an early generalization of a crude metaphysical concept such as is found in several other savage words also, extremely important for our knowledge of primitive mentality but, as far as our present data go, opening only a problem as to the relation between the early concepts of "force," "the supernatural," and "the virtue of magic." It is impossible to decide, with the summary information at our disposal, what is the primary meaning of these compound concepts: that of physical force and that of supernatural efficiency. In the American concepts the emphasis seems to be on the former, in the Oceanic on the latter. What I want to make clear is that in all the attempts to understand native mentality it is necessary to study and describe the types of behavior first and to explain their vocabulary by their customs and their life. There is no more fallacious guide of knowledge than language, and in anthropology the "ontological argument" is specially dangerous.

It was necessary to enter into this problem in detail, for the theory of *mana* as the essence of primitive magic and religion has been so brilliantly advocated and so recklessly handled that it must be realized first that our knowledge of the *mana*, notably in Melanesia, is somewhat contradictory, and especially that we have hardly any data at all showing just how this conception enters into religious or magical cult and belief.

One thing is certain: magic is not born of an abstract conception of universal power, subsequently applied to concrete cases. It has undoubtedly arisen independently in a number of actual situations. Each type of magic, born of its own situation and of the emotional tension thereof, is due to the spontaneous flow of ideas and the spontaneous reaction of man. It is the uniformity of the mental process in each case which has led to certain universal features of magic and to the general conceptions which we find at the basis of man's magical thought and behavior. It will be necessary to give now an analysis of the situations of magic and the experiences which they provoke.

4. MAGIC AND EXPERIENCE   So far we have been dealing mainly with native ideas and with native views of magic. This has led us to a point where the savage simply affirms that magic gives man the power over certain things. Now we must analyze this belief from the point of view of the sociological observer. Let us realize once more the type of situation in which we find magic. Man, engaged in a series of practical activities, comes to a gap; the hunter is disappointed by his quarry, the sailor misses propitious winds, the canoe builder has to deal with some material of which he is never certain that it will stand the strain, or the healthy person suddenly feels his strength failing. What does man do naturally under such conditions, setting aside all magic, belief and ritual? Forsaken by his knowledge, baffled by his past experience and by his technical skill, he realizes his impotence. Yet his desire grips him only the more strongly; his anxiety, his fears and hopes, induce a tension in his organism which drives him to some sort of activity. Whether he be savage or civilized, whether in possession of magic or entirely ignorant of its existence, passive inaction, the only thing dictated by reason, is the last thing in which he can acquiesce. His nervous system and his whole organism drive him to some substitute activity. Obsessed by the idea of the desired end, he sees it and feels it. His organism reproduces the acts suggested by the anticipations of hope, dictated by the emotion of passion so strongly felt.

The man under the sway of impotent fury or dominated by thwarted hate spontaneously clenches his fist and carries out imaginary thrusts at his enemy, muttering imprecations, casting words of hatred and anger against him. The lover aching for his unattainable or irresponsive beauty sees her in his visions, addresses her, and entreats and com-

mands her favors, feeling himself accepted, pressing her to
his bosom in his dreams. The anxious fisherman or hunter
sees in his imagination the quarry enmeshed in the nets,
the animal attained by the spear; he utters their names,
describes in words his visions of the magnificent catch, he
even breaks out into gestures of mimic representation of
what he desires. The man lost at night in the woods or the
jungle, beset by superstitious fear, sees around him the
haunting demons, addresses them, tries to ward off, to
frighten them, or shrinks from them in fear, like an animal
which attempts to save itself by feigning death.

These reactions to overwhelming emotion or obsessive
desire are natural responses of man to such a situation,
based on a universal psycho-physiological mechanism. They
engender what could be called extended expressions of
emotion in act and in word, the threatening gestures of
impotent anger and its maledictions, the spontaneous enactment of the desired end in a practical impasse, the passionate fondling gestures of the lover, and so on. All these
spontaneous acts and spontaneous works make man forecast
the images of the wished-for results, or express his passion
in uncontrollable gestures, or break out into words which
give vent to desire and anticipate its end.

And what is the purely intellectual process, the conviction formed during such a free outburst of emotion in
words and deeds? First there surges a clear image of the
desired end, of the hated person, of the feared danger or
ghost. And each image is blended with its specific passion,
which drives us to assume an active attitude towards that
image. When passion reaches the breaking point at which
man loses control over himself, the words which he utters,
his blind behavior, allow the pent-up physiological tension
to flow over. But over all this outburst presides the image of
the end. It supplies the motive-force of the reaction, it
apparently organizes and directs words and acts towards a
definite purpose. The substitute action in which the passion
finds its vent, and which is due to impotence, has sub-

jectively all the value of a real action, to which emotion would, if not impeded, naturally have led.

As the tension spends itself in these words and gestures the obsessing visions fade away, the desired end seems nearer satisfaction, we regain our balance, once more at harmony with life. And we remain with a conviction that the words of malediction and the gestures of fury have traveled towards the hated person and hit their target; that the imploration of love, the visionary embraces, cannot have remained unanswered, that the visionary attainment of success in our pursuit cannot have been without a beneficial influence on the pending issue. In the case of fear, as the emotion which has led us to frenzied behavior gradually subsides, we feel that it is this behavior that has driven away the terrors. In brief, a strong emotional experience, which spends itself in a purely subjective flow of images, words, and acts of behavior, leaves a very deep conviction of its reality, as if of some practical and positive achievement, as if of something done by a power revealed to man. This power, born of mental and physiological obsession, seems to get hold of us from outside, and to primitive man, or to the credulous and untutored mind of all ages, the spontaneous spell, the spontaneous rite, and the spontaneous belief in their efficiency must appear as a direct revelation from some external and no doubt impersonal sources.

When we compare this spontaneous ritual and verbiage of overflowing passion or desire with traditionally fixed magical ritual and with the principles embodied in magical spells and substances, the striking resemblance of the two products shows that they are not independent of each other. Magical ritual, most of the principles of magic, most of its spells and substances, have been revealed to man in those passionate experiences which assail him in the impasses of his instinctive life and of his practical pursuits, in those gaps and breaches left in the ever-imperfect wall of culture which he erects between himself and the besetting temptations and dangers of his destiny. In this I think we have to recognize not only one of the sources but the very fountainhead of magical belief.

To most types of magical ritual, therefore, there corresponds a spontaneous ritual of emotional expression or of a forecast of the desired end. To most features of magical spell, to the commands, invocations, metaphors, there corresponds a natural flow of words, in malediction, in entreaty, in exorcism, and in the descriptions of unfulfilled wishes. To every belief in magical efficiency there can be laid in parallel one of those illusions of subjective experience, transient in the mind of the civilized rationalist, though even there never quite absent, but powerful and convincing to the simple man in every culture, and, above all, to the primitive savage mind.

Thus the foundations of magical belief and practice are not taken from the air, but are due to a number of experiences actually lived through, in which man receives the revelation of his power to attain the desired end. We must now ask: What is the relation between the promises contained in such experience and their fulfillment in real life? Plausible though the fallacious claims of magic might be to primitive man, how is it that they have remained so long unexposed?

The answer to this is that, first, it is a well-known fact that in human memory the testimony of a positive case always overshadows the negative one. One gain easily outweighs several losses. Thus the instances which affirm magic always loom far more conspicuously than those which deny it. But there are other facts which endorse by a real or apparent testimony the claims of magic. We have seen that magical ritual must have originated from a revelation in a real experience. But the man who from such an experience conceived, formulated, and gave to his tribesmen the nucleus of a new magical performance—acting, be it remembered, in perfect good faith—must have been a man of genius. The men who inherited and wielded his magic after him, no doubt always building it out and developing it, while believing that they were simply following up the tradition, must have been always men of great intelligence, energy, and power of enterprise. They would be the men successful in all emergencies. It is an empirical fact that in all savage societies magic and outstanding personality go hand in hand. Thus magic also coincides with personal success, skill, courage, and mental power. No wonder that it is considered a source of success.

This personal renown of the magician and its importance in enhancing the belief about the efficiency of magic are the cause of an interesting phenomenon: what may be called the *current mythology* of magic. Round every big magician there arises a halo made up of stories about his wonderful cures or kills, his catches, his victories, his conquests in love. In every savage society such stories form the backbone of belief in magic, for, supported as they are by the emotional experiences which everyone has had himself, the running chronicle of magical miracles establishes its claims beyond any doubt or cavil. Every eminent practitioner, besides his traditional claim, besides the filiation with his predecessors, makes his personal warrant of wonder-working.

Thus myth is not a dead product of past ages, merely surviving as an idle narrative. It is a living force, constantly producing new phenomena, constantly surrounding magic by new testimonies. Magic moves in the glory of past tradition, but it also creates its atmosphere of ever-nascent myth. As there is the body of legends already fixed, standardized, and constituting the folklore of the tribe, so there is always a stream of narratives in kind to those of the mythological time. Magic is the bridge between the golden age of primeval craft and the wonder-working power of to-day. Hence the formulas are full of mythical allusions, which, when uttered, unchain the powers of the past and cast them into the present.

With this we see also the role and meaning of mythology in a new light. Myth is not a savage speculation about origins of things born out of philosophic interest. Neither is it the result of the contemplation of nature—a sort of symbolical representation of its laws. It is the historical statement of one of those events which once for all vouch for the truth of a certain form of magic. Sometimes it is the actual record of a magical revelation coming directly from the first man to whom magic was revealed in some dramatic occurrence. More often it bears on its surface that it is merely a statement of how magic came into the possession of a clan or a community or a tribe. In all cases it is a warrant of its truth, a pedigree of its filiation, a charter of its claims to validity. And as we have seen, myth is the natural result of human faith, because every power must give signs of its efficiency, must act and be known to act, if people are to believe in its virtue. Every belief engenders its mythology, for there is no faith without miracles, and the main myth recounts simply the primeval miracle of the magic.

Myth, it may be added at once, can attach itself not only to magic but to any form of social power or social claim. It is used always to account for extraordinary privileges or duties, for great social inequalities, for severe burdens of rank, whether this be very high or very low. Also the beliefs and powers of religion are traced to their sources by mythological accounts. Religious myth, however, is rather an explicit dogma, the belief in the nether world, in creation, in the nature of divinities, spun out into a story. Sociological myth, on the other hand, especially in primitive cultures, is usually blended with legends about the sources of magical power. It can be said without exaggeration that the most typical, most highly developed, mythology in primitive societies is that of magic, and the function of myth is not to explain but to vouch for, not to satisfy curiosity but to give confidence in power, not to spin out yarns but to establish the flowing freely from present-day occurrences, frequently similar validity of belief. The deep connection between myth and cult, the pragmatic function of myth in enforcing belief, has been so persistently overlooked in favor of the etiological or explanatory theory of myth that it was necessary to dwell on this point.

5. MAGIC AND SCIENCE   We have had to make a digression on mythology since we found that myth is engendered by the real or imaginary success of witchcraft. But what about its failures? With all the strength which magic draws from the spontaneous belief and spontaneous ritual of intense desire or thwarted emotion, with all the force given it by the personal prestige, the social power and success common in the magician and practitioner—still there are failures and breakdowns, and we should vastly underrate the savage's intelligence, logic, and grasp of experience if we assumed that he is not aware of it and that he fails to account for it.

First of all, magic is surrounded by strict conditions: exact remembrance of a spell, unimpeachable performance of the rite, unswerving adhesion to the taboos and observances which shackle the magician. If any one of these is neglected, failure of magic follows. And then, even if magic be done in the most perfect manner, its effects can be equally well undone: for against every magic there can be also counter-magic. If magic, as we have shown, is begotten by the union of man's steadfast desire with the wayward whim of chance, then every desire, positive or negative, may—nay, must—have its magic. Now in all his social and worldly ambitions, in all his strivings to catch good fortune and trap propitious luck, man moves in an atmosphere of rivalry, of envy, and of spite. For luck, possessions, even health, are matters of degree and of comparison, and if your neighbor owns more cattle, more wives, more health, and more power than yourself, you feel dwarfed in all you own and all you are. And such is human nature that a man's desire is as much satisfied by the thwarting of others as by the advancement of himself. To this sociological play of desire and counter-desire, of ambition and spite, of success and envy, there corresponds the play of magic and counter-magic, or of magic white and black.

In Melanesia, where I have studied this problem at first-hand, there is not one single magical act which is not firmly believed to possess a counter-act which, when stronger, can completely annihilate its effects. In certain types of magic, as for instance, that of health and disease, the formulas actually go in couples. A sorcerer who learns a performance by which to cause a definite disease will at the same time learn the formula and the rite which can annul completely the effects of his evil magic. In love, again, not only does there exist a belief that, when two formulas are performed to win the same heart, the stronger will override the weaker one, but there are spells uttered directly to alienate the affections of the sweetheart or wife of another. Whether this duality of magic is as consistently carried out all the world over as in the Trobriands it is difficult to say, but that the twin forces of white and black, of positive and negative, exist everywhere is beyond doubt. Thus the failures of magic can always be accounted for by the slip of memory, by slovenliness in performance or in observance of a taboo, and, last not least, by the fact that someone else has performed some counter-magic.

We are now in a position to state more fully the relation between magic and science already outlined above. Magic is akin to science in that it always has a definite aim intimately associated with human instincts, needs, and pursuits. The magic art is directed towards the attainment of practical aims. Like the other arts and crafts, it is also governed by a theory, by a system of principles which dictate the manner in which the act has to be performed in order to be effective. In analyzing magical spells, rites, and substances we have found that there are a number of general principles which govern them. Both science and magic develop a special technique. In magic, as in the other arts, man can undo what he has done or mend the damage which he has wrought. In fact, in magic, the quantitive equivalents of black and white seem to be much more exact and the effects of witchcraft much more completely eradicated by counter-witchcraft than is possible in any practical art or craft. Thus both magic and science show certain similarities, and, with Sir James Frazer, we can appropriately call magic a pseudo-science.

And the spurious character of this pseudo-science is not hard to detect. Science, even as represented by the primitive knowledge of savage man, is based on the normal universal experience of everyday life, experience won in man's struggle with nature for his subsistence and safety, founded on observation, fixed by reason. Magic is based on specific experience of emotional states in which man observes not nature but himself, in which the truth is revealed not by reason but by the play of emotions upon the human organism. Science is founded on the conviction that experience, effort, and reason are valid; magic on the belief that hope cannot fail nor desire deceive. The theories of knowledge are dictated by logic, those of magic by the association of ideas under the influence of desire. As a matter of empirical fact the body of rational knowledge and the body of magical lore are incorporated each in a different tradition, in a different social setting and in a different type of activity, and all these differences are clearly recognized by the savages. The one constitutes the domain of the profane; the other, hedged round by observances, mysteries, and taboos, makes up half of the domain of the sacred.

6. MAGIC AND RELIGION   Both magic and religion arise and function in situations of emotional stress: crises of life, lacunae in important pursuits, death and initiation into tribal mysteries, unhappy love and unsatisfied hate. Both magic and religion open up escapes from such situations and such impasses as offer no empirical way out except by ritual and belief into the domain of the supernatural. This domain embraces, in religion, beliefs in ghosts, spirits, the primitive forebodings of providence, the guardians of tribal mysteries; in magic, the primeval force and virtue of magic. Both magic and religion are based strictly on mythological tradition, and they also both exist in the atmosphere of the miraculous, in a constant revelation of their wonder-

working power. They both are surrounded by taboos and observances which mark off their acts from those of the profane world.

Now what distinguishes magic from religion? We have taken for our starting-point a most definite and tangible distinction: we have defined, within the domain of the sacred, magic as a practical art consisting of acts which are only means to a definite end expected to follow later on; religion as a body of self-contained acts being themselves the fulfillment of their purpose. We can now follow up this difference into its deeper layers. The practical art of magic has its limited, circumscribed technique: spell, rite, and the condition of the performer form always its trite trinity. Religion, with its complex aspects and purposes, has no such simple technique, and its unity can be seen neither in the form of its acts nor even in the uniformity of its subject matter, but rather in the function which it fulfills and in the value of its belief and ritual. Again, the belief in magic, corresponding to its plain practical nature, is extremely simple. It is always the affirmation of man's power to cause certain definite effects by a definite spell and rite. In religion, on the other hand, we have a whole supernatural world of faith: the pantheon of spirits and demons, the benevolent powers of totem, guardian spirit, tribal all-father, the vision of the future life, create a second supernatural reality for primitive man. The mythology of religion is also more varied and complex as well as more creative. It usually centers round the various tenets of belief, and it develops them into cosmogonies, tales of culture heroes, accounts of the doings of gods and demigods. In magic, important as it is, mythology is an ever-recurrent boasting about man's primeval achievements.

Magic, the specific art for specific ends, has in every one of its forms come once into the possession of man, and it had to be handed over in direct filiation from generation to generation. Hence it remains from the earliest times in the hands of specialists, and the first profession of mankind is that of a wizard or witch. Religion, on the other hand, in primitive conditions is an affair of all, in which everyone takes an active and equivalent part. Every member of the tribe has to go through initiation, and then himself initiates others. Everyone wails, mourns, digs the grave and commemorates, and in due time everyone has his turn in being mourned and commemorated. Spirits are for all, and everyone becomes a spirit. The only specialization in religion—that is, early spiritualistic mediumism—is not a profession but a personal gift. One more difference between magic and religion is the play of black and white in witchcraft, while religion in its primitive stages has but little of the contrast between good and evil, between the beneficent and malevolent powers. This is due also to the practical character of magic, which aims at direct quantitative results, while early religion, though essentially moral, has to deal with fateful, irremediable happenings and supernatural forces and beings, so that the undoing of things done by man does not enter into it. The maxim that fear first made gods in the universe is certainly not true in the light of anthropology.

In order to grasp the difference between religion and magic and to gain a clear vision of the three-cornered constellation of magic, religion, and science, let us briefly realize the cultural function of each. The function of primitive knowledge and its value have been assessed already and indeed are not difficult to grasp. By acquainting man with his surroundings, by allowing him to use the forces of nature, science, primitive knowledge, bestows on man an immense biological advantage, setting him far above all the rest of creation. The function of religion and its value we have learned to understand in the survey of savage creeds and cults given above. We have shown there that religious faith establishes, fixes, and enhances all valuable mental attitudes, such as reverence for tradition, harmony with environment, courage and confidence in the struggle with difficulties and at the prospect of death. This belief, embodied and maintained by cult and ceremonial, has an immense biological value, and so reveals to primitive man truth in the wider, pragmatic sense of the word.

What is the cultural function of magic? We have seen that all the instincts and emotions, all practical activities, lead man into impasses where gaps in his knowledge and the limitations of his early power of observation and reason betray him at a crucial moment. Human organism reacts to this in spontaneous outbursts, in which rudimentary modes of behavior and rudimentary beliefs in their efficiency are engendered. Magic fixes upon these beliefs and rudimentary rites and standardizes them into permanent traditional forms. Thus magic supplies primitive man with a number of ready-made ritual acts and beliefs, with a definite mental and practical technique which serves to bridge over the dangerous gaps in every important pursuit or critical situation. It enables man to carry out with confidence his important tasks, to maintain his poise and his mental integrity in fits of anger, in the throes of hate, of unrequited love, of despair and anxiety. The function of magic is to ritualize man's optimism, to enhance his faith in the victory of hope over fear. Magic expresses the greater value for man of confidence over doubt, of steadfastness over vacillation, of optimism over pessimism.

Looking from far and above, from our high places of safety in developed civilization, it is easy to see all the crudity and irrelevance of magic. But without its power and guidance early man could not have mastered his practical difficulties as he has done, nor could man have advanced to the higher stages of culture. Hence the universal occurrence of magic in primitive societies and its enormous sway. Hence do we find magic an invariable adjunct of all important activities. I think we must see in it the embodiment of the sublime folly of hope, which has yet been the best school of man's character.[1]

[1] *Bibliographical Note.* The most important works on Primitive Religion, Magic and Knowledge, referred to in the text, directly or implicitly, are: E. B. Tylor, *Primitive Culture*, 4th ed., 2 vols., 1903; J. F. McLennan, *Studies in*

Ancient History, 1886; W. Robertson Smith, *Lectures on the Religion of the Semites*, 1889; A. Lang, *The Making of Religion*, 1889, and *Magic and Religion*, 1901. These, though out of date as regards material and some of their conclusions, are still inspiring and deserve study. Entirely fresh and representing the most modern points of view are the classical works of J. G. Frazer, *The Golden Bough*, 3rd ed., in 12 vols., 1911–14 (also abridged edition, 1 vol.) *Totemism and Exogamy*, 4 vols., 1910; *Folk-Lore in the Old Testament*, 3 vols., 1919; *The Belief in Immortality and the Worship of the Dead*, so far 3 vols., 1913–24. With Frazer's works should be read the two excellent contributions of E. Crawley, *The Mystic Rose*, 1902 (out of print, new edition forthcoming), and *The Tree of Life*, 1905. Also on the subject of the history of morals, the two extremely important works: E. Westermarck, *The Origin and Development of the Moral Ideas*, 2 vols., 1905, and L. T. Hobhouse, *Morals in Evolution*, 2nd ed., 1915. Further: D. G. Brinton, *Religions of Primitive Peoples*, 1899; K. Th. Preuss, *Der Ursprung der Religion und Kunst*, 1904 (in "Globus," serially); R. R. Marett, *The Threshold of Religion*, 1909; H. Hubert et M. Mauss, *Mélanges d'histoire des religions*, 1909; A. van Gennep, *Les Rites de passage*, 1909; J. Harrison, *Themis* 1910–12; I. King, *The Development of Religion*, 1910; W. Schmidt, *Der Ursprung der Gottesidee*, 1912; E. Durkheim, *Les Formes élementaires de la Vie religieuse*, 1912 (also English translation); P. Ehrenreich, *Die Allgemeine Mythologie*, 1910; R. H. Lowie, *Primitive Religion*, 1925. An encyclopedic survey of facts and opinions will be found in Wilh. Wundt's voluminous *Volkerpsychologie*, 1904 ff.; J. Hastings' *Encyclopedia of Religion and Ethics* is excellent and indispensable to the serious student. Primitive Knowledge in particular is discussed by Lévy-Bruhl in *Les fonctions mentales dans les sociétés inférieures*, 1910; F. Boas, *The Mind of Primitive Man*, 1910; R. Thurnwald, *Psychologie des Primitiven Menschen*, in the *Handbuch der vergl. Psychol.*, edited by G. Kafka, 1922; A. A. Goldenwasser, *Early Civilization*, 1923. Cf. also R. H. Lowie, *Primitive Society*, 1920; and A. L. Kroeber, *Anthropology*, 1923. For fuller information upon the natives of Melanesia, who loom largely in the foregoing descriptions, cf. R. H. Codrington, *The Melanesians*, 1891; C. G. Seligman, *The Melanesians of British New Guinea*, 1910; R. Thurnwald, *Forschungen auf den Solominseln und Bismarckarchipel*, 2 vols., 1912, and *Die Gemeinde der Bánaro*, 1921; B. Malinowski, *The*

Natives of Mailu, 1915 (in Trans. of the R. Soc. of S. Australia, vol. xxxix); *Baloma,* article in the Journ. of the R. Anthrop. Institute, 1916; *Argonauts of the Western Pacific,* 1922; and three articles in *Psyche*, III., 2; IV., 4; V., 3, 1923–5.

Myth in Primitive Psychology

DEDICATION TO SIR JAMES FRAZER If I had the power of evoking the past, I should like to lead you back some twenty years to an old Slavonic university town—I mean the town of Cracow, the ancient capital of Poland and the seat of the oldest university in eastern Europe. I could then show you a student leaving the medieval college buildings, obviously in some distress of mind, hugging, however, under his arm, as the only solace of his troubles, three green volumes with the well-known golden imprint, a beautiful conventional-ized design of mistletoe—the symbol of *The Golden Bough*.

I had just then been ordered to abandon for a time my physical and chemical research because of ill-health, but I was allowed to follow up a favorite side line of study, and I decided to make my first attempt to read an English masterpiece in the original. Perhaps my mental distress would have been lessened, had I been allowed to look into the future and to foresee the present occasion, on which I have the great privilege of delivering an address in honor of Sir James Frazer to a distinguished audience, in the language of *The Golden Bough* itself.

For no sooner had I begun to read this great work, than I became immersed in it and enslaved by it. I realized then that anthropology, as presented by Sir James Frazer, is a great science, worthy of as much devotion as any of her elder and more exact sister studies, and I became bound to the service of Frazerian anthropology.

We are gathered here to celebrate the annual totemic festival of *The Golden Bough*; to revive and strengthen the bonds of anthropological union; to commune with the source and symbol of our anthropological interest and affection. I am but your humble spokesman, in expressing our joint admiration to the great writer and his classical works; *The Golden Bough, Totemism and Exogamy, Folklore in the Old Testament, Psyche's Task,* and *The Belief in Immortality.* As a true officiating magician in a savage tribe would have to do, I have to recite the whole list, so that the spirit of the works (their 'mana') may dwell among us.

In all this, my task is pleasant and in a way easy, for implicit in whatever I may say is a tribute to him, whom I have always regarded as the 'Master.' On the other hand this very circumstance also makes my task difficult, for having received so much, I fear I may not have enough to show in return. I have therefore decided to keep my peace even while I am addressing you—to let another one speak through my mouth, another one who has been to Sir James Frazer an inspiration and a lifelong friend, as Sir James has been to us. This other one, I need hardly tell you, is the modern representative of primitive man, the contemporary savage, whose thoughts, whose feelings, whose very life breath pervades all that Frazer has written.

In other words, I shall not try to serve up any theories of my own, but instead I shall lay before you some results of my anthropological field work, carried out in northwest

Melanesia. I shall restrict myself, moreover, to a subject upon which Sir James Frazer has not directly concentrated his attention, but in which, as I shall try to show you, his influence is as fruitful as in those many subjects that he has made his own.

[The above formed the opening passages of an address delivered in honor of Sir James Frazer at the University of Liverpool, in November, 1925.]

By the examination of a typical Melanesian culture and by a survey of the opinions, traditions, and behavior of these natives, I propose to show how deeply the sacred tradition, the myth, enters into their pursuits, and how strongly it controls their moral and social behavior. In other words, the thesis of the present work is that an intimate connection exists between the word, the mythos, the sacred tales of a tribe, on the one hand, and their ritual acts, their moral deeds, their social organization, and even their practical activities, on the other.

In order to gain a background for our description of the Melanesian facts, I shall briefly summarize the present state of the science of mythology. Even a superficial survey of the literature would reveal that there is no monotony to complain of as regards the variety of opinions or the acrimony of polemics. To take only the recent up-to-date theories advanced in explanation of the nature of myth, legend, and fairy tale, we should have to head the list, at least as regards output and self-assertion, by the so-called school of Nature-mythology which flourishes mainly in Germany. The writers of this school maintain that primitive man is highly interested in natural phenomena, and that his interest is predominantly of a theoretical, contemplative, and poetical character. In trying to express and interpret the phases of the moon, or the regular and yet changing path of the sun across the skies, primitive man constructs symbolic personified rhapsodies. To writers of this school every myth possesses as its kernel or ultimate reality some natural phenomenon or other, elaborately woven into a tale to an extent which sometimes almost masks and obliterates it. There is not much agreement among these students as to what type of natural phenomenon lies at the bottom of most mythological productions. There are extreme lunar mythologists so completely moonstruck with their idea that they will not admit that any other phenomenon could lend itself to a savage rhapsodic interpretation except that of earth's nocturnal satellite. The Society for the Comparative Study of Myth, founded in Berlin in 1906, and counting among its supporters such famous scholars as Ehrenreich, Siecke, Winckler, and many others, carried on their business under the sign of the moon. Others, like Frobenius for instance, regard the sun as the only subject around which primitive man has spun his symbolic tales. Then there is the school of meteorological interpreters who regard wind, weather, and colors of the skies as the essence of myth. To this belonged such well-known writers of the older generation as Max Müller and Kuhn. Some of these departmental mythologists fight fiercely for their heavenly body or principle; others have a more catholic taste, and prepare to agree that primeval man has made his mythological brew from all the heavenly bodies taken together.

I have tried to state fairly and plausibly this naturalistic interpretation of myths, but as a matter of fact this theory seems to me to be one of the most extravagant views ever advanced by an anthropologist or humanist—and that means a great deal. It has received an absolutely destructive criticism from the great psychologist Wundt, and appears absolutely untenable in the light of any of Sir James Frazer's writings. From my own study of living myths among savages, I should say that primitive man has to a very limited extent the purely artistic or scientific interest in nature; there is but little room for symbolism in his ideas and tales; and myth, in fact, is not an idle rhapsody, not an aimless outpouring of vain imaginings, but a hard-working, extremely important cultural force. Besides ignoring the cultural function of myth, this theory imputes to primitive man a number of imaginary interests, and it confuses several clearly distinguishable types of story, the fairy tale, the legend, the saga, and the sacred tale or myth.

In strong contrast to this theory which makes myth naturalistic, symbolic, and imaginary, stands the theory which regards a sacred tale as a true historical record of the past. This view, recently supported by the so-called Historical School in Germany and America, and represented in England by Dr. Rivers, covers but part of the truth. There is no denying that history, as well as natural environment, must have left a profound imprint on all cultural achievements, hence also on myths. But to take all mythology as mere chronicle is as incorrect as to regard it as the primitive naturalist's musings. It also endows primitive man with a sort of scientific impulse and desire for knowledge. Although the savage has something of the antiquarian as well as of the naturalist in his composition, he is, above all, actively engaged in a number of practical pursuits, and has to struggle with various difficulties; all his interests are tuned up to this general pragmatic outlook. Mythology, the sacred lore of the tribe, is, as we shall see, a powerful means of assisting primitive man, of allowing him to make the two ends of his cultural patrimony meet. We shall see, moreover, that the immense services to primitive culture performed by myth are done in connection with religious ritual, moral influence, and sociological principle. Now religion and morals draw only to a very limited extent upon an interest in science or in past history, and myth is thus based upon an entirely different mental attitude.

The close connection between religion and myth which has been overlooked by many students has been recognized by others. Psychologists like Wundt, sociologists like Durkheim, Hubert, and Mauss, anthropologists like Crawley, classical scholars like Miss Jane Harrison have all understood the intimate association between myth and ritual, between sacred tradition and the norms of social structure. All of these writers have been to a greater or lesser extent influenced by the work of Sir James Frazer. In spite of the fact that the great British anthropologist, as well as most of his followers, have a clear vision of the sociological and ritual importance of myth, the facts which I shall present will allow us to clarify and formulate more precisely the main principles of a sociological theory of myth.

I might present an even more extensive survey of the opinions, divisions, and controversies of learned mythologists. The science of mythology has been the meeting point of various scholarships: the classical humanist must decide for himself whether Zeus is the moon, or the sun, or a strictly historical personality; and whether his ox-eyed spouse is the morning star, or a cow, or a personification of the wind—the loquacity of wives being proverbial. Then all these questions have to be rediscussed upon the stage of mythology by the various tribes of archaeologists, Chaldean and Egyptian, Indian and Chinese, Peruvian and Mayan. The historian and the sociologist, the student of literature, the grammarian, the Germanist and the Romanist, the Celtic scholar and the Slavist discuss, each little crowd among themselves. Nor is mythology quite safe from logicians and psychologists, from the metaphysician and the epistemologist—to say nothing of such visitors as the theosophist, the modern astrologist, and the Christian Scientist. Finally, we have the psychoanalyst who has come at last to teach us that the myth is a daydream of the race, and that we can only explain it by turning our back upon nature, history, and culture, and diving deep into the dark pools of the subconscious, where at the bottom there lie the usual paraphernalia and symbols of psychoanalytic exegesis. So that when at last the poor anthropologist and student of folklore come to the feast, there are hardly any crumbs left for them!

If I have conveyed an impression of chaos and confusion, if I have inspired a sinking feeling towards the incredible mythological controversy with all the dust and din which it raises, I have achieved exactly what I wanted. For I shall invite my readers to step outside the closed study of the theorist into the open air of the anthropological field, and to follow me in my mental flight back to the years which I spent among a Melanesian tribe of New Guinea. There, paddling on the lagoon, watching the natives under the blazing sun at their garden work, following them through the patches of jungle, and on the winding beaches and reefs, we shall learn about their life. And again, observing their ceremonies in the cool of the afternoon or in the shadows of the evening, sharing their meals round their fires, we shall be able to listen to their stories.

For the anthropologist—one and only among the many participants in the mythological contest—has the unique advantage of being able to step back behind the savage whenever he feels that his theories become involved and the flow of his argumentative eloquence runs dry. The anthropologist is not bound to the scanty remnants of culture, broken tablets, tarnished texts, or fragmentary inscriptions. He need not fill out immense gaps with voluminous, but conjectural, comments. The anthropologist has the myth-maker at his elbow. Not only can he take down as full a text as exists, with all its variations, and control it over and over; he has also a host of authentic commentators to draw upon; still more he has the fullness of life itself from which the myth has been born. And as we shall see, in this live context there is as much to be learned about the myth as in the narrative itself.

Myth as it exists in a savage community, that is, in its living primitive form, is not merely a story told but a reality lived. It is not of the nature of fiction, such as we read today in a novel, but it is a living reality, believed to have once happened in primeval times, and continuing ever since to influence the world and human destinies. This myth is to the savage what, to a fully believing Christian, is the Biblical story of Creation, of the Fall, of the Redemption by Christ's Sacrifice on the Cross. As our sacred story lives in our ritual, in our morality, as it governs our faith and controls our conduct, even so does his myth for the savage.

The limitation of the study of myth to the mere examination of texts has been fatal to a proper understanding of its nature. The forms of myth which come to us from classical antiquity and from the ancient sacred books of the East and other similar sources have come down to us without the context of living faith, without the possibility of obtaining comments from true believers, without the concomitant knowledge of their social organization, their practiced morals, and their popular customs—at least without the full information which the modern fieldworker can easily obtain. Moreover, there is no doubt that in their present literary form these tales have suffered a very considerable transformation at the hands of scribes, commentators, learned priests, and theologians. It is necessary to go back to primitive mythology in order to learn the secret of its life in the study of a myth which is still alive—before, mummified in priestly wisdom, it has been enshrined in the indestructible but lifeless repository of dead religions.

Studied alive, myth, as we shall see, is not symbolic, but a direct expression of its subject matter; it is not an explanation in satisfaction of a scientific interest, but a narrative resurrection of a primeval reality, told in satisfaction of deep religious wants, moral cravings, social submissions, assertions, even practical requirements. Myth fulfills in primitive culture an indispensable function: it expresses, enhances, and codifies belief; it safeguards and enforces morality; it vouches for the efficiency of ritual and contains practical rules for the guidance of man. Myth is thus a vital ingredient of human civilization; it is not an idle tale, but a hard-worked active force; it is not an intellectual explanation or an artistic imagery, but a pragmatic charter of primitive faith and moral wisdom.

I shall try to prove all these contentions by the study of various myths; but to make our analysis conclusive it will first be necessary to give an account not merely of myth, but also of fairy tale, legend, and historical record.

Let us then float over in spirit to the shores of a Trobriand[1] lagoon, and penetrate into the life of the natives

[1] The Trobriand Islands are a coral archipelago lying to the northeast of New Guinea. The natives belong to the Papuo-Melanesian race, and in their physical appearance, mental equipment, and social organization they show a combination of the Oceanic characteristics mixed with some features of the more backward Papuan culture from the mainland of New Guinea.

For a full account of the Northern Massim, of which the Trobrianders form a section, see the classical treatise of

—see them at work, see them at play, and listen to their stories. Late in November the wet weather is setting in. There is little to do in the gardens, the fishing season is not in full swing as yet, overseas sailing looms ahead in the future, while the festive mood still lingers after the harvest dancing and feasting. Sociability is in the air, time lies on their hands, while bad weather keeps them often at home. Let us step through the twilight of the approaching evening into one of their villages and sit at the fireside, where the flickering light draws more and more people as the evening falls and the conversation brightens. Sooner or later a man will be asked to tell a story, for this is the season of *fairy tales*. If he is a good reciter, he will soon provoke laughter, rejoinders, and interruptions, and his tale will develop into a regular performance.

At this time of the year folk tales of a special type called *kukwanebu* are habitually recited in the villages. There is a vague belief, not very seriously taken, that their recital has has a beneficial influence on the new crops recently planted in the gardens. In order to produce this effect, a short ditty in which an allusion is made to some very fertile wild plants, the *kasiyena*, must always be recited at the end.

Every story is 'owned' by a member of the community. Each story, though known by many, may be recited only by the 'owner'; he may, however, present it to someone else by teaching that person and authorizing him to retell it. But not all the 'owners' know how to thrill and to raise a hearty laugh, which is one of the main ends of such stories. A good raconteur has to change his voice in the dialogue, chant the ditties with due temperament, gesticulate, and in general play to the gallery. Some of these tales are certainly 'smoking-room' stories, of others I will give one or two examples.

Professor C. G. Seligman, *Melanesians of British New Guinea* (Cambridge, 1910). This book shows also the relation of the Trobrianders to the other races and cultures on and around New Guinea. A short account will also be found in *Argonauts of the Western Pacific*, by the present author (London, 1922).

Thus there is the maiden in distress and the heroic rescue. Two women go out in search of birds' eggs. One discovers a nest under a tree, the other warns her: "These are eggs of a snake, don't touch them." "Oh, no! They are eggs of a bird," she replies and carries them away. The mother snake comes back, and finding the nest empty starts in search of the eggs. She enters the nearest village and sings a ditty:—

"I wend my way as I wriggle along,
The eggs of a bird it is licit to eat;
The eggs of a friend are forbidden to touch."

This journey lasts long, for the snake is traced from one village to the other and everywhere has to sing her ditty. Finally, entering the village of the two women, she sees the culprit roasting the eggs, coils around her, and enters her body. The victim is laid down helpless and ailing. But the hero is nigh; a man from a neighboring village dreams of the dramatic situation, arrives on the spot, pulls out the snake, cuts it to pieces, and marries both women, thus carrying off a double prize for his prowess.

In another story we learn of a happy family, a father and two daughters, who sail from their home in the northern coral archipelagoes, and run to the southwest till they come to the wild steep slopes of the rock island Gumasila. The father lies down on a platform and falls asleep. An ogre comes out of the jungle, eats the father, captures and ravishes one of the daughters, while the other succeeds in escaping. The sister from the woods supplies the captive one with a piece of lawyer cane, and when the ogre lies down and falls asleep they cut him in half and escape.

A woman lives in the village of Okopukopu at the head of a creek with her five children. A monstrously big stingaree paddles up the creek, flops across the village, enters the hut, and to the tune of a ditty cuts off the woman's finger. One son tries to kill the monster and fails. Every day the same performance is repeated till on the fifth day the youngest son succeeds in killing the giant fish.

A louse and a butterfly embark on a bit of aviation, the louse as a passenger, the butterfly as aeroplane and pilot. In the middle of the performance, while flying overseas just between the beach of Wawela and the island of Kitava, the louse emits a loud shriek, the butterfly is shaken, and the louse falls off and is drowned.

A man whose mother-in-law is a cannibal is sufficiently careless to go away and leave her in charge of his three children. Naturally she tries to eat them; they escape in time, however, climb a palm, and keep her (through a somewhat lengthy story) at bay, until the father arrives and kills her. There is another story about a visit to the Sun, another about an ogre devastating gardens, another about a woman who was so greedy that she stole all food at funeral distributions, and many similar ones.

In this place, however, we are not so much concentrating our attention on the text of the narratives, as on their socio-logical reference. The text, of course, is extremely impor-tant, but without the context it remains lifeless. As we have seen, the interest of the story is vastly enhanced and it is given its proper character by the manner in which it is told. The whole nature of the performance, the voice and the mimicry, the stimulus and the response of the audience mean as much to the natives as the text; and the sociologist should take his cue from the natives. The performance, again, has to be placed in its proper time setting—the hour of the day, and the season, with the background of the sprouting gardens awaiting future work, and slightly in-fluenced by the magic of the fairy tales. We must also bear in mind the sociological context of private ownership, the sociable function and the cultural role of amusing fiction. All these elements are equally relevant; all must be studied as well as the text. The stories live in native life and not on paper, and when a scholar jots them down without being able to evoke the atmosphere in which they flourish he has given us but a mutilated bit of reality.

I pass now to another class of stories. These have no spe-cial season, there is no stereotyped way of telling them, and the recital has not the character of a performance, nor has it any magical effect. And yet these tales are more important than the foregoing class; for they are believed to be true, and the information which they contain is both more valuable and more relevant than that of the *kukwanebu*. When a party goes on a distant visit or sails on an expedition, the younger members, keenly interested in the landscape, in new communities, in new people, and perhaps even new customs, will express their wonder and make inquiries. The older and more experienced will supply them with information and comment, and this always takes the form of a concrete narrative. An old man will perhaps tell his own experiences about fights and expeditions, about famous magic and extraordinary economic achievements. With this he may mix the reminiscences of his father, hearsay tales and legends, which have passed through many generations. Thus memories of great droughts and devastating famines are conserved for many years, together with the descriptions of the hardships, struggles, and crimes of the exasperated population.

A number of stories about sailors driven out of their course and landing among cannibals and hostile tribes are remembered, some of them set to song, others formed into historic legends. A famous subject for song and story is the charm, skill, and performance of famous dancers. There are tales about distant volcanic islands; about hot springs in which once a party of unwary bathers were boiled to death; about mysterious countries inhabited by entirely different men or women; about strange adventures which have happened to sailors in distant seas; monstrous fish and octopi, jumping rocks and disguised sorcerers. Stories again are told, some recent, some ancient, about seers and visitors to the land of the dead, enumerating their most famous and significant exploits. There are also stories associated with natural phenomena; a petrified canoe, a man changed into a rock, and a red patch on the coral rock left by a party who ate too much betel nut.

We have here a variety of tales which might be subdivided into *historical accounts* directly witnessed by the narrator, or at least vouched for by someone within living memory; *legends,* in which the continuity of testimony is broken, but which fall within the range of things ordinarily experienced by the tribesmen; and *hearsay tales* about distant countries and ancient happenings of a time which falls outside the range of present-day culture. To the natives, however, all these classes imperceptibly shade into each other; they are designated by the same name, *libwogwo;* they are all regarded as true; they are not recited as a performance, nor told for amusement at a special season. Their subject matter also shows a substantial unity. They all refer to subjects intensely stimulating to the natives; they all are connected with activities such as economic pursuits, warfare, adventure, success in dancing and in ceremonial exchange. Moreover, since they record singularly great achievements in all such pursuits, they redound to the credit of some individual and his descendants or of a whole community; and hence they are kept alive by the ambition of those whose ancestry they glorify. The stories told in explanation of peculiarities of features of the landscape frequently have a sociological context, that is, they enumerate whose clan or family performed the deed. When this is not the case, they are isolated fragmentary comments upon some natural feature, clinging to it as an obvious survival.

In all this it is once more clear that we can neither fully grasp the meaning of the text, nor the sociological nature of the story, nor the natives' attitude towards it and interest in it, if we study the narrative on paper. These tales live in the memory of man, in the way in which they are told, and even more in the complex interest which keeps them alive, which makes the narrator recite with pride or regret, which makes the listener follow eagerly, wistfully, with hopes and ambitions roused. Thus the essence of a *legend,* even more than that of a *fairy tale,* is not to be found in a mere perusal of the story, but in the combined study of the narrative and its context in the social and cultural life of the natives.

But it is only when we pass to the third and most important class of tales, the *sacred tales* or *myths*, and contrast them with the legends, that the nature of all three classes comes into relief. This third class is called by the natives *liliu*, and I want to emphasize that I am reproducing prima facie the natives' own classification and nomenclature, and limiting myself to a few comments on its accuracy. The third class of stories stands very much apart from the other two. If the first are told for amusement, the second to make a serious statement and satisfy social ambition, the third are regarded, not merely as true, but as venerable and sacred, and they play a highly important cultural part. The *folk tale*, as we know, is a seasonal performance and an act of sociability. The *legend*, provoked by contact with unusual reality, opens up past historical vistas. The *myth* comes into play when rite, ceremony, or a social or moral rule demands justification, warrant of antiquity, reality, and sanctity.

In the subsequent chapters of this book we will examine a number of myths in detail, but for the moment let us glance at the subjects of some typical myths. Take, for instance, the annual feast of the return of the dead. Elaborate arrangements are made for it, especially an enormous display of food. When this feast approaches, tales are told of how death began to chastise man, and how the power of eternal rejuvenation was lost. It is told why the spirits have to leave the village and do not remain at the fireside, finally why they return once in a year. Again, at certain seasons in preparation for an overseas expedition, canoes are overhauled and new ones built to the accompaniment of a special magic. In this there are mythological allusions in the spells, and even the sacred acts contain elements which are only comprehensible when the story of the flying canoe, its ritual, and its magic are told. In connection with ceremonial trading, the rules, the magic, even the geographical routes are associated with corresponding mythology. There is no important magic, no ceremony, no ritual without belief; and the belief is spun out into accounts of concrete precedent. The union is very intimate, for myth is not only looked upon as a commentary of additional information, but it is a warrant, a charter, and often even a practical guide to the activities with which it is connected. On the other hand the rituals, ceremonies, customs, and social organization contain at times direct references to myth, and they are regarded as the results of mythical event. The cultural fact is a monument in which the myth is embodied; while the myth is believed to be the real cause which has brought about the moral rule, the social grouping, the rite, or the custom. Thus these stories form an integral part of culture. Their existence and influence not merely transcend the act of telling the narrative, not only do they draw their substance from life and its interests—they govern and control many cultural features, they form the dogmatic backbone of primitive civilization.

This is perhaps the most important point of the thesis which I am urging: I maintain that there exists a special class of stories, regarded as sacred, embodied in ritual, morals, and social organization, and which form an integral and active part of primitive culture. These stories live not by idle interest, not as fictitious or even as true narratives; but are to the natives a statement of a primeval, greater, and more relevant reality, by which the present life, fates, and activities of mankind are determined, the knowledge of which supplies man with the motive for ritual and moral actions, as well as with indications as to how to perform them.

In order to make the point at issue quite clear, let us once more compare our conclusions with the current views of modern anthropology, not in order idly to criticize other opinions, but so that we may link our results to the present state of knowledge, give due acknowledgment for what we have received, and state where we have to differ clearly and precisely.

It will be best to quote a condensed and authoritative statement, and I shall choose for this purpose of definition an analysis given in *Notes and Queries on Anthropology*, by the late Miss C. S. Burne and Professor J. L. Myres.

Under the heading "Stories, Sayings, and Songs," we are informed that "this section includes many *intellectual* efforts of peoples" which "represent the earliest attempt to exercise reason, imagination, and memory." With some apprehension we ask where is left the emotion, the interest, and ambition, the social role of all the stories, and the deep connection with cultural values of the more serious ones? After a brief classification of stories in the usual manner we read about the sacred tales: "*Myths* are stories which, however marvelous and improbable to us, are nevertheless related in all good faith, because they are intended, or believed by the teller, to explain by means of something concrete and intelligible an abstract idea or such vague and difficult conceptions as Creation, Death, distinctions of race or animal species, the different occupations of men and women; the origins of rites and customs, or striking natural objects or prehistoric monuments; the meaning of the names of persons or places. Such stories are sometimes described as *etiological*, because their purpose is to explain why something exists or happens." [2]

Here we have in a nutshell all that modern science at its best has to say upon the subject. Would our Melanesians agree, however, with this opinion? Certainly not. They do not want to 'explain,' to make 'intelligible' anything which happens in their myths—above all not an abstract idea. Of that there can be found to my knowledge no instance either in Melanesia or in any other savage community. The few abstract ideas which the natives possess carry their concrete commentary in the very word which expresses them. When being is described by verbs to lie, to sit, to stand, when cause and effect are expressed by words signifying foundation and the past standing upon it, when various concrete nouns tend towards the meaning of space, the word and the relation to concrete reality make the abstract idea sufficiently 'intelligible.' Nor would a Trobriander or any other native agree with the view that "Creation, Death, distinctions of race or

[2] Quoted from *Notes and Queries on Anthropology*, pp. 210 and 211.

animal species, the different occupations of men and
women" are "vague and difficult conceptions." Nothing is
more familiar to the native than the different occupations
of the male and female sex; there is nothing to be *explained*
about it. But though familiar, such differences are at times
irksome, unpleasant, or at least limiting, and there is the
need to justify them, to vouch for their antiquity and reality, in short to buttress their validity. Death, alas, is not
vague, or abstract, or difficult to grasp for any human being.
It is only too hauntingly real, too concrete, too easy to
comprehend for anyone who has had an experience affecting
his near relatives or a personal foreboding. If it were vague
or unreal, man would have no desire so much as to mention
it; but the idea of death is fraught with horror, with a desire
to remove its threat, with the vague hope that it may be,
not explained, but rather explained away, made unreal, and
actually denied. Myth, warranting the belief in immortality, in eternal youth, in a life beyond the grave, is not
an intellectual reaction upon a puzzle, but an explicit act
of faith born from the innermost instinctive and emotional
reaction to the most formidable and haunting idea. Nor are
the stories about "the origins of rites and customs" told
in mere explanation of them. They never explain in any
sense of the word; they always state a precedent which
constitutes an ideal and a warrant for its continuance, and
sometimes practical directions for the procedure.

We have, therefore, to disagree on every point with this
excellent though concise statement of present-day mythological opinion. This definition would create an imaginary,
non-existent class of narrative, the etiological myth, corresponding to a non-existent desire to explain, leading a
futile existence as an 'intellectual effort,' and remaining
outside native culture and social organization with their
pragmatic interests. The whole treatment appears to us
faulty, because myths are treated as mere stories, because
they are regarded as a primitive intellectual armchair occupation, because they are torn out of their life context, and
studied from what they look like on paper, and not from

what they do in life. Such a definition would make it impossible either to see clearly the nature of myth or to reach a satisfactory classification of folk tales. In fact we would also have to disagree with the definition of legend and of fairy tale given subsequently by the writers in *Notes and Queries on Anthropology*.

But above all, this point of view would be fatal to efficient field work, for it would make the observer satisfied with the mere writing down of narratives. The intellectual nature of a story is exhausted with its text, but the functional, cultural, and pragmatic aspect of any native tale is manifested as much in its enactment, embodiment, and contextual relations as in the text. It is easier to write down the story than to observe the diffuse, complex ways in which it enters into life, or to study its function by the observation of the vast social and cultural realities into which it enters. And this is the reason why we have so many texts and why we know so little about the very nature of myth.

We may, therefore, learn an important lesson from the Trobrianders, and to them let us now return. We will survey some of their myths in detail, so that we can confirm our conclusions inductively, yet precisely.

II. MYTHS OF ORIGIN

We may best start with the beginning of things, and examine some of the myths of origin. The world, say the natives, was originally peopled from underground. Humanity had there led an existence similar in all respects to the present life on earth. Underground, men were organized in villages, clans, districts; they had distinctions of rank, they knew privileges and had claims, they owned property, and were versed in magic lore. Endowed with all this, they emerged, establishing by this very act certain rights in land and citizenship, in economic prerogative and magical pursuit. They brought with them all their culture to continue it upon this earth.

There are a number of special spots—grottoes, clumps of trees, stone heaps, coral outcrops, springs, heads of creeks—called 'holes' or 'houses' by the natives. From such 'holes' the first couples (a sister as the head of the family and the brother as her guardian) came and took possession of the lands, and gave the totemic, industrial, magical, and sociological character to the communities thus begun.

The problem of rank which plays a great role in their sociology was settled by the emergence from one special hole, called Obukula, near the village of Laba'i. This event was notable in that, contrary to the usual course (which is: one original 'hole,' one lineage), from this hole of Laba'i there emerged representatives of the four main clans one after the other. Their arrival, moreover, was followed by an apparently trivial but, in mythical reality, a most important event. First there came the *Kaylavasi* (iguana), the animal of the Lukulabuta clan, which scratched its way through the earth as iguanas do, then climbed a tree, and remained there as a mere onlooker, following subsequent events. Soon there came out the Dog, totem of the Lukuba clan, who originally had the highest rank. As a third came the Pig, representative of the Malasi clan, which now holds the highest rank. Last came the Lukwasisiga totem, represented in some versions by the Crocodile, in others by the Snake, in others by the Opossum, and sometimes completely ignored. The Dog and Pig ran round, and the Dog, seeing the fruit of the *noku* plant, nosed it, then ate it. Said the Pig: "Thou eatest *noku*, thou eatest dirt; thou art a low-bred, a commoner; the chief, the *guya'u*, shall be I." And ever since, the highest subclan of the Malasi clan, the Tabalu, have been the real chiefs.

In order to understand this myth, it is not enough to follow the dialogue between the Dog and the Pig which might appear pointless or even trivial. Once you know the native sociology, the extreme importance of rank, the fact that food and its limitations (the taboos of rank and clan) are the main index of man's social nature, and finally the psychology of totemic identification—you begin to under-

stand how this incident, happening as it did when humanity was *in statu nascendi*, settled once for all the relation
between the two rival clans. To understand this myth you
must have a good knowledge of their sociology, religion,
customs, and outlook. Then, and only then, can you appreciate what this story means to the natives and how it
can live in their life. If you stayed among them and learned
the language you would constantly find it active in discussion and squabbles in reference to the relative superiority
of the various clans, and in the discussions about the various
food taboos which frequently raise fine questions of casu-
istry. Above all, if you were brought into contact with
communities where the historical process of the spread of
influence of the Malasi clan is still in evolution, you would
be brought face to face with this myth as an active force.

Remarkably enough the first and last animals to come out,
the iguana and the Lukwasisiga totem, have been from the
beginning left in the cold: thus the numerical principle
and the logic of events is not very strictly observed in the
reasoning of the myth.

If the main myth of Laba'i about the relative superiority
of the four clans is very often alluded to throughout the
tribe, the minor local myths are not less alive and active,
each in its own community. When a party arrives at some
distant village they will be told not only the legendary
historical tales, but above all the mythological charter of
that community, its magical proficiencies, its occupational
character, its rank and place in totemic organization. Should
there arise land quarrels, encroachment in magical matters,
fishing rights, or other privileges the testimony of myth
would be referred to.

Let me show concretely the way in which a typical myth
of local origins would be retailed in the normal run of
native life. Let us watch a party of visitors arriving in one
or the other of the Trobriand villages. They would seat
themselves in front of the headman's house, in the central
place of the locality. As likely as not the spot of origins is
nearby, marked by a coral outcrop or a heap of stones.

This spot would be pointed out, the names of the brother and sister ancestors mentioned, and perhaps it would be said that the man built his house on the spot of the present headman's dwelling. The native listeners would know, of course, that the sister lived in a different house nearby, for she could never reside within the same walls as her brother.

As additional information, the visitors might be told that the ancestors had brought with them the substances and paraphernalia and methods of local industry. In the village of Yalaka, for instance, it would be the processes for burning lime from shells. In Okobobo, Obweria, and Obowada the ancestors brought the knowledge and the implements for polishing hard stone. In Bwoytalu the carver's tool, the hafted shark tooth, and the knowledge of the art came out from underground with the original ancestors. In most places the economic monopolies are thus traced to the autochthonous emergence. In villages of higher rank the insignia of hereditary dignity were brought; in others some animal associated with the local subclan came out. Some communities started on their political career of standing hostility to one another from the very beginning. The most important gift to this world carried from the one below is always magic; but this will have to be treated later on and more fully.

If a European bystander were there and heard nothing but the information given from one native to the other, it would mean very little to him. In fact, it might lead him into serious misunderstandings. Thus the simultaneous emergence of brother and sister might make him suspicious either of a mythological allusion to incest, or else would make him look for the original matrimonial pair and inquire about the sister's husband. The first suspicion would be entirely erroneous, and would shed a false light over the specific relation between brother and sister, in which the former is the indispensable guardian, and the second, equally indispensable, is responsible for the transmission of the line. Only a full knowledge of the matrilineal ideas and institutions gives body and meaning to the bare men-

tion of the two ancestral names, so significant to a native listener. If the European were to inquire who was the sister's
husband and how she came to have children, he would soon
find himself once more confronted by an entirely foreign
set of ideas—the sociological irrelevance of the father, the
absence of any ideas about physiological procreation, and
the strange and complicated system of marriage, matrilineal
and patrilocal at the same time.[1]

The sociological relevance of these accounts of origins
would become clear only to a European inquirer who had
grasped the native legal ideas about local citizenship and
the hereditary rights to territory, fishing grounds, and local
pursuits. For according to the legal principles of the tribe
all such rights are the monopolies of the local community,
and only people descendent in the female line from the
original ancestress are entitled to them. If the European
were told further that, besides the first place of emergence,
there are several other 'holes' in the same village, he would
become still more baffled until, by a careful study of concrete details and the principles of native sociology, he became acquainted with the idea of compound village communities, i.e., communities in which several subclans have
merged.

It is clear, then, that the myth conveys much more to the
native than is contained in the mere story; that the story
gives only the really relevant concrete local differences; that
the real meaning, in fact the full account, is contained in
the traditional foundations of social organization; and that
this the native learns, not by listening to the fragmentary
mythical stories, but by living within the social texture of
his tribe. In other words, it is the context of social life, it is

[1] For a full statement of the psychology and sociology
of kinship and descent see articles on "The Psychology of
Sex and the Foundations of Kinship in Primitive Societies",
"Psycho-analysis and Anthropology", "Complex and Myth
in Mother Right", all three in the psychological journal,
Psyche, Oct. 1923, April, 1924, and Jan. 1925. The first
article is included in *The Father in Primitive Psychology*
(Psyche Miniature, 1926).

the gradual realization by the native of how everything
which he is told to do has its precedent and pattern in
bygone times, which brings home to him the full account
and the full meaning of his myths of origin.

For an observer, therefore, it is necessary to become fully
acquainted with the social organization of the natives if he
wants really to grasp its traditional aspect. The short accounts, such as those which are given about local origins,
will then become perfectly plain to him. He will also clearly
see that each of them is only a part, and a rather insignificant
one, of a much bigger story, which cannot be read except
from native life. What really matters about such a story
is its social function. It conveys, expresses, and strengthens
the fundamental fact of the local unity and of the kinship
unity of the group of people descendent from a common
ancestress. Combined with the conviction that only common
descent and emergence from the soil give full rights to it,
the story of origin literally contains the legal charter of the
community. Thus, even when the people of a vanquished
community were driven from their grounds by a hostile
neighbor their territory always remained intact for them;
and they were always, after a lapse of time and when their
peace ceremony had been concluded, allowed to return to
the original site, rebuild their village, and cultivate their
gardens once more.[2] The traditional feeling of a real and
intimate connection with the land; the concrete reality of
seeing the actual spot of emergence in the middle of the
scenes of daily life; the historical continuity of privileges,
occupations, and distinctive characters running back into
the mythological first beginnings—all this obviously makes
for cohesion, for local patriotism, for a feeling of union and
kinship in the community. But although the narrative of
original emergence integrates and welds together the historical tradition, the legal principles, and the various cus-

[2] *Cf.* The account given of these facts in the article on
"War and Weapons among the Trobriand Islanders", *Man*,
Jan. 1918; and in Professor Seligman's *Melanesians*, pp.
663–68.

toms, it must also be clearly kept in mind that the original
myth is but a small part of the whole complex of traditional
ideas. Thus on the one hand the reality of myth lies in its
social function; on the other hand, once we begin to study
the social function of myth, and so to reconstruct its full
meaning, we are gradually led to build up the full theory
of native social organization.

One of the most interesting phenomena connected with
traditional precedent and charter is the adjustment of myth
and mythological principle to cases in which the very
foundation of such mythology is flagrantly violated. This
violation always takes place when the local claims of an
autochthonous clan, i.e., a clan which has emerged on the
spot, are overridden by an immigrant clan. Then a conflict
of principles is created, for obviously the principle that land
and authority belong to those who are literally born out
of it does not leave room for any newcomers. On the other
hand, members of a subclan of high rank who choose to
settle down in a new locality cannot very well be resisted
by the autochthons—using this word again in the literal
native mythological sense. The result is that there come into
existence a special class of mythological stories which justify
and account for the anomalous state of affairs. The strength
of the various mythological and legal principles is manifested in that the myths of justification still contain the
antagonistic and logically irreconcilable facts and points of
view, and only try to cover them by facile reconciliatory
incident, obviously manufactured *ad hoc*. The study of such
stories is extremely interesting, both because it gives us a
deep insight into the native psychology of tradition, and
because it tempts us to reconstruct the past history of the
tribe, though we must yield to the temptation with due
caution and scepticism.

In the Trobriands we find that the higher the rank of a
totemic subclan, the greater its power of expansion. Let us
first state the facts and then proceed to their interpretation.
The subclan of the highest rank, the Tabalu subclan of the
Malasi clan, are found now ruling over a number of

villages: Omarakana, their main capital; Kasanayi, the twin village of the capital; and Olivilevi, a village founded some three 'reigns' ago after a defeat of the capital. Two villages, Omlamwaluwa, now extinct, and Dayagila, no longer ruled by the Tabalu, also once belonged to them. The same sub-clan, bearing the same name and claiming the same descent, but not keeping all the taboos of distinction and not entitled to all the insignia, is found ruling in the villages of Oyweyowa, Gumilababa, Kavataria, and Kadawaga, all in the western part of the archipelago, the last mentioned on the small island Kayleula. The village of Tukwa'ukwa was but recently taken over by the Tabalu some five 'reigns' ago. Finally, a subclan of the same name and claiming affinity rules over the two big and powerful communities of the South, Sinaketa and Vakuta.

The second fact of importance referring to these villages and their rulers is that the ruling clan does not pretend to have emerged locally in any of those communities in which its members own territory, carry on local magic, and wield power. They all claim to have emerged, accompanied by the original pig, from the historical hole of Obukula on the northwestern shore of the island near the village of Laba'i. From there they have, according to their tradition, spread all over the district.[3]

In the traditions of this clan there are certain definitely historical facts which must be clearly disentangled and registered; the foundation of the village of Olivilevi three 'reigns' ago, the settlement of the Tabalu in Tukwa'ukwa five 'reigns' ago, the taking over of Vakuta some seven or eight 'reigns' ago. By 'reign' I mean the life rule of one individual chief. Since in the Trobriands, as no doubt in most matrilineal tribes, a man is succeeded by his younger brother, the average 'reign' is obviously much shorter than the span of a generation and also much less reliable as a measure of time, since in many cases it need not be shorter.

[3] The reader who wants to grasp these historical and geographical details should consult the map facing p. 51 of the writer's *Argonauts of the Western Pacific*.

These particular historical tales, giving a full account of how, when, by whom, and in what manner the settlement was effected, are sober matter-of-fact statements. Thus it is possible to obtain from independent informants the detailed account of how, in the time of their fathers or grandfathers respectively, the chief Bugwabwaga of Omarakana, after an unsuccessful war, had to flee with all his community far south, to the usual spot where a temporary village was erected. After a couple of years he returned to perform the peace-making ceremony and to rebuild Omarakana. His younger brother, however, did not return with him, but erected a permanent village, Olivilevi, and remained there. The account, which can be confirmed in the minutest detail from any intelligent adult native in the district, is obviously as reliable an historical statement as one can obtain in any savage community. The data about Tukwa'ukwa, Vakuta, and so on are of similar nature.

What lifts the trustworthiness of such accounts above any suspicion is their sociological foundation. The flight after defeat is a general rule of tribal usage; and the manner in which the other villages become the seat of the highest rank people, i.e., intermarriage between Tabalu women and head men of other villages, is also characteristic of their social life. The technique of this proceeding is of considerable importance and must be described in detail. Marriage is patrilocal in the Trobriands, so that the woman always moves to her husband's community. Economically, marriage entails the standing exchange of food given by the wife's family for valuables supplied by the husband. Food is especially plentiful in the central plains of Kiriwina, ruled over by the chiefs of highest rank from Omarakana. The valuable shell ornaments, coveted by the chiefs, are produced in the coastal districts to the west and south. Economically, therefore, the tendency always has been, and still is, for women of high rank to marry influential headmen in such villages as Gumilababa, Kavataria, Tukwa'ukwa, Sinaketa, and Vakuta.

So far everything happens according to the strict letter of

tribal law. But once a Tabalu woman has settled in her husband's village, she overshadows him by rank and very often by influence. If she has a son or sons these are, until puberty, legal members of their father's community. They are the most important males in it. The father, as things are in the Trobriands, always wishes to keep them even after puberty for reasons of personal affection; the community feels that their whole status is being raised thereby. The majority desire it; and the minority, the rightful heirs to the headmen, his brothers and his sisters' sons, do not dare to oppose. If, therefore, the sons of high rank have no special reasons for returning to their rightful village, that of their mother, they remain in the father's community and rule it. If they have sisters these may also remain, marry within the village, and thus start a new dynasty. Gradually, though perhaps not at once, they succeed to all the privileges, dignities, and functions vested till then in the local headman. They are styled 'masters' of the village and of its lands, they preside over the formal councils, they decide upon all communal matters where a decision is needed, and above all they take over the control of local monopolies and local magic.

All the facts I have just reviewed are strictly empirical observations; let us now look at the legends adduced to cover them. According to one story two sisters, Botabalu and Bonumakala, came out of the original hole near Laba'i. They went at once to the central district of Kiriwina, and both settled in Omarakana. Here they were welcomed by the local lady in charge of magic and all the rights, and thus the mythological sanction of their claims to the capital was established. (To this point we shall have to return again.) After a time they had a quarrel about some banana leaves pertaining to the beautiful fiber petticoats used for dress. The elder sister then ordered the younger to go, which among the natives is a great insult. She said: "I shall remain here and keep all the strict taboos. You go and eat bush-pig, *katakayluva* fish." This is the reason why the chiefs in the coastal district, though in reality they have the same rank, do not keep the same taboos. The same story is told by natives of the coastal villages with the difference, however, that it is the younger sister who orders her senior to remain in Omarakana and keep all the taboos, while she herself goes to the west.

According to a Sinaketan version, there were three original women of the Tabalu subclan, the eldest remained in Kiriwina, the second settled in Kuboma, the youngest came to Sinaketa and brought with her the *Kaloma* shell discs, which started the local industry.

All these observations refer only to one subclan of the Malasi clan. The other subclans of this clan, of which I have some dozen on record, are all of low rank; are all local, that is have not immigrated into their present territory; and some of them, those of Bwoytalu, belong to what might be called the pariah or specially despised category of people. Although they all bear the same generic name, have the same common totem, and on ceremonial occasions would range themselves side by side with the people of the highest rank, they are regarded by the natives as belonging to an entirely different class.

Before I pass to the reinterpretation or historical reconstruction of these facts, I shall present the facts referring to the other clans. The Lukuba clan is perhaps the next in importance. They count among their subclans two or three which immediately follow in rank the Tabalu of Omarakana. The ancestors of these subclans are called Mwauri, Mulobwaima, and Tudava; and they all three came out from the same main hole near Laba'i, out of which the four totemic animals emerged. They moved afterwards to certain important centers in Kiriwina and in the neighboring islands of Kitava and Vakuta. As we have seen, according to the main myth of emergence, the Lukuba clan had the highest rank at first, before the dog and pig incident reversed the order. Moreover, most mythological personalities or animals belong to the Lukuba clan. The great mythological culture hero Tudava, reckoned also as ancestor by the subclan of that name, is a Lukuba. The majority of the mythical heroes in connection with the intertribal relations and the ceremonial forms of trading belong also to the same clan.[4] Most of the economic magic of the tribe also belongs to people of this clan. In Vakuta, where they have been recently overshadowed, if not displaced, by the Tabalu, they are still able to assert themselves; they have still retained the monopoly in magic; and, taking their stand upon mythological tradition, the Lukuba still affirm their real superiority to the usurpers. There are far fewer subclans of low rank among them than among the Malasi.

About the third large totemic division, the Lukwasisiga, there is much less to be said as regards mythology and cultural or historic role. In the main emergence myth they are either completely left out, or else their ancestral animal or person is made to play an entirely insignificant part. They do not own any specially important forms of magic and are conspicuously absent from any mythological reference. The only important part which they play is in the great Tudava cycle in which the ogre Dokonikan is made to belong to the Lukwasisiga totem. To this clan belongs the headman of the village Kabwaku, who is also the chief of the district of Tilataula. This district was always in a relation of potential hostility to the district of Kiriwina proper, and the chiefs of Tilataula were the political rivals of the Tabalu, the people of the highest rank. From time to time the two would wage war. No matter which side was defeated and had to fly, peace was always restored by a ceremonial reconciliation, and the same relative status once more obtained between the two provinces. The chiefs of Omarakana always retained superiority of rank and a sort of general control over the hostile district, even after this had been victorious. The chiefs of Kabwaku were to a certain extent bound to execute their orders; and more especially if a direct capital punishment had to be meted out in olden days the chief of Omarakana would delegate

[4] Cf. *Argonauts of the Western Pacific*, p. 321.

his potential foe to carry it out. The real superiority of the chiefs of Omarakana was due to their rank. But to a great extent their power and the fear with which they inspired all the other natives was derived from the important sun and rain magic which they wielded. Thus members of a subclan of the Lukwasisiga were the potential foes and the executive vassals, but in war the equals, of the highest chiefs. For, as in peace times the supremacy of the Tabalu would remain unchallenged, so in war the Toliwaga of Kabwaku were considered generally the more efficient and redoubtable. The Lukwasisiga clan were also on the whole regarded as landlubbers (*Kulita'odila*). One or two other subclans of this clan were of rather high rank and intermarried rather frequently with the Tabalu of Omarakana.

The fourth clan, the Lukulabuta, includes only subclans of low rank among its numbers. They are the least numerous clan, and the only magic with which they are associated is sorcery.

When we come to the historical interpretation of these myths a fundamental question meets us at the outset: must we regard the subclans which figure in legend and myth as representing merely the local branches of a homogeneous culture, or can we ascribe to them a more ambitious significance and regard them as standing for representatives of various cultures, that is, as units of different migration waves. If the first alternative is accepted then all the myths, historical data, and sociological facts refer simply to small internal movements and changes, and there is nothing to be added to them except what we have said.

In support of the more ambitious hypothesis, however, it might be urged that the main legend of emergence places the origins of the four clans in a very suggestive spot. Laba'i lies on the northwestern beach, the only place open to sailors who would have come from the direction of the prevailing monsoon winds. Moreover, in all the myths the drift of a migration, the trend of cultural influence, the travels of culture heroes, take place from north to south and generally, though less uniformly, from west to east. This is the direction which obtains in the great cycle of Tudava stories; this is the direction which we have found in the migration myths; this is the direction which obtains in the majority of the Kula legends. Thus the assumption is plausible that a cultural influence has been spreading from the northern shores of the archipelago, an influence which can be traced as far east as Woodlark Island, and as far south as the D'Entrecasteaux Archipelago. This hypothesis is suggested by the conflict element in some of the myths, such as that between the dog and the pig, between Tudava and Dokonikan, and between the cannibal and non-cannibal brother. If we then accept this hypothesis for what it is worth, the following scheme emerges. The oldest layer would be represented by the Lukwasisiga and Lukulabuta clans. The latter is the first to emerge mythologically; while both are relatively autochthonous in that they are not sailors, their communities usually lie inland, and their occupation is mainly agriculture. The generally hostile attitude of the main Lukwasisiga subclan, the Toliwaga, to what would be obviously the latest immigrants, the Tabalu, might also be made to fit into this hypothesis. It is again plausible that the cannibal monster who is fought by the innovator and cultural hero, Tudava, belongs to the Lukwasisiga clan.

I have expressly stated that the subclans and not the clans must be regarded as migration units. For it is an incontrovertible fact that the big clan, which comprises a number of subclans, is but a loose social unit, split by important cultural rifts. The Malasi clan, for instance, includes the highest subclan, the Tabalu, as well as the most despised subclans, Wabu'a and Gumsosopa of Bwoytalu. The historical hypothesis of migratory units would still have to explain the relation between subclans and clan. It seems to me that the minor subclans must also have been of a previous arrival, and that their totemic assimilations is a by-product of a general process of sociological reorganization which took place after the strong and influential immigrants of the Tudava and Tabalu type had arrived.

The historical reconstruction requires, therefore, a number of auxiliary hypotheses, each of which must be regarded as plausible, but must remain arbitrary; while each assumption adds a considerable element of uncertainty. The whole reconstruction is a mental game, attractive and absorbing, often sponstaneously obtruding itself upon a fieldworker, but always remaining outside the field of observation and sound conclusion—that is, if the fieldworker keeps his powers of observation and his sense of reality under control. The scheme which I have here developed is the one into which the facts of Trobriand sociology, myth, and custom naturally arrange themselves. Nevertheless, I do not attach any serious importance to it, and I do not believe that even a very exhaustive knowledge of a district entitles the ethnographer to anything but tentative and cautious reconstructions. Perhaps a much wider collation of such schemes might show their value, or else prove their utter futility. It is only perhaps as working hypotheses, stimulating to more careful and minute collection of legend, of all tradition, and of sociological difference, that such schemes possess any importance whatever.

As far as the sociological theory of these legends goes the historical reconstruction is irrelevant. Whatever the hidden reality of their unrecorded past may be, myths serve to cover certain inconsistencies created by historical events, rather than to record these events exactly. The myths associated with the spread of the powerful subclans show on certain points a fidelity to life in that they record facts inconsistent with one another. The incidents by which this inconsistency is obliterated, if not hidden, are most likely fictitious; we have seen certain myths vary according to the locality in which they are told. In other cases the incidents bolster up non-existent claims and rights.

The historical consideration of myth is interesting, therefore, in that it shows that myth, taken as a whole, cannot be sober dispassionate history, since it is always made *ad hoc* to fulfill a certain sociological function, to glorify a certain group, or to justify an anomalous status. These considerations show us also that to the native mind immediate history, semi-historic legend, and unmixed myth flow into one another, form a continuous sequence, and fulfill really the same sociological function.

And this brings us once more to our original contention that the really important thing about the myth is its character of a retrospective, ever-present, live actuality. It is to a native neither a fictitious story, nor an account of a dead past; it is a statement of a bigger reality still partially alive. It is alive in that its precedent, its law, its moral, still rule the social life of the natives. It is clear that myth functions especially where there is a sociological strain, such as in matters of great difference in rank and power, matters of precedence and subordination, and unquestionably where profound historical changes have taken place. So much can be asserted as a fact, though it must always remain doubtful how far we can carry out historical reconstruction from the myth.

We can certainly discard all explanatory as well as all symbolic interpretations of these myths of origin. The personages and beings which we find in them are what they appear to be on the surface, and not symbols of hidden realities. As to any explanatory function of these myths, there is no problem which they cover, no curiosity which they satisfy, no theory which they contain.

III. MYTHS OF DEATH AND OF THE RECURRENT CYCLE OF LIFE

In certain versions of origin myths the existence of humanity underground is compared to the existence of human spirits after death in the present-day spirit world. Thus a mythological rapprochement is made between the primeval past and the immediate destiny of each man, another of those links with life which we find so important in the understanding of the psychology and the cultural value of myth.

The parallel between primeval and spiritual existence can be drawn even further. The ghosts of the deceased move after death to the island of Tuma. There they enter the earth through a special hole—a sort of reversed proceeding to the original emergence. Even more important is the fact that after a span of spiritual existence in Tuma, the nether world, an individual grows old, grey, and wrinkled; and that then he has to rejuvenate by sloughing his skin. Even so did human beings in the old primeval times, when they lived underground. When they first came to the surface they had not yet lost this ability; men and women could live eternally young.

They lost the faculty, however, by an apparently trivial, yet important and fateful event. Once upon a time there lived in the village of Bwadela an old woman who dwelt with her daughter and granddaughter; three generations of genuine matrilineal descent. The grandmother and granddaughter went out one day to bathe in the tidal creek. The girl remained on the shore, while the old woman went away some distance out of sight. She took off her skin, which, carried by the tidal current, floated along the creek until it stuck on a bush. Transformed into a young girl, she came back to her granddaughter. The latter did not recognize her; she was afraid of her, and bade her begone. The old woman, mortified and angry, went back to her bathing place, searched for her old skin, put it on again, and returned to her granddaughter. This time she was recognized and thus greeted: "A young girl came here; I was afraid; I chased her away." Said the grandmother: "No, you didn't want to recognize me. Well, you will become old—I shall die." They went home to where the daughter was preparing the meal. The old woman spoke to her daughter: "I went to bathe; the tide carried my skin away; your daughter did not recognize me; she chased me away. I shall not slough my skin. We shall all become old. We shall all die."

After that men lost the power of changing their skin and of remaining youthful. The only animals who have retained the power of changing the skin are the 'animals of the

below'—snakes, crabs, iguanas, and lizards: this is because
men also once lived under the ground. These animals come
out of the ground and they still can change their skin. Had
men lived above, the 'animals of the above'—birds, flying
foxes, and insects—would also be able to change their skins
and renew their youth.

Here ends the myth as it is usually told. Sometimes the
natives will add other comments drawing parallels between
spirits and primitive humanity; sometimes they will emphasize the regeneration motive of the reptiles; sometimes
tell only the bare incident of the lost skin. The story is, in
itself, trivial and unimportant; and it would appear so to
anyone who did not study it against the background of the
various ideas, customs, and rites associated with death and
future life. The myth is obviously but a developed and
dramatized belief in the previous human power of rejuvenation and in its subsequent loss.

Thus, through the conflict between granddaughter and
grandmother, human beings, one and all, had to submit to
the process of decay and debility brought on by old age.
This, however, did not involve the full incidence of the
inexorable fate which is the present lot of man; for old age,
bodily decay, and debility do not spell death to the natives.
In order to understand the full cycle of their beliefs it is
necessary to study the factors of illness, decay, and death.
The native of the Trobriands is definitely an optimist in
his attitude to health and illness. Strength, vigor, and bodily
perfection are to him the natural status which can only be
affected or upset by an accident or by a supernatural cause.
Small accidents such as excessive fatigue, sunstroke, overeating, or exposure may cause minor and temporary ailments. By a spear in battle, by poison, by a fall from a
rock or a tree a man may be maimed or killed. Whether
these accidents and others, such as drowning and the attack of a crocodile or a shark, are entirely free from sorcery
is ever a debatable question to a native. But there is no
doubt whatever to him that all serious and especially all
fatal illnesses are due to various forms and agencies of

witchcraft. The most prevalent of these is the ordinary sorcery practiced by wizards, who can produce by their spells and rites a number of ailments covering well-nigh the whole domain of ordinary pathology, with the exception of very rapid fulminating diseases and epidemics.

The source of witchcraft is always sought in some influence coming from the south. There are two points in the Trobriand Archipelago at which sorcery is said to have originated, or rather to have been brought over from the D'Entrecasteaux Archipelago. One of these is the grove of Lawaywo between the villages of Ba'u and Bwoytalu, and the other is the southern island of Vakuta. Both these districts are still considered the most redoubtable centers of witchcraft.

The district of Bwoytalu occupies a specially low social position in the island, inhabited as it is by the best wood-carvers, the most expert fiber plaiters, and the eaters of such abominations as stingaree and bush pig. These natives have been endogamous for a long time, and they probably represent the oldest layer of indigenous culture in the island. To them sorcery was brought from the southern archipelago by a crab. This animal is either depicted as emerging out of a hole in the Lawaywo grove, or else as traveling by the air and dropping from above at the same place. About the time of its arrival a man and a dog went out. The crab was red, for it had the sorcery within it. The dog saw it and tried to bite it. Then the crab killed the dog, and having done this, proceeded to kill the man. But looking at him the crab became sorry, 'its belly was moved,' and it brought him back to life. The man then offered his murderer and savior a large payment, a *pokala*, and asked the crustacean to give him the magic. This was done. The man immediately made use of his sorcery to kill his benefactor, the crab. He then proceeded to kill, according to a rule observed or believed to have been observed until now, a near maternal relative. After that he was in full possession of witchcraft. The crabs at present are black, for sorcery

has left them; they are, however, slow to die for once they
were the masters of life and of death.

A similar type of myth is told in the southern island of
Vakuta. They tell how a malicious being of human shape,
but not of human nature, went into a piece of bamboo
somewhere on the northern shore of Normanby Island.
The piece of bamboo drifted northwards till it was washed
ashore near the promontory of Yayvau or Vakuta. A man
from the neighboring village of Kwadagila heard a voice in
the bamboo and opened it. The demon came out and taught
him sorcery. This, according to the informants in the south,
is the real starting point of black magic. It went to the
district of Ba'u in Bwoytalu from Vakuta and not directly
from the southern archipelagoes. Another version of the
Vakuta tradition maintains that the *tauva'u* came to Vakuta
not in a bamboo but by a grander arrangement. At
Sewatupa on the northern shore of Normanby Island there
stood a big tree in which many of the malignant beings used
to reside. It was felled, and it tumbled right across the sea,
so that while its base remained on Normanby Island the
trunk and the branches came across the sea and the top
touched Vakuta. Hence sorcery is most rampant in the
southern archipelago; the intervening sea is full of fish who
live in the branches and boughs of the tree; and the place
whence sorcery came to the Trobriands is the southern beach
of Vakuta. For in the top of the tree there were three
malignant beings, two males and a female, and they gave
some magic to the inhabitants of the island.

In these mythical stories we have but one link in the
chain of beliefs which surround the final destiny of human
beings. The mythical incidents can be understood and their
importance realized only in connection with the full beliefs
in the power and nature of witchcraft, and with the feelings
and apprehensions regarding it. The explicit stories about
the advent of sorcery do not quite exhaust or account for
all the supernatural dangers. Rapid and sudden disease and
death are, in native belief, brought about, not by the male
sorcerers, but by flying witches who act differently and

possess altogether a more supernatural character. I was unable to find any initial myth about the origin of this type of witchcraft. On the other hand, the nature and the whole proceedings of these witches are surrounded by a cycle of beliefs which form what might be called a standing or current myth. I shall not repeat them with detail, for I have given a full account in my book, the *Argonauts of the Western Pacific*.[1] But it is important to realize that the halo of supernatural powers surrounding individuals who are believed to be witches gives rise to a continuous flow of stories. Such stories can be regarded as minor myths generated by the strong belief in the supernatural powers. Similar stories are also told about the male sorcerers, the *bwaga'u*.

Epidemics, finally, are ascribed to the direct action of the malignant spirits, the *tauva'u*, who, as we saw, are mythologically often regarded as the source of all witchcraft. These malignant beings have a permanent abode in the south. Occasionally they will move to the Trobriand Archipelago, and, invisible to ordinary human beings, they walk at night through the villages rattling their lime gourds and clanking their wooden sword clubs. Wherever this is heard fear falls upon the inhabitants, for those whom the *tauva'u* strike with their wooden weapons die, and such an invasion is always associated with death in masses. *Leria*, epidemic disease, obtains then in the villages. The malignant spirits can sometimes change into reptiles and then become visible to human eyes. It is not always easy to distinguish such a reptile from an ordinary one, but it is very important to do so, for a *tauva'u*, injured or ill-treated, revenges itself by death.

Here, again, around this standing myth, around this domestic tale of a happening which is not placed in the past but still occurs, there cluster innumerable concrete stories. Some of them even occurred while I was in the Trobriands; there was a severe dysentery once, and the first outbreak of

[1] Chap. X, *passim:* especially pp. 236–48, also pp. 320, 321, 393.

what probably was Spanish influenza in 1918. Many natives
reported having heard the *tauva'u*. A giant lizard was seen
in Wawela; the man who killed it died soon after, and the
epidemic broke out in the village. While I was in Oburaku,
and sickness was rife in the village, a real *tauva'u* was seen
by the crew of the boat in which I was being paddled; a
large multicolored snake appeared on a mangrove, but
vanished mysteriously as we came near. It was only through
my short-sightedness, and perhaps also my ignorance of how
to look for a *tauva'u* that I failed to observe this miracle
myself. Such and similar stories can be obtained by the
score from natives in all localities. A reptile of this type
should be put on a high platform and valuables placed in
front of it; and I have been assured by natives who have
actually witnessed it that this is not infrequently done,
though I never have seen this myself. Again, a number of
women witches are said to have had intercourse with
tauva'u, and of one living at present this is positively affirmed.

In the case of this belief we see how minor myths are
constantly generated by the big schematic story. Thus with
regard to all the agencies of disease and death the belief,
and the explicit narratives which cover part of it, the small
concrete supernatural events constantly registered by the
natives, form one organic whole. These beliefs are obviously
not a theory or explanation. On the one hand, they are the
whole complex of cultural practices, for sorcery is not only
believed to be practiced, but actually is practiced, at least
in its male form. On the other hand, the complex under
discussion covers the whole pragmatic reaction of man towards disease and death; it expresses his emotions, his forebodings; it influences his behavior. The nature of myth
again appears to us as something very far removed from
a mere intellectual explanation.

We are now in full possession of the native ideas about
the factors which in the past cut short man's power of
rejuvenation, and which at present cut short his very existence. The connection, by the way, between the two losses

is only indirect. The natives believe that although any form of sorcery can reach the child, the youth, or the man in the prime of life, as well as the aged, yet old people are more easily stricken. Thus the loss of rejuvenation at least prepared the ground for sorcery.

But although there was a time when people grew old and died, and thus became spirits, they yet remained in the villages with the survivors—even as now they stay around the dwellings when they return to their village during the annual feast of the *milamala*. But one day an old woman spirit who was living with her people in the house crouched on the floor under one of the bedstead platforms. Her daughter, who was distributing food to the members of the family, spilled some broth out of the coconut cup and burnt the spirit, who expostulated and reprimanded her daughter. The latter replied: "I thought you had gone away; I thought you were only coming back at one time in the year during the *milamala*." The spirit's feelings were hurt. She replied: "I shall go to Tuma and live underneath." She then took up a coconut, cut it in half, kept the half with the three eyes, and gave her daughter the other. "I am giving you the half which is blind, and therefore you will not see me. I am taking the half with the eyes, and I shall see you when I come back with other spirits." This is the reason why the spirits are invisible, though they themselves can see human beings.

This myth contains a reference to the seasonal feast of *milamala*, the period at which the spirits return to their villages while festive celebrations take place. A more explicit myth gives an account of how the *milamala* was instituted. A woman of Kitava died leaving a pregnant daughter behind her. A son was born, but his mother had not enough milk to feed him. As a man of a neighboring island was dying, she asked him to take a message to her own mother in the land of spirits, to the effect that the departed one should bring food to her grandson. The spirit woman filled her basket with spirit food and came back wailing as follows: "Whose food am I carrying? That of my grandson to

whom I am going to give it; I am going to give him his
food." She arrived on Bomagema beach in the island of
Kitava and put down the food. She spoke to her daughter:
"I bring the food; the man told me I should bring it. But I
am weak; I fear that people may take me for a witch." She
then roasted one of the yams and gave it to her grandson.
She went into the bush and made a garden for her daughter. When she came back, however, her daughter received a
fright for the spirit looked like a sorceress. She ordered her
to go away saying: "Return to Tuma, to the spiritland;
people will say that you are a witch." The spirit mother
complained: "Why do you chase me away? I thought I
would stay with you and make gardens for my grandchild."
The daughter only replied: "Go away, return to Tuma."
The old woman then took up a coconut, split it in half,
gave the blind half to her daughter, and kept the half with
the eyes. She told her that once a year, she and other spirits
would come back during the *milamala* and look at the people in the villages, but remain invisible to them. And this
is how the annual feast came to be what it is.

In order to understand these mythological stories, it is
indispensable to collate them with native beliefs about the
spirit world, with the practices during the *milamala* season,
and with the relations between the world of the living and
the world of the dead, such as exist in native forms of
spiritism.[2] After death every spirit goes to the nether world
in Tuma. He has to pass at the entrance Topileta, the
guardian of the spirit world. The newcomer offers some
valuable gift, the spiritual part of the valuables with which
he had been bedecked at the time of dying. When he arrives among the spirits he is received by his friends and
relatives who have previously died, and he brings the news
from the upper world. He then settles down to spirit life,
which is similar to earthly existence, though sometimes its

[2] An account of these facts has been already given in an
article on "Baloma; the Spirits of the Dead in the Trobriand Islands" in the *Journal of the Royal Anthropological
Institute*, 1916. *Cf.* below p. 149.

description is colored by hopes and desires and made into a sort of real Paradise. But even those natives who describe it thus never show any eagerness to reach it.

Communication between spirits and the living is carried out in several ways. Many people have seen spirits of their deceased relatives or friends, especially in or near the island of Tuma. Again, there are now, and seem to have been from time immemorial, men and women who in trances, or sometimes in sleep, go on long expeditions to the nether world. They take part in the life of the spirits, and carry back and forth news, items of information, and important messages. Above all they are always ready to convey gifts of food and valuables from the living to the spirits. These people bring home to other men and women the reality of the spirit world. They also give a great deal of comfort to the survivors who are ever eager to receive news from their dear departed.

To the annual feast of the *milamala*, the spirits return from Tuma to their villages. A special high platform is erected for them to sit upon, from which they can look down upon the doings and amusements of their brethren. Food is displayed in big quantities to gladden their hearts, as well as those of the living citizens of the community. During the day valuables are placed on mats in front of the headman's hut and the huts of important and wealthy people. A number of taboos are observed in the village to safeguard the invisible spirits from injury. Hot fluids must not be spilled, as the spirits might be burned like the old woman in the myth. No native may sit, cut wood within the village, play about with spears or sticks, or throw missiles, for fear of injuring a *Baloma*, a spirit. The spirits, moreover, manifest their presence by pleasant and unpleasant signs, and express their satisfaction or the reverse. Slight annoyance is sometimes shown by unpleasant smells, more serious ill humor is displayed in bad weather, accidents, and damage to property. On such occasions—as well as when an important medium goes into a trance, or someone is near to death—the spirit world seems very near and real to the natives. It is clear that myth fits into these beliefs as an integral part of them. There is a close and direct parallel between, on the one hand, the relations of man to spirit, as expressed in present-day religious beliefs and experiences, and, on the other hand, the various incidents of the myth. Here again the myth can be regarded as constituting the furthest background of a continuous perspective which ranges from an individual's personal concerns, fears, and sorrows at the one end, through the customary setting of belief, through the many concrete cases told from personal experience and memory of past generations, right back into the epoch where a similar fact is imagined to have occurred for the first time.

I have presented the facts and told the myths in a manner which implies the existence of an extensive and coherent scheme of beliefs. This scheme does not exist, of course, in any explicit form in the native folklore. But it does correspond to a definite cultural reality, for all the concrete manifestations of the natives' beliefs, feelings, and forebodings with reference to death and afterlife hang together and form a great organic unit. The various stories and ideas just summarized shade into one another, and the natives spontaneously point out the parallels and bring out the connections between them. Myths, religious beliefs, and experiences in connection with spirits and the supernatural are really all parts of the same subject; the corresponding pragmatic attitude is expressed in conduct by the attempts to commune with the nether world. The myths are but a part of the organic whole; they are an explicit development into narrative of certain crucial points in native belief. When we examine the subjects which are thus spun into stories we find that they all refer to what might be called the specially unpleasant or negative truths; the loss of rejuvenation, the onset of disease, the loss of life by sorcery, the withdrawal of the spirits from permanent contact with men, and finally the partial communication re-established with them. We see also that the myths of this cycle are more dramatic, they also form a more consecutive, yet complex, account than was the case with the myths of origins. Without laboring the point, I think that this is due to a deeper metaphysical reference, in other words, to a stronger emotional appeal in stories which deal with human destiny, as compared with sociological statements or charters.

In any case we see that the point where myth enters in these subjects is not to be explained by any greater amount of curiosity or any more problematic character, but rather by emotional coloring and pragmatic importance. We have found that the ideas elaborated by myth and spun out into narrative are especially painful. In one of the stories, that of the institution of the *milamala* and the periodical return of the spirits, it is the ceremonial behavior of man, and the taboos observed with regard to the spirits, which are in question. The subjects developed in these myths are clear enough in themselves; there is no need to 'explain' them, and the myth does not even partially perform this function. What it actually does is to transform an emotionally overwhelming foreboding, behind which, even for a native, there lurks the idea of an inevitable and ruthless fatality. Myth presents, first of all, a clear realization of this idea. In the second place, it brings down a vague but great apprehension to the compass of a trivial, domestic reality. The longed-for power of eternal youth and the faculty of rejuvenation which gives immunity from decay and age, have been lost by a small accident which it would have been in the power of a child and a woman to prevent. The separation from the beloved ones after death is conceived as due to the careless handling of a coconut cup and to a small altercation. Disease, again, is conceived as something which came out of a small animal, and originated through an accidental meeting of a man, a dog, and a crab. Elements of human error, of guilt, and of mischance assume great proportions. Elements of fate, of destiny, and of the inevitable are, on the other hand, brought down to the dimension of human mistakes.

In order to understand this, it is perhaps well to realize

that in his actual emotional attitude towards death, whether his own or that of his loved ones, the native is not completely guided by his belief and his mythological ideas. His intense fear of death, his strong desire to postpone it, and his deep sorrow at the departure of beloved relatives belie the optimistic creed and the easy reach of the beyond which is inherent in native customs, ideas, and ritual. After death has occurred, or at a time when death is threatening, there is no mistaking the dim division of shaking faith. In long conversations with several seriously ill natives, and especially with my consumptive friend Bagido'u, I felt, half-expressed and roughly formulated, but still unmistakable in them all, the same melancholy sorrow at the transience of life and all its good things, the same dread of the inevitable end, and the same questioning as to whether it could be staved off indefinitely or at least postponed for some little time. But again, the same people would clutch at the hope given to them by their beliefs. They would screen, with the vivid texture of their myths, stories, and beliefs about the spirit world, the vast emotional void gaping beyond them.

IV. MYTHS OF MAGIC

Let me discuss in more detail another class of mythical stories, those connected with magic. Magic, from many points of view, is the most important and the most mysterious aspect of primitive man's pragmatic attitude towards reality. It is one of the problems which are engaging at present the most vivid and most controversial interests of anthropologists. The foundations of this study have been laid by Sir James Frazer who has also erected a magnificent edifice thereon in his famous theory of magic.

Magic plays such a great part in northwest Melanesia that even a superficial observer must soon realize its enormous sway. Its incidence, however, is not very clear at first sight. Although it seems to crop up everywhere, there are certain highly important and vital activities from which magic is conspicuously absent.

No native would ever make a yam or taro garden without magic. Yet certain important types of planting, such as the raising of the coconut, the cultivation of the banana, of the mango, and of the breadfruit, are devoid of magic. Fishing, the economic activity only second in importance to agriculture, has in some of its forms a highly developed magic. Thus the dangerous fishing of the shark, the pursuit of the uncertain *kalala* or of the *to'ulam* are smothered in magic. The equally vital, but easy and reliable method of fishing by poison has no magic whatever. In the construction of the canoe—an enterprise surrounded with technical difficulties, requiring organized labor, and leading to an ever-dangerous pursuit—the ritual is complex, deeply associated with the work, and regarded as absolutely indispensable. In the construction of houses, technically quite as difficult a pursuit, but involving neither danger, nor chance, nor yet such complex forms of co-operation as the canoe, there is no magic whatever associated with the work. Wood-carving, an industrial activity of the greatest importance, is carried on in certain communities as a universal trade, learnt in childhood, and practiced by everyone. In these communities there is no magic of carving at all. A different type of artistic sculpture in ebony and hardwood, practiced only by people of special technical and artistic ability all over the district, has, on the other hand, its magic, which is considered as the main source of skill and inspiration. In trade, a ceremonial form of exchange known as the *Kula* is surrounded by important magical ritual; while on the other hand, certain minor forms of barter of a purely commercial nature are without any magic at all. Pursuits such as war and love, as well as certain forces of destiny and nature such as disease, wind, and weather are in native belief almost completely governed by magical forces.

Even this rapid survey leads us to an important generalization which will serve as a convenient starting point. We find magic wherever the elements of chance and accident, and the emotional play between hope and fear have a wide and extensive range. We do not find magic wherever the pursuit is certain, reliable, and well under the control of rational methods and technological processes. Further, we find magic where the element of danger is conspicuous. We do not find it wherever absolute safety eliminates any elements of foreboding. This is the psychological factor. But magic also fulfills another and highly important sociological function. As I have tried to show elsewhere, magic is an active element in the organization of labor and in its systematic arrangement. It also provides the main controlling power in the pursuit of game. The integral cultural function of magic, therefore, consists in the bridging-over of gaps and inadequacies in highly important activities not yet completely mastered by man. In order to achieve this end, magic supplies primitive man with a firm belief in his power of succeeding; it provides him also with a definite mental and pragmatic technique wherever his ordinary means fail him. It thus enables man to carry out with confidence his most vital tasks, and to maintain his poise and his mental integrity under circumstances which, without the help of magic, would demoralize him by despair and anxiety, by fear and hatred, by unrequited love and impotent hate.

Magic is thus akin to science in that it always has a definite aim intimately associated with human instincts, needs, and pursuits. The magic art is directed towards the attainment of practical ends; like any other art or craft it is also governed by theory, and by a system of principles which dictate the manner in which the act has to be performed in order to be effective. Thus magic and science show a number of similarities, and with Sir James Frazer, we can appropriately call magic a pseudo science.

Let us look more closely at the nature of the magic art. Magic, in all its forms, is composed of three essential ingredients. In its performance there always enter certain words, spoken or chanted; certain ceremonial actions are always carried out; and there is always an officiating minister of the ceremony. In analyzing, therefore, the nature of magic, we have to distinguish the formula, the rite, and the condition of the performer. It may be said at once that in the part of Melanesia with which we are concerned, the spell is by far the most important constituent of magic. To the natives, knowledge of magic means the knowledge of the spell; and in any act of witchcraft the ritual centers round the utterance of the spell. The rite and the competence of the performer are merely conditioning factors which serve for the proper preservation and launching of the spell. This is very important from the point of view of our present discussion, for the magical spell stands in close relation to traditional lore and more especially to mythology.[1]

In the case of almost all types of magic we find some story accounting for its existence. Such a story tells when and where that particular magical formula entered the possession of man, how it became the property of a local group, how it passed from one to another. But such a story is not the story of magical origins. Magic never 'originated'; it never was created or invented. All magic simply *was* from the beginning, as an essential adjunct to all those things and processes which vitally interest man and yet elude his normal rational efforts. The spell, the rite, and the object which they govern are coeval.

Thus the essence of all magic is its traditional integrity. Magic can only be efficient if it has been transmitted without loss and without flaw from one generation to the other, till it has come down from primeval times to the present performer. Magic, therefore, requires a pedigree, a sort of traditional passport in its travel across time. This is supplied by the myth of magic. The manner in which myth endows the performance of magic with worth and validity, in which

[1] Cf. *Argonauts of the Western Pacific*, pp. 329, 401, et seq., and pp. 69–78 of "Magic, Science and Religion" in *Science, Religion and Reality*, Essays by Various Authors (1925). In this volume pp. 74–84.

myth blends with the belief in magical efficiency, will be best illustrated by a concrete example.

As we know, love and the attractions of the other sex play an important role in the life of these Melanesians. Like many races of the South Seas they are very free and easy in their conduct, especially before marriage. Adultery, however, is a punishable offense, and relations with the same totemic clan are strictly forbidden. But the greatest crime in the eyes of the natives is any form of incest. Even the bare idea of such a trespass between brother and sister fills them with violent horror. Brother and sister, united by the nearest bond of kinship in this matriarchal society, may not even converse freely, must never joke or smile at one another, and any allusion to one of them in the presence of the other is considered extremely bad taste. Outside the clan, however, freedom is great, and the pursuit of love assumes a variety of interesting and even attractive forms.

All sexual attraction and all power of seduction are believed to reside in the magic of love. This magic the natives regard as founded in a dramatic occurrence of the past, told in a strange, tragic myth of brother and sister incest, to which I can only refer briefly here.[2] The two young people lived in a village with their mother, and by an accident the girl inhaled a strong love decoction, prepared by her brother for someone else. Mad with passion, she chased him and seduced him on a lonely beach. Overcome by shame and remorse, they forsook food and drink, and died together in a grotto. An aromatic herb grew through their inlaced skeletons, and this herb forms the most powerful ingredient in the substances compounded together and used in love magic.

It can be said that the myth of magic, even more than the other types of savage myth, justifies the sociological claims of the wielder, shapes the ritual, and vouches for

[2] For the complete account of this myth see the author's *Sex and Repression in Primitive Society* (1926), where its full sociological bearings are discussed.

the truth of the belief in supplying the pattern of the subsequent miraculous confirmation.

Our discovery of this cultural function of magical myth fully endorses the brilliant theory of the origins of power and kingship developed by Sir James Frazer in the early parts of his *Golden Bough*. According to Sir James, the beginnings of social supremacy are due primarily to magic. By showing how the efficacy of magic is associated with local claims, sociological affiliation, and direct descent, we have been able to forge another link in the chain of causes which connect tradition, magic, and social power.

V. CONCLUSION

Throughout this book I have attempted to prove that myth is above all a cultural force; but it is not only that. It is obviously also a narrative, and thus it has its literary aspect—an aspect which has been unduly emphasized by most scholars, but which, nevertheless, should not be completely neglected. Myth contains germs of the future epic, romance, and tragedy; and it has been used in them by the creative genius of peoples and by the conscious art of civilization. We have seen that some myths are but dry and succinct statements with scarcely any nexus and no dramatic incident; others, like the myth of love or the myth of canoe magic and of overseas sailing, are eminently dramatic stories. Did space permit, I could repeat a long and elaborate saga of the culture hero Tudava, who slays an ogre, avenges his mother, and carries out a number of cultural tasks.[1] Comparing such stories, it might be possible to show why myth lends itself in certain of its forms to subsequent literary elaboration, and why certain other of its forms remain artistically sterile. Mere sociological precedence, legal title, and vindication of lineage and local claims

[1] For one of the main episodes of the myth of Tudava, see pp. 209–210 of the author's "Complex and Myth in Mother Right" in *Psyche*, Vol. V., Jan. 1925.

do not lead far into the realm of human emotions, and therefore lack the elements of literary value. Belief, on the other hand, whether in magic or in religion, is closely associated with the deepest desires of man, with his fears and hopes, with his passions and sentiments. Myths of love and of death, stories of the loss of immortality, of the passing of the Golden Age, and of the banishment from Paradise, myths of incest and of sorcery play with the very elements which enter into the artistic forms of tragedy, of lyric, and of romantic narrative. Our theory, the theory of the cultural function of myth, accounting as it does for its intimate relation to belief and showing the close connection between ritual and tradition, could help us to deepen our understanding of the literary possibilities of savage story. But this subject, however fascinating, cannot be further elaborated here.

In our opening remarks, two current theories of myth were discredited and discarded: the view that myth is a rhapsodic rendering of natural phenomena, and Andrew Lang's doctrine that myth is essentially an explanation, a sort of primitive science. Our treatment has shown that neither of these mental attitudes is dominant in primitive culture; that neither can explain the form of primitive sacred stories, their sociological context, or their cultural function. But once we have realized that myth serves principally to establish a sociological charter, or a retrospective moral pattern of behavior, or the primeval supreme miracle of magic—it becomes clear that elements both of explanation and of interest in nature must be found in sacred legends. For a precedent accounts for subsequent cases, though it does so through an order of ideas entirely different from the scientific relation of cause and effect, of motive and consequence. The interest in nature, again, is obvious if we realize how important is the mythology of magic, and how definitely magic clings to the economic concerns of man. In this, however, mythology is very far from a disinterested and contemplative rhapsody about natural phenomena. Between myth and nature two links must be interpolated:

man's pragmatic interest in certain aspects of the outer world, and his need of supplementing rational and empirical control of certain phenomena by magic.

Let me state once more that I have dealt in this book with savage myth, and not with the myth of culture. I believe that the study of mythology as it functions and works in primitive societies should anticipate the conclusions drawn from the material of higher civilizations. Some of this material has come down to us only in isolated literary texts, without its setting in actual life, without its social context. Such is the mythology of the ancient classical peoples and of the dead civilizations of the Orient. In the study of myth the classical scholar must learn from the anthropologist.

The science of myth in living higher cultures, such as the present civilization of India, Japan, China, and last but not least, our own, might well be inspired by the comparative study of primitive folklore; and in its turn civilized culture could furnish important additions and explanations to savage mythology. This subject is very much beyond the scope of the present study. I do, however, want to emphasize the fact that anthropology should be not only the study of savage custom in the light of our mentality and our culture, but also the study of our own mentality in the distant perspective borrowed from Stone Age man. By dwelling mentally for some time among people of a much simpler culture than our own, we may be able to see ourselves from a distance, we may be able to gain a new sense of proportion with regard to our own institutions, beliefs, and customs. If anthropology could thus inspire us with some sense of proportion, and supply us with a finer sense of humor, it might justly claim to be a very great science.

I have now completed the survey of facts and the range of conclusions; it only remains to summarize them briefly. I have tried to show that folklore, these stories handed on in a native community, live in the cultural context of tribal life and not merely in narrative. By this I mean that the ideas, emotions, and desires associated with a given story are experienced not only when the story is told, but also when in certain customs, moral rules, or ritual proceedings, the counterpart of the story is enacted. And here a considerable difference is discovered between the several types of story. While in the mere fireside *tale* the sociological context is narrow, the *legend* enters much more deeply into the tribal life of the community, and the *myth* plays a most important function. Myth, as a statement of primeval reality which still lives in present-day life and as a justification by precedent, supplies a retrospective pattern of moral values, sociological order, and magical belief. It is, therefore, neither a mere narrative, nor a form of science, nor a branch of art or history, nor an explanatory tale. It fulfills a function *sui generis* closely connected with the nature of tradition, and the continuity of culture, with the relation between age and youth, and with the human attitude towards the past. The function of myth, briefly, is to strengthen tradition and endow it with a greater value and prestige by tracing it back to a higher, better, more supernatural reality of initial events.

Myth is, therefore, an indispensable ingredient of all culture. It is, as we have seen, constantly regenerated; every historical change creates its mythology, which is, however, but indirectly related to historical fact. Myth is a constant by-product of living faith, which is in need of miracles; of sociological status, which demands precedent; of moral rule, which requires sanction.

We have made, perhaps, a too ambitious attempt to give a new definition of myth. Our conclusions imply a new method of treating the science of folklore, for we have shown that it cannot be independent of ritual, of sociology, or even of material culture. Folk tales, legends, and myths must be lifted from their flat existence on paper, and placed in the three-dimensional reality of full life. As regards anthropological field work, we are obviously demanding a new method of collecting evidence. The anthropologist must relinquish his comfortable position in the long chair on the veranda of the missionary compound, Government station, or planter's bungalow, where, armed with pencil and note-book and at times with a whisky and soda, he has been accustomed to collect statements from informants, write down stories, and fill out sheets of paper with savage texts. He must go out into the villages, and see the natives at work in gardens, on the beach, in the jungle; he must sail with them to distant sandbanks and to foreign tribes, and observe them in fishing, trading, and ceremonial overseas expeditions. Information must come to him full-flavored from his own observations of native life, and not be squeezed out of reluctant informants as a trickle of talk. Field work can be done first or secondhand even among the savages, in the middle of pile dwellings, not far from actual can-nibalism and head-hunting. Open-air anthropology, as op-posed to hearsay note-taking, is hard work, but it is also great fun. Only such anthropology can give us the all-round vision of primitive man and of primitive culture. Such an-thropology shows us, as regards myth, that far from being an idle mental pursuit, it is a vital ingredient of practical relation to the environment.

The claims and merits, however, are not mine, but are due once more to Sir James Frazer. The Golden Bough contains the theory of the ritual and sociological function of myth, to which I have been able to make but a small con-tribution, in that I could test, prove, and document in my field work. This theory is implied in Frazer's treatment of magic; in his masterly exposition of the great importance of agricultural rites; in the central place which the cults of vegetation and fertility occupy in the volumes of Adonis, Attis, Osiris, and in those on the Spirits of the Corn and of the Wild. In these works, as in so many of his other writings, Sir James Frazer has established the intimate relation be-tween the word and the deed in primitive faith; he has shown that the words of the story and of the spell, and the acts of ritual and ceremony are the two aspects of primitive belief. The deep philosophic query propounded by Faust, as to the primacy of the word or of the deed, appears to us fallacious. The beginning of man is the beginning of articulate thought and of thought put into action. Without words, whether framed in sober rational conversation, or launched in magical spells, or used to entreat superior divinities, man would not have been able to embark upon his great Odyssey of cultural adventure and achievement.

Baloma; the Spirits of the Dead in the Trobriand Islands[1]

I.

Among the natives of Kiriwina, death is the starting point of two series of events which run almost independently of each other. Death affects the deceased individual; his soul (*baloma* or *bulum*) leaves the body and goes to another world, there to lead a shadowy existence. His passing is also a matter of concern to the bereft community. Its members wail for him, mourn for him, and celebrate an endless series of feasts. These festivities consist, as a rule, in the distribution of uncooked food; while less frequently they are actual feasts in which cooked food is eaten on the spot. They center around the dead man's body, and are closely connected with the duties of mourning, wailing and sorrowing for the dead individual. But—and this is the important point for the present description—these social activities and ceremonies have no connection with the spirit. They are not performed, either to send a message of love and regret to the *baloma* (spirit), or to deter him from returning; they do not influence his welfare, nor do they affect his relation to the survivors.

It is possible, therefore, to discuss the native beliefs in

afterlife without touching the subject of mourning and mortuary ceremonies. The latter are extremely complex, and, in order to be properly described, a thorough knowledge of the native social system would be required.[2] In this article the beliefs concerning the spirits of the dead and afterlife will be described.

A remarkable thing happens to the spirit immediately after its exodus from the body. Broadly speaking, it may be described as a kind of splitting up. In fact, there are two beliefs, which, being obviously incompatible, yet exist side by side. One of them is, that the *baloma* (which is the main form of the dead man's spirit) goes "to Tuma, a small island lying some ten miles to the northwest of the Trobriands."[3] This island is inhabited by living man as well, who dwell in one large village, also called Tuma; and it is often visited by natives from the main island. The other belief affirms that the spirit leads a short and precarious existence after death near the village, and about the usual haunts of the dead man, such as his garden, or the seabeach, or the waterhole. In this form, the spirit is called *kosi* (sometimes pronounced *kos*). The connection between the *kosi* and the *Baloma* is not very clear, and the natives do not trouble to reconcile any inconsistencies with regard to this matter. The more intelligent informants are able to explain away the inconsistencies, but such "theological" attempts do not agree with each other, and there does not seem to be any predominantly orthodox version.[4] The two beliefs, however, exist side by side in dogmatic strength; they are known to be true, and they influence the actions of men and regulate their behavior; thus the people are genuinely, though not very deeply, frightened of the *kosi*, and some of the actions observed in mourning, and the disposal of the dead, imply belief in the spirit's journey to Tuma, with some of its details.

The dead man's body is adorned with all his valuable ornaments, and all the articles of native wealth he possessed are laid beside it. This is done in order that he may carry the "essence" or "spirit part" of his riches to the other world. These proceedings imply the belief in Topileta, the native Charon, who receives his "fare" from the spirit (see below).

The *kosi*, the ghost of the dead man, may be met on a road near the village, or be seen in his garden, or heard knocking at the houses of his friends and relatives, for a few days after death. People are distinctly afraid of meeting the *kosi*, and are always on the lookout for him, but they are not in really deep terror of him. The *kosi* seems always to be in the mood of a frivolous, yet harmless, hobgoblin, playing small tricks, making himself a nuisance, and frightening people, as one man might frighten another in the darkness for a practical joke. He may throw small stones or gravel at anyone passing his haunt of an evening; or call out his name; or laughter may be heard coming out of the night. But he will never do any actual harm. Nobody has ever been hurt, still less killed, by a *kosi*. Nor do the *kosi* ever employ any of those ghastly, hair-raising methods of frightening people, so well known from our own ghost stories.

I remember well the first time I heard the *kosi* mentioned. It was a dark night, and I, in the company of three natives, was returning from a neighboring village, where a man had died that afternoon and been buried in our presence. We were marching in Indian file, when suddenly one of the natives stopped, and they all began to talk, looking around with evident curiosity and interest, but without a trace of terror. My interpreter explained that the *kosi* was heard in the yam garden which we were just crossing. I was struck by the frivolous way in which the natives treated this gruesome incident, and tried to make out how far they were serious about the alleged appearance, and in what manner they reacted to it emotionally. There seemed to be not the slightest doubt about the reality of the occurrence, and I afterwards learned that although the *kosi* is quite commonly seen or heard, no one is afraid to go alone into the darkness of the garden where the *kosi* has just been heard, nor is anyone in the least under the influence of the heavy, oppressing, almost paralyzing fear so well known to all those who have experienced or studied the fear of ghosts, as these are conceived by us in Europe. The natives have absolutely no "ghost stories" to relate about the *kosi* beyond insignificant pranks, and even little children do not seem to be afraid of him.

In general, there is a remarkable absence of superstitious fear of darkness, and no reluctance to go about alone at night. I have sent out boys, of certainly not more than ten years of age, a good distance alone at night, to fetch some object left on purpose, and I found that they were remarkably fearless, and for a small bit of tobacco quite ready to go. Men and youths will walk alone at night from one village to another, often a couple of miles, without the chance of meeting anyone. In fact, as such excursions are usually carried out in connection with some love adventure, often illicit, the man would avoid meeting anybody by stepping aside into the bush. I well remember having met on the road in the dusk solitary women, though only old ones. The road from Omarakana (and a whole series of other villages lying not far from the eastern shore) to the beach passes through the *raiboag*, a well-wooded coral ridge, where the path winds through boulders and rocks, over crevasses and near caves, at night a very uncanny type of surrounding; but the natives often go there and back at night, quite alone; of course, individuals differ, some being more afraid than others, but in general there is very little of the universally reported native's dread of darkness among the Kiriwinians.[5]

Nevertheless, when death occurs in a village, there is an enormous increase of superstitious fear. This fear is not, however, aroused by the *kosi* but by much less "supernatural" beings, *i.e.*, by invisible sorceresses called *mulukuausi*. These are actual living women who may be known and talked with in ordinary life, but who are supposed to possess the power of making themselves invisible, or of despatching a "sending" from their bodies, or of traveling vast distances through the air. In this disembodied form they are extremely virulent, powerful, and also ubiquitous.[6]

Anyone who chances to be exposed to them is sure to be attacked.

They are especially dangerous at sea, and whenever there is a storm, and a canoe is threatened, the *mulukuausi* are there looking out for prey. Nobody, therefore, would dream of going on any more distant voyage such as south to the D'Entrecasteaux group, or east to the Marshall Bennets, or still further, to Woodlark Island, without knowing the *kaiga'u*, a powerful magic, designed to ward off and bewilder the *mulukuausi*. Even when building a sea-going *waga* (canoe) of the large type, called *masawa*, spells must be uttered to reduce the danger from these terrible women.

They are also dangerous on land, where they attack people and eat away tongues, eyes, and lungs (*lopoulo*, translated "lungs," also denotes the "insides" in general). But all these data really belong to the chapter about sorcery and evil magic, and have only been mentioned here, where the *mulukuausi* interest us, as especially connected with the dead. For they are possessed of truly ghoulish instincts. Whenever a man dies, they simply swarm and feed on his insides. They eat away his *lopoulo*, his tongue, his eyes, and, in fact, all his body, after which they become more than ever dangerous to the living. They assemble all round the house where the dead man lived and try to enter it. In the old days, when the corpse was exposed in the middle of the village in a half-covered grave, the *mulukuausi* used to congregate on the trees in and around the village.⁷ When the body is carried into the grave to be buried, magic is used to ward off the *mulukuausi*.

The *mulukuausi* are intimately connected with the smell of carrion, and I have heard many natives affirm that at sea, when in danger, they were distinctly conscious of the smell of *burapuase* (carrion), which was a sign that the evil women were there.

The *mulukuausi* are objects of real terror. Thus the immediate neighborhood of the grave is absolutely deserted when night approaches. I owe my first acquaintance with the *mulukuausi* to an actual experience. Quite at the beginning of my stay in Kiriwina, I had been watching the wailing round a freshly made grave. After sunset, all the mourners retired into the village, and when they tried to beckon me away, I insisted on remaining behind, thinking that there might be some ceremony which they wanted to perform in my absence. After I had maintained my vigil for some ten minutes, a few men returned with my interpreter, who had previously gone to the village. He explained the matter to me, and was very serious about the danger from the *mulukuausi*, though, knowing white men and their ways, he was not so much concerned for me.[8]

Even in and around the village where a death has occurred there is the greatest fear of the *mulukuausi*, and at night the natives refuse to go about the village or to enter the surrounding grove and gardens. I have often questioned natives as to the real danger of walking about alone at night soon after a man had died, and there was never the slightest doubt that the only beings to be dreaded were the *mulukuausi*.

II.

Having dealt with the *kosi*, the frivolous and meek ghost of the deceased who vanishes after a few days of irrelevant existence, and with the *mulukuausi*, the ghoulish, dangerous women who feed on carrion and attack the living, we may pass to the main form of the spirit, the *baloma*. I call this the main form because the *baloma* leads a positive, well-defined existence in Tuma; because he returns from time to time to his village; because he has been visited and seen in Tuma by men awake and men asleep, and by those who were almost dead, yet returned to life again; because he plays a notable part in native magic, and even receives offerings and a kind of propitiation; finally, because he asserts his reality in the most radical manner by returning to the place of life, by reincarnation, and thus leads a continuous existence.

The *baloma* leaves the body immediately after death has occurred and goes to Tuma. The route taken and the mode of transit are essentially the same as those which a living person would take in order to go from his village to Tuma. Tuma is an island; one must therefore sail in a canoe. A *baloma* from a coastal village would embark and cross over to the island. A spirit from one of the inland villages would go to one of the coastal villages whence it is customary to embark for Tuma. Thus from Omarakana, a village situated almost in the center of the northern part of Boiowa (the main island of the Trobriand group), the spirit would go to Kaibuola, a village on the north coast, from whence it is easy to sail to Tuma, especially during the southeast season, when the southeast trade wind would be dead fair, and carry the canoe over in a few hours. At Olivilevi, a large village on the east coast, which I visited during the *milamala* (the annual feast of the spirits), the *baloma* were supposed to be encamped on the beach, where they had arrived in their canoes, the latter being of a "spiritual" and "immaterial" quality, though perhaps such expressions imply more than the natives conceive. One thing is certain, that no ordinary man under ordinary circumstances would see such a canoe or anything belonging to a *baloma*.

As we have seen at the outset, when a *baloma* leaves the village and the people who wail for him, his connection with them is severed; for a time, at least, their wailings do not reach him or in any way influence his welfare. His own heart is sore, and he grieves for those left behind. On the beach at Tuma there is a stone called Modawosi, on which the spirit sits down and wails, looking back towards the shores of Kiriwina. Soon other *baloma* hear him. All his kinsmen and friends come towards him, squat down with him, and join in his lamentations. Their own departure is brought home to them, and they are sorry to think of their homes and of all those they left behind. Some of the *baloma* wail, some sing a monotonous chant, exactly as is done during the great mortuary vigil (*iawali*) after a man's death. Then the *baloma* goes to a well, called Gilala,[9] and washes his eyes, which renders him invisible.[10] From here the spirit proceeds to Dukupuala, a spot in the *raiboag* where there are two stones called Dikumaio'i. The *balom* knocks these two stones in turn. The first responds with a loud sound (*kakupuana*), but when the second is hit the earth trembles (*ioiu*). The *baloma* hear this sound, and they all congregate round the newcomer and welcome him to Tuma.[11]

Somewhere during this ingress the spirit has to face Topileta, the headman of the villages of the dead. At what stage exactly Topileta meets the stranger my informants were unable to say, but it must be somewhere in the early part of his adventures in Tuma, because Topileta lives not far from the Modawosi stone, and acts as a kind of Cerberus or St. Peter in so far as he admits the spirit into the nether world, and is even supposed to be able to refuse admission. His decision does not, however, rest on moral considerations of any description: it is simply conditioned by his satisfaction with the payment made by the newcomer. After death the bereaved relatives adorn the corpse with all the native ornaments which the deceased had possessed. They also put on his body all his other *vaigu'a* (valuables),[12] in the first place his ceremonial axe blades (*beku*). The spirit is supposed to carry these away with him to Tuma—in their "spiritual" aspect, of course. As the natives explain simply and exactly: "As the man's *baloma* goes away and his body remains, so the *baloma* of the jewels and axe blades go away to Tuma, though the objects remain."[13] The spirit carries these valuables in a small basket and makes an appropriate present to Topileta.

This payment is said to be made for showing the proper way to Tuma. Topileta asks the newcomer the cause of his death. There are three classes—death as the result of evil magic, death by poison, and death in warfare. There are also three roads leading to Tuma, and Topileta indicates the proper road according to the form of death suffered. There is no special virtue attached to any of these roads, though my informants were unanimous in saying that death in war was a "good death," that by poison not so good, while death by sorcery is the worst. These qualifications meant that a man would prefer to die one death rather than another; and though they did not imply any moral attribute attached to any of these forms, a certain glamor attached to death in war, and the dread of sorcery and sickness seem certainly to cause those preferences.

With death in warfare is classed one form of suicide, that in which a man climbs a tree and throws himself down (native name, *lo'u*). This is one of the two forms of suicide extant in Kiriwina, and it is practiced by both men and women. Suicide seems to be very common.[14] It is performed as an act of justice, not upon oneself, but upon some person of near kindred who has caused offense. As such it is one of the most important legal institutions among these natives. The underlying psychology is, however, not so simple, and this remarkable group of facts cannot be discussed here in detail.

Besides the *lo'u*, suicide is also accomplished by taking poison, for which purpose the fish poison (*tuva*) is used.[15] Such people, together with those murdered by the gall bladder of the poisonous fish, *soka*, go the second road, that of poison.

People who have died by drowning go the same road as those killed in war, and drowning was said to be also a "good death."

Finally comes the group of all those who have been killed by evil sorcery. The natives admit that there may be illness from natural causes, and they distinguish it from bewitchment by evil magic. But, according to the prevalent view, only the latter can be fatal. Thus the third road to Tuma includes all the cases of "natural death," in our sense of the word, of death not due to an obvious accident. To the native minds such deaths are, as a rule, due to sorcery.[16] The female spirits go the same three ways as the male. They are shown the way by Topileta's wife, called Bomiamuia. So much about the various classes of death.

A man or woman unable to pay the necessary fee to the

gatekeeper of the Underworld would fare very badly. Such a spirit, turned out of Tuma, would be banished into the sea and changed into a *vaiaba*, a mythical fish possessing the head and tail of a shark and the body of a stingaree. However, the danger of being turned into a *vaiaba* does not appear to loom conspicuously in the native mind; on the contrary, on inquiry I gathered that such a disaster rarely, if ever, happens, and my informants were unable to quote any instance. When asked whence they knew about such things, they gave the usual answer, "ancient talk" (*tokunabogu livala*). Thus there are no ordeals after death, no accounts of one's life to give to anyone, no tests to undergo, and in general no difficulties whatever on the road from this life to the other.

As to the nature of Topileta, Professor Seligman writes: "Topileta resembles a man in every way except that he has huge ears, which flap continually; he is, according to one account, of the Malasi clan, and seems to lead very much the ordinary life of a Trobriand Islander." This information was collected on a neighboring island, Kaileula (called by Professor Seligman, Kadawaga), but it entirely agrees with what I was told on Kiriwina about Topileta. Professor Seligman further writes: "He (Topileta) has certain magical powers, causing earthquakes at will, and when he becomes old, making medicine which restores youth to himself, his wife and children.

"Chiefs still retain their authority in Tuma, and Topileta, though himself the most important being in Tuma . . . is so obviously regarded as different from all dead chiefs that he cannot, in the ordinary sense, be said to rule over the dead; indeed, it was difficult to discover that Topileta exerted any authority in the other world." [17]

In fact, Topileta is an intrinsic accessory of Tuma, but, beyond his initial meeting with all spirits, he does not in any way interfere with their doings. Chiefs do, indeed, retain their rank, though whether they exercise any authority was not clear to my informants.[18] Topileta is, moreover, the real owner or master of the spiritland on Tuma and of the

villages.[19] There are three villages in the nether world—
Tuma proper, Wabuaima, and Walisiga. Topileta is the
tolivalu (master of village) of all three, but whether this is
a mere title or whether he has anything to say in important
matters was not known to any of my informants. It was
also unknown whether the three villages had any connection
with the three roads leading to the nether world.

Having passed Topileta, the spirit enters the village in
which he will dwell henceforth. He always finds some of
his relatives, and these may stay with him till a house is
found or built for him. The natives imagine this exactly
as happens in this world when a man has to move to another
village—a by no means rare event in the Trobriands. For
a time the stranger is very sad, and weeps. There are,
however, decided attempts on the part of the other *baloma*,
especially those of the opposite sex, to make him comfortable in his new existence, and to induce him to form new
ties and attachments and forget the old ones. My informants
(who were all men) were unanimous in declaring that a
man coming to Tuma is simply pestered by the advances of
the fair, and, in this world, bashful, sex. At first the spirit
wants to weep for those left behind; his relative *baloma*
protect him, saying, "Wait, let him have a spell; let him
cry." If he has been happily married, and has left a widow
for whom he cares, he naturally wants to be left for a somewhat longer time to his grief. All in vain! It seems (this is
again the male opinion only) that there are many more
women in the other world than men, and that they are
very impatient of any prolonged mourning. If they cannot
succeed otherwise, they try magic, the all-powerful means
of gaining another person's affection. The spirit women on
Tuma are not less expert, and no more scrupulous, in
using love charms than the living women in Kiriwina. The
stranger's grief is very soon overcome, and he accepts the
offering called *nabuoda'u*—a basket filled with *bu'a* (betel
nut), *mo'i* (betel pepper), and scented herbs. This is offered to him with the words "*Kam paku*," and if accepted,
the two belong to each other.[20] A man may wait for his

widow to join him in Tuma, but my informants did not seem inclined to think that many would do this. The blame for this rests, however, entirely on the Tuma belles, who use such potent magic that not even the strongest fidelity can possibly resist it.

The spirit, in any case, settles down to a happy existence in Tuma, where he spends another lifetime,[21] until he dies again. But this new death is again not complete annihilation, as we shall see hereafter.

III.

Until this occurs the *baloma* is by no means entirely out of touch with the living world. He visits his native village from time to time, and he is visited by his surviving friends and relatives. Some of these latter possess the faculty of getting right into the shadowy world of spirits. Others are able to get glimpses only of the *baloma*, to hear them, to see them from a distance or in the dark—just sufficiently clearly to recognize them, and to be absolutely sure that they are *baloma*.

Tuma—the place of the living—is a village where the natives of Kiriwina go from time to time. In Tuma and the adjoining islands turtle shell and the large white cowrie shells (*Ovulum ovum*) are very plentiful; in fact, this small island is the main source of those important articles of decoration for the northern and eastern villages of Kiriwina.[22] Therefore Tuma is often visited by men from the main island.

All my informants from Omarakana and the neighboring villages knew Tuma quite well. And there was hardly anybody who had not had some experience of the *baloma*. One man saw a shadow in the twilight receding at his approach; another heard a well-known voice, etc., etc. Bagido'u, an exceptionally intelligent man of the Tabalu subclan, the garden magician of Omarakana, and my best informant on all matters of ancient lore and tradition, has

seen any number of spirits, and had not the slightest doubt
that a man staying in Tuma for some length of time would
have no difficulty in seeing any of his deceased friends.
One day he (Bagido'u) was getting water out of a well in
the *raiboag* (stony woodland) on Tuma, when a *baloma*
hit him on the back, and, on turning round, Bagido'u
just saw a shadow retreating into the bush, and heard a
smacking sound, such as is usually made with the lips if a
native wants to attract somebody's attention. Again, one
night, Bagido'u was sleeping in Tuma on a bed. Suddenly
he found himself lifted out of it and put on the ground.

A large party of men, with To'uluwa, the chief of Omarakana, went to Tuma. They landed not far from the
Modawosi stone, when they saw a man standing there. They
immediately identified him as Gi'iopeulo, a great warrior
and a man of indomitable strength and courage, who had
died recently in a village not more than five minutes distance from Omarakana. When they approached, he dis-
appeared, but they heard distinctly "*Bu kusisusi bala* [You
remain, I shall go]"—the usual form of "Good-by." Another
of my informants was in Tuma drinking water in one of
the large water grottoes, so typical of the *raiboag*. He heard
a girl called Buava'u Lagim cry out to him, calling him by
name, out of this waterhole.

I have heard of many more such incidents. It is worthy of
note that in all these cases the *baloma* are distinct from the
kosi—that is, the natives are sure that it is a *baloma*, and
not a *kosi*, that is seen or heard, though their slightly
frivolous behavior (like the throwing of a respectable man
out of his bed, or hitting him on the back) does not differ
from that of the *kosi* in any essential respect. Again, the
natives do not seem to regard any of those appearances or
pranks of the *baloma* with any sort of "creepy" feeling; they
do not seem to be afraid of them, as Europeans are of
ghosts, any more than they are of the *kosi*.

Besides these intermittent glimpses of the spirit life, the
living are brought into touch with the *baloma* in a much
more intimate manner, through the mediation of those

privileged people who visit in their own person the land of the dead. Professor Seligman writes: "There are individuals who say that they have visited Tuma and returned to the upper world." [23] Such people are by no means rare, and are of both sexes, though, of course, they differ vastly in renown. In Omarakana, the village where I was living, the most renowned person of this sort was a woman, Bwoilagesi, a daughter of the late chief Numakala, brother and predecessor of To'uluwa, the present ruler of Omarakana. She has visited, and apparently continues to visit, Tuma, where she sees and speaks with the *baloma*. She has also brought back a *baloma* song from Tuma, which is sung very often by the women of Omarakana.

There is also a man, Moniga'u, who goes to Tuma from time to time and brings news from the spirits. Although I knew both those people very well, I was not able to get from them any detailed information as to their wanderings in Tuma. They were both very uneasy on this subject, and returned my questions with half-hearted and obvious answers. I was strongly under the impression that they were unable to give any detailed statements, and that all they knew was told by them to everybody, and was thus public property. Such public property was the song above mentioned,[24] and also personal messages from various spirits to their families. Bwoilagesi—with whom I talked once on this subject in the presence of her son, Tukulubakiki, one of the most friendly, decent and intelligent natives I met—stated that she never remembers what she saw, though she remembers what was told to her. She does not walk or sail to Tuma; she falls asleep and just finds herself among the *baloma*. She and her son were quite positive that the song was given her by the *baloma*. But it was evident that the subject was painful to Tukulubakiki, especially when I pressed about details. I was unable to find any instance in which my lady informant derived actual economic benefit from her exploits in Tuma, though her prestige was immensely enhanced, in spite of the existence of sporadic, yet unmistakable, scepticism.

Thus I was told by two of my informants that all such claims about seeing the *Baloma* are downright lies. One of them, Gomaia, a boy of Sinaketa (a village on the southern half of the island) told me that one of the most remarkable men who used to visit Tuma was one Mitakai'io, of Oburaku; but even he was a humbug. He used to boast that he could go to Tuma in order to eat. "I want to eat now; I shall go to Tuma; there is plenty of food there: ripe bananas, yams and taro, ready to eat; fish and pigs; there is plenty of areca nut and betel pepper, too; all the time I go to Tuma I eat." It may be easily imagined how strongly these pictures would appeal to the natives' fancy, how they would enhance the personal prestige of the boaster and arouse the envy of the more ambitious. Boasting about food is the most prevalent form of native vanity or ambition. A commoner might pay with his life if he had too much food or too good a garden, and especially if he displayed it too boastfully.

Gomaia apparently did not like Mitakai'io's boastings, and tried to get at the truth. He offered one pound. "I'll give you one pound if you take me to Tuma." But Mitakai'io was satisfied with much less. "Your father and mother cry for you all the time; they want to see you; give me two sticks of tobacco and I shall go, see them, give them the tobacco. Your father saw me; he told me, 'Bring the tobacco from Gomaia.'" But Mitakai'io was not in a hurry to take Gomaia to the other world. Gomaia gave him the two sticks, and these were smoked by the wizard himself. Gomaia found it out and was very indignant, and insisted on getting to Tuma, promising to give the pound as soon as he returned from there again. Mitakai'io gave him three kinds of leaves, which he ordered him to rub all over his body, and to swallow another small parcel. This was done, and Gomaia lay down and went to sleep—but he never reached Tuma. This made him sceptical, but, though Mitakai'io never got the promised pound, he retained his general prestige.

The same Mitakai'io exposed another minor Tuma seer,

by name Tomuaia Lakuabula. There was a chronic controversy between the two, Mitakai'io often expressing a
contemptuous opinion about Tomuaia. Finally the matter
had to be settled by a test. Tomuaia promised to go to
Tuma and to bring some token from there. As a matter of
fact, he went to the bush and stole a bunch of betel nuts
belonging to Mourada the *tokaraiwaga valu* (village headman) of Oburaku. He consumed plenty of the nuts himself,
keeping one, however, for future use. In the evening he said
to his wife, "Prepare my mat on the couch; I hear the
baloma singing; I shall soon be with them; I must lie
down." Then he began to sing in his house. All the men
outside heard him and said to each other: "It is Tomuaia
who sings alone and none else." They told him so the next
day, but he said they could not have heard him, but many
of the *baloma* were singing, and he had joined them.

When day was approaching, he put the one betel nut,
kept for the purpose, into his mouth, and at daybreak he
got up, went out of his house, and, taking the betel nut
from his mouth, cried: "I have been to Tuma; I have
brought a betel nut from there." All the people were highly
impressed with the token, but Mourada and Mitakai'io,
who had watched him carefully on the previous day, knew
that he had stolen the bunch of nuts, and they exposed
him. From that time Tomuaia did not talk about Tuma.
I have noted this story exactly as I heard it from Gomaia,
and I am telling it in the same form. The natives in their
narrative very often do not preserve the right perspective,
however. It seems to me probable that my informant has
condensed into his account different occurrences; but in
this place it is the main fact of the natives' psychological
attitude towards "spiritism" that is interesting; I mean the
pronounced scepticism of some individuals on this subject
and the tenacity of belief among the majority. It is also
obvious from these stories—and it was stated outright by
my sceptical friends—that the chief element in all wanderings to Tuma is the material benefit derived from this by
the seers.

A slightly different form of communication with spirits is that of the men who have short fits, in which they talk to the *baloma*. I am not able even approximately to define the psychological or pathological basis of such phenomena. Unfortunately, they were only brought to my notice towards the end of my stay—in fact, about a fortnight before my departure, and then only by accident. One morning I heard loud and, it seemed to me, quarrelsome vociferation from the other side of the village, and, being always on the alert for some sociological "document," I inquired from the natives in my hut what it was. They replied that Gumguya'u —a respectable and quiet man—was talking to the *baloma*. I hurried to the spot, but, arriving too late, found the man exhausted on his bed, apparently asleep. The incident did not arouse any excitement, because, as they said, it was his habit to talk to the *baloma*. The conversation was carried on by Gumguya'u in a loud and high-pitched tone that sounded like an abusive monologue, and it was said to have reference to a big ceremonial boat race which had taken place two days before. Such a race is always held when a new canoe is built, and it is the duty of the chief, who organizes it, to arrange a big *sagali* (ceremonial distribution of food) in connection with the festivities. The *baloma* are in some impersonal and vague manner always interested in festivities, and they watch to ensure plenty of food. Any scarcity, caused either by slackness or the bad luck of the organizer, is resented by the *baloma*, who blame him for it, whether it be his fault or not. Thus, in this case, the *baloma* had approached Gumguya'u with the intention of expressing their strong disapproval of the meager character of the *sagali* made the other day on the beach. The organizer of the feast was, of course, To'uluwa, the chief of Omarakana.

Dreams also seem to play some part in the commerce between the *baloma* and the living. Perhaps the cases in which principally the *baloma* thus appear to the living occur immediately after death, when the spirit comes and tells the news to any near friend or relative who is not on the spot. Again, *baloma* often come to women in dreams to tell them that they will become enceinte. During the *milamala*, the annual feast, people are frequently visited by dead relatives in dreams. In the first of the cases mentioned (when spirits after death come to absent friends or relatives) there is some latitude and some "symbolizing," such as has been assumed in the interpretation of dreams throughout all ages and civilizations. Thus a large party of Omarakana boys went away to work on a plantation in Milne Bay, on the extreme east end of the mainland of New Guinea. Among them was Kalogusa, a son of To'uluwa, the chief, and Gumigawa'ia, a commoner from Omarakana. One night Kalogusa dreamt that his mother, an old woman, one of the sixteen wives of To'uluwa, now living in Omarakana, came to him and told him that she had died. He was very sad, and apparently showed his grief by wailing. (The story was told to me by one of the party.) All the others knew that "something must have happened in Omarakana." When they learned on their way home that the mother of Gumigawa'ia had died, they were not at all astonished, and found in this the explanation of Kalogusa's dream.

This seems to be the proper place to discuss the nature of the *baloma* and their relation to the *kosi*. Of what stuff are they made? Of the same or of different substance? Are they shades, or spirits, or are they conceived materially? It is possible to put all these questions to the natives, the most intelligent of whom will grasp them without difficulty and discuss them with the ethnographer, showing a considerable amount of insight and interest. But such discussions have proved to me unmistakably that in dealing with these and similar questions one leaves behind the domain of belief proper and approaches quite a different class of native ideas. Here the native speculates rather than positively believes, and his speculations are not a very serious matter to him, nor does he trouble at all as to whether they are orthodox or not. Only exceptionally intelligent natives will enter into such questions at all, and these express rather their private opinion than positive tenets. Even the exceptionally intelligent natives have nothing in their vocabulary or store

of ideas that would correspond even approximately to our
ideas of "substance" or "nature," though there is a word,
u'ula, corresponding approximately to "cause," "origin."

You may ask: "What is the *baloma* like? Is its body like
ours, or different? And in what manner is it different?" You
may further point out to the native the problem of the
body remaining and the disembodied *baloma* going away.
To such questions the answer will be almost invariably that
the *baloma* is like a reflection (*saribu*) in water (or mirror
for the modern Kiriwinian), and that the *kosi* is like a
shadow (*kaikuabula*). This distinction—the "reflection"
character of the *baloma* and the shadowy nature of the
kosi—is the usual, but by no means the exclusive opinion.
At times both are said to be like *saribu* or like *kaikuabula*.
I was always under the impression that such answers were
not so much a definition as a simile. By that I mean that
the natives were not at all certain that a *baloma* is made of
the same matter as a reflection; they knew, in fact, that
a reflection is "nothing," that it is a *sasopa* (lie), that there
is no *baloma* in it, but the *baloma* is just "something
like a reflection" (*baloma makawala saribu*). When forced
against a metaphysical wall by such questions, "How can a
baloma call out, and eat, and make love if it is like a *saribu*?
How can a *kosi* hammer against a house, or throw stones, or
strike a man if it is like a shadow?" the more intelligent
replied more or less to the effect: "Well the *baloma* and the
kosi are like the reflection and like the shadow, but they are
also like men, and they behave all the same as men do."
And it was difficult to argue with them.[25] The less intelligent or less patient informants were inclined to shrug their
shoulders over such questions; others, again, would obviously become interested in the speculations, and produce
extempore opinions, and ask your view, and just enter into
a metaphysical discussion of a sort. Such extemporized
opinions, however, never amounted to very far-reaching
speculations; they just turned round the general views above
mentioned.

It must be clearly understood that there were certain

tenets which my informants one and all would endorse.
There is not the slightest doubt that a *baloma* retains the
semblance of the man he represents, so that if you see the
baloma, you recognize the man that was. The *baloma* live
the life of men; they get older; they eat, sleep, love, both
whilst in Tuma and on visits which they pay to their villages. All these were points on which the natives had not
the slightest doubts. It will be remarked that these tenets
refer to actions of the *baloma,* describe their behavior, and
also that some of them—such as the belief in the *baloma's*
need of food, for instance—imply certain behavior on the
part of men (compare below, description of the *milamala*).
The only almost general tenet concerning the *baloma* and
kosi was that the former are like reflections, the latter like
shadows. It is noteworthy that this double simile corresponds respectively to the open, defined, permanent nature
of the *baloma* and to the vague, precarious, nocturnal character of the *kosi.*

But even as to the fundamental relations between the
baloma and *kosi* there exist essential discrepancies—discrepancies which bear not merely on their nature, but even
upon their relative existence. By far the more general view
is that the *baloma* goes straight to Tuma and that another
spirit, the *kosi,* roams about for a short time. This view
admits of two interpretations: either there are two spirits
in the living man, and they both leave the body at death,
or else the *kosi* is a kind of secondary spirit, appearing only
at death and absent in a living body. The natives understood this question if I put it in this form: "Do the *baloma*
and *kosi* stop in the body all the time? Or, on the contrary, does the *baloma* alone stop in the body and the *kosi*
only appear at death?" But the answers were all vacillating
and contradictory, the same man giving different answers
at various times, the best proof that one was in the domain
of pure extempore speculation.

Besides this more general view, I found several men who
repeatedly maintained that the *kosi* is the first stage of a
development, and that subsequently, after a few days, the

kosi is transformed into a *baloma*. Here we would have, therefore, only one spirit, who lingers for a time after death round and near his home and then departs. In spite of its greater simplicity and logical plausibility, this belief was by far the less pronounced. It was, however, independent and developed enough to prevent the former belief being assumed as exclusive or even orthodox.

An interesting variation of the first version (that of a parallel existence of both *baloma* and *kosi*) was that given by Gomaia, one of my best informants. He was positive that only such men as had been sorcerers (*bwoga'u*) during their life would produce a *kosi* after death. To be a *bwoga'u* is not very difficult, however. Any man who knows any of the *silami* (evil spells), and who is in the habit of practicing them, is a *bwoga'u*. According to Gomaia, the others (the ordinary persons) would not become *kosi*; they would become *baloma* only, and go to Tuma. In all other particulars—such as the respective nature of *baloma* and *kosi*, and the behavior as well as the precarious existence—Gomaia agreed with the general views. His version is noteworthy, because he is a very intelligent native and his father was a great wizard and *bwoga'u*, and his *kadala* (maternal uncle) is also a sorcerer. Moreover, this version agrees very well with the fact that the *bwoga'u* is always imagined as prowling at night, and, in fact, except for the *mulukuausi*, he presents the only serious terror of the night. Again, the *mulukuausi*, though not the *bwoga'u* (a still more virulent form of evil-minded human being, wise in sorcery), have, as we saw above, a "double" or "sending" called *kakuluwala*, which leaves their body and travels invisibly. This belief in a "double" or "sending" is parallel to another, which affirms that the *mulukuausi* travel bodily.

These remarks show that, generally speaking, the question as to the nature of the *baloma* and *kosi* and of their mutual relationship has not crystallized into any orthodox and definite doctrine.

The relation of the *baloma* to the body of the living man is still less clear to the natives. They are unable to give any definite answers to such questions as: "Does the *baloma* stop in any part of the body (head, belly, lungs)? Can it leave it during life? Is it the *baloma* that walks in dreams? Is it the *baloma* of some people that go to Tuma?" Though the two last-mentioned questions are usually answered by "yes," it is a very unconvincing affirmation, and it is obvious that these speculations are not backed up by orthodox tradition. Intelligence, memory, wisdom they localize in the body, and know the seat of each of those faculties of the mind; but the *baloma* they are not able to locate, and, indeed, I rather think they imagine that it is a double that detaches itself from the body at death, and not a soul that dwells in the body during life. I am only sure, however, that their ideas are in an uncrystallized form, rather felt than formulated, rather referring to activities of the *baloma* than analytically discussing his nature and various conditions of existence.

Another point about which there appears to be no one definite, dogmatic answer is the actual abode of the spirits. Do they reside on the surface of earth, on the island of Tuma, or do they live underground or elsewhere? There are several opinions, and the respective supporters were quite definite in upholding their views. Thus from a number of informants, including Bagido'u, a very serious and reliable man, I received the answer that the *baloma* live on the island of Tuma, that their villages are somewhere there, exactly as the *baloma* camp somewhere in the neighborhood of a village in Kiriwina on their annual return during the *milamala*. The above-mentioned three villages of the dead share the surface of the island with Tuma, the village of the living. The *baloma* are invisible, and so is everything that belongs to them, and that is the reason why their villages can be there without being in anybody's way.

Another view is that the *baloma* descend underground to a real "nether world," and live there in Tumaviaka (Great Tuma). This view was expressed in two different versions, one of which speaks of a kind of two-storied underworld. When the *baloma* dies at the close of his first spiritual existence he descends to the lower story, or stratum, from whence only he is able to return to the material world (*cf. infra*, VI, Reincarnation). The majority reject this theory, and say that there is only one tier of nether world, which agrees with Professor Seligman's statement: "The spirits of the dead do not stay in the upper world with the living, but descend into the other world below the earth." [26] Again, this view of an underground Tuma seems to harmonize better with the prevalent idea on Kiriwina that the first human beings emerged from holes in the ground. Professor Seligman even obtained the account that "the world was originally colonized from Tuma, men and women being sent to the upper world by Topileta, who himself stopped underground." [27] That I did not come across this statement is not astonishing in consideration of the great diversity of views on certain matters, the nature of Tuma and its relation to the world of the living being one of them. Seligman's statement corroborates the opinion that "underground Tuma" is the most orthodox version, though, as already stated, the whole question is not dogmatically settled in native belief.

IV.

Let us return to the intercourse between living men and the spirits. All that was said above on this subject refers to what takes place in dreams or visions or to what is effected by furtive, short glimpses of spirits, as seen by men while awake and in a normal state of mind. All this kind of intercourse may be described as private and accidental. It is not regulated by customary rules, though, of course, it is subject to a certain frame of mind, and it has to conform with a certain type of belief. It is not public: the whole community does not share in it collectively, and there is no ceremonial associated with it. But there are occasions on which the *baloma* visit the village or take part in certain public functions—occasions on which they are received by the community collectively, when they obtain certain attentions, strictly official and regulated by custom, when they act and play their role in magical activities.

Thus every year, after the garden crops have been harvested and there is a marked pause in the gardening, because the new gardens cannot be seriously tackled yet, the natives have a time of dancing, feasting, and general rejoicing called *milamala*. During the *milamala* the *baloma* are present in the village. They return in a body from Tuma to their own village, where preperations are made to receive them, where special platforms are erected to accommodate them, and where customary gifts are offered to them, and whence, after the full moon is over, they are ceremonially but unceremoniously driven away.

Again, the *baloma* play an important part in magic. Names of ancestral spirits are recited in the magical spells; in fact, these invocations are perhaps the most prominent and persistent feature of the magical spells. Moreover, in some magical performances offerings are made to the *baloma*. There are traces of the belief that the ancestral spirits have some share in fostering the ends of the given magical performances; indeed, those offerings to the *baloma* are the only ceremonial element (in the narrower sense) in magical performances I was able to detect.[28]

I wish to add in this place that there is no association between the *baloma* of a dead man and the relics of his body, such as his skull, jawbone, arm and leg bones, and hair, which are carried about by the relatives and used as lime pot, necklace, and lime spatulae respectively, a connection which exists among some other tribes of New Guinea.[29]

The facts connected with the *milamala* and with the magical role of spirits must now be considered in detail.

The annual feast, *milamala*, is a very complex social and magico-religious phenomenon. It may be called a "harvest festival," as it is held after the yam crops have been harvested and the food houses are full. But, remarkably enough, there is no direct, or even indirect, reference to field activities in the *milamala*. There is nothing in this feast, held after the old gardens have yielded their results and the new ones are waiting to be made, which would imply any retrospective consideration of the past year's gardening or a prospect of the future year's husbandry. The *milamala* is the dancing period. Dancing usually lasts through the moon of *milamala* only, but it may be extended for another moon, or even for two. Such an extension is called *usigula*. No dancing proper takes place at other times of the year. The *milamala* is opened by certain ceremonial performances connected with dancing and with the first beating of the drums. This annual period of feasting and dancing is, of course, also accompanied by a distinct heightening of sexual life. Again, there are certain ceremonial visits paid by one village community to another, and return visits associated with gifts and with such transactions as buying and selling of dances.

Before proceeding to the proper theme of the present section—the description of the part played by the *baloma* in the *milamala*—it seems necessary to give a picture of the general aspect of the festive period, otherwise the detail about the *baloma* would perhaps appear out of focus.

The *milamala* comes in immediate succession to the harvesting activities, which themselves present a distinctly festive character, though they lack the fundamental element of enjoyment for the Kiriwinian. The native finds, however, an enormous amount of joy and amusement in bringing home the harvest. He loves his garden and takes a genuine pride in his crops. Before they are finally stacked in the special storehouses, which are by far the most conspicuous and picturesque buildings in a village, he takes several opportunities of displaying them. Thus, when the tubers of *taitu* (a species of yam)—much the most important crop in that part of the world—are taken out of the ground, they are properly cleaned of all earth, the hair with which they are covered is shaved off with a shell, and the tubers are piled in large conical heaps. Special huts or shelters are constructed in the garden to protect the *taitu* from the sun, and under these shelters the tubers are displayed—a large conical heap in the middle, representing the choice of the yield, and round it several smaller heaps, in which inferior grades of *taitu* are stacked, as well as the tubers to be used for seed. Days and weeks are spent in cleaning the tubers and piling them artistically into heaps, so that the geometrical form may be perfect and none but the very best tubers be visible on the surface. The work is done by the owner and his wife, if he has one, but parties from the village walk about the garden, paying each other visits and admiring the yams. Comparisons and praises are the theme of conversation.

The yams may remain thus for a couple of weeks in the garden, after which time they are carried into the village. These proceedings have a pronouncedly festive character, the carriers decorating themselves with leaves, scented herbs, facial paint, though not with the "full dress" of the dancing time. When the *taitu* is brought into the village the party shout a litany, one man saying the words and the others responding in one strident scream. Usually they come in running to the villages; then the whole party busy themselves arranging the *taitu* into conical heaps exactly similar to those from which it has just been taken in the garden. These heaps are made in the large circular space being put up in front of the yam house, where the tubers will be finally stored.

But before that happens the yams will have to spend another fortnight or so on the ground, and be counted and admired again. They are covered with palm leaves as a protection against the sun. Finally, there is another festive day in the village, when all the heaps are put into the yam houses. This is done in one day, though the bringing of the yams into the village covers several days. This description may give some idea of the considerable heightening of the *tempo* in village life at the time of the harvest, especially as the *taitu* is often brought in from other villages, and the harvest is a time when even distant communities pay each other visits.[30]

When the food is finally in the storehouses there is a pause in native gardening, and this pause is filled by the *milamala*. The ceremony which inaugurates the whole festive period is at the same time a "consecration" of the drums. Previous to this no drums may be beaten publicly. After the inauguration the drums can be used, and the dancing begins. The ceremony consists, like the majority of ceremonies in Kiriwina, of a distribution of food (*sagali*). The food is put in heaps, and in this particular ceremony it is cooked and the heaps placed on wooden dishes or in baskets. Then a man comes along, and in a loud voice calls out a name at each heap.[31] The wife or other female relative of the man named takes the food and carries it to his house, where it is eaten. Such a ceremony (called distribution of *sagali*) does not seem to us much of a feast, especially as the climax—as we understand the climax of a feast, *i.e.*, the eating—is never reached communally, but only in the family circle. But the festive element lies in the preparations, in the collection of the prepared food, in making it all a common property (for each has to contribute his share to the general stock, which is to be equally divided among all the participants), and finally in the public distribution. This distribution is the opening ceremony of the *milamala*; the men dress in the afternoon and perform the first dance.

Now life in the village changes distinctly. People do not go to the gardens any more, nor do they perform any other regular work, such as fishing or canoe building. In the morning the village is alive with all the inmates who have not gone to work, and often with visitors from other villages. But the real festivities begin later in the day. When the hottest hours of the day are over, at about three to four o'clock in the afternoon, the men put on their headdresses. These consist of a great number of white cockatoo feathers, stuck into the thick black hair, from which they protrude in all directions, like the quills of a porcupine, forming large white haloes around their heads. A certain accent of color and finish is given to the whole by a plume of red feathers that overtops the white sphere. In contrast to the gorgeous variety of feather headdresses found in many other districts of New Guinea, the Kiriwinians have only this one type of decoration, which is repeated invariably by all individuals and in all forms of dance. Nevertheless, in conjunction with the cassowary tufts tipped with red feathers, and inserted into belt and armlets, the general appearance of the dancer has a fantastic charm. In the regular rhythmic movement of the dance, the dress seems to blend with the dancer, the colors of the red-tipped black tufts toning well with the brown skin. The white headdress and the brown figure seem to be transformed into a harmonious and fantastic whole, somewhat savage, but in no way grotesque, rhythmically moving against the background to a monotonous and melodious chant and the overbearing beat of the drums.

In some dances a painted dancing shield is used, in others they hold in their hands streamers of pandanus leaves. These latter dances, always of much slower rhythm, are disfigured (to the European taste) by the custom of men wearing women's grass petticoats. The majority of dances are circular, the drumbeaters and singers standing in the middle, while the dancers move round them in a ring.

Ceremonial dances in full ornamentation are never held at night. When the sun goes down, the men disperse and take off their feathers. The drums stop for a while—it is the time when the natives have their main repast of the day. When night has fallen the drums are sounded again, and the performers, now wearing no ornaments, step into the ring. Sometimes they sing a genuine dancing song, and sound a proper dancing beat, and then the people perform a regular dance. But usually, especially later in the night, the singing ceases, the dancing is given up, and only the continued beat of the drums rings through the night. The people, men, women and children, now join and walk round the central group of drumbeaters in twos and threes, women with small children in arms or at the breast, old men and women leading their grandchildren by the hand, all walking with an untiring perserverance one after the other, fascinated by the rhythmical beat of the drums, pursuing the aimless and endless round of the ring. From time to time the dancers intone a long drawn "Aa . . . a; Eee. . . . e," with a sharp accent at the end; simultaneously the drums cease to beat, and the indefatigable carousal seems for a moment to be freed from its spell, without, however, breaking up or ceasing to move. Soon, however, the drummers take up their interrupted music no doubt to the delight of the dancers, but to the despair of the ethnographer, who sees a lugubriously sleepless night before him. This *karibom*, as it is called, gives the small children the opportunity to play, hopping about and across the slowly moving chain of grown-ups; it allows the old people and the women actively to enjoy, at least, a kind of imitation of dancing; it is also the proper time for amorous advances among the young people.

The dancing and the *karibom* are repeated day after day and night after night. As the moon waxes, the festive character, the frequency and care with which ornamental dances are held, and their duration, increases; the dances begin earlier, the *karibom* lasts well-nigh throughout the night. The whole life in the villages is modified and heightened. Large parties of young people of both sexes visit neighboring villages. Presents of food are brought from far away, and on the road people may be met loaded with bananas, coconuts, bunches of areca nut, and of taro. Some important ceremonial visits are paid, in which a whole village calls on another officially, under the leadership of the chief. Such visits are sometimes connected with momentous transactions, such as the buying of dances, for these are always monopolies, and have to be bought at a considerable price. Such a transaction is a bit of native history, and will be spoken of for years and generations. I was fortunate enough to assist at one visit connected with such a transaction, which always consists of several visits, on each of which the visiting party (who are always the sellers) perform the dance officially, the onlookers learning the dance in this way, and some of them joining in the performance.

All big official visits are celebrated with considerable presents, which are always given to the guests by the hosts. The latter, in their turn, will visit their former guests and receive the return gifts.

Towards the end of the *milamala*, visits are received almost daily from quite distant villages. Such visits in olden days had a very compound character. They were undoubtedly friendly, and were intended to be so, but there was always danger lurking behind the official friendliness. The visiting parties were always armed, and it was on such occasions that the whole array of "ceremonial" arms came into display. Indeed, even now the carrying of arms is not entirely suppressed, though at present they are nothing more than articles of decoration and display, owing to the white man's influence. All the large wooden sword clubs, some of which are beautifully carved in heavy hardwood; the carved walking sticks and short, ornamental spears, all so well known from the New Guinea collections in the museums, belong to this class of weapon. They serve equally the purposes of vanity and of business. Vanity, display of wealth, of valuable, finely ornamented objects, is one of the ruling passions of the Kiriwinian. To "swagger" with a large wooden sword, murderous looking, yet nicely carved and painted white and red, is an essential element of the fun to a Kiriwinian youth in festive paint, with a white nose sticking out of a completely blackened face, or one "black eye," or some rather complex curves running all across his face. In olden days he was often called upon to use such weapons, and even now may resort to them in the white heat of passion. Either he fancies a girl, or he is fancied by one, and his advances, unless very skillfully conducted, are sure to be resented. Women and the suspicion of magical practices are the main causes of quarrels and village brawls, which, in accordance with the general quickening of tribal life at the *milamala*, were, and are, very much in season at these times.

Towards the time of full moon, when enthusiasm begins to reach its high-water mark, the villages are decorated with as large a display of food as possible. The *taitu* is not taken out of the yam houses, though it is visible there, through the large interstices of the beams, forming the wells of the storehouses. Bananas, taro, coconuts, etc., are laid out in a manner which will be described in detail hereafter. There is also a display of *vaigu'a*, the native articles of value.

The *milamala* ends on the night of the full moon. The drums do not cease to be used immediately afterwards, but all dancing proper is absolutely stopped, except when the *milamala* is prolonged into a special period of extra dancing, called *usigula*. Usually the monotonous and insipid *karibom* is performed night after night, for months after the *milamala*.

I have been through the *milamala* season twice: once in Olivilevi, the "capital" village of Luba, a district in the southern part of the island, where the *milamala* takes place a month sooner than in Kiriwina proper. Here I saw only the last five days of the *milamala*, but in Omarakana, the main village of Kiriwina, I watched the whole proceedings from beginning to end. There I saw, among other features, one big visit, when To'uluwa went with all the men from Omarakana to the village of Liluta, in connection with the purchase of the *rogaiewo* dance by the latter community from the former.

Let us now pass to that aspect of the *milamala* which really bears upon the subject treated in this article, namely, to the part played in the festivities by the *baloma*, who at this time pay their regular yearly visit to their native villages.

The *baloma* know when the feast approaches, because it is held always at the same time of the year, in the first half of the moon, which is also called *milamala*. This moon is determined—as their calendar in general—by the position of the stars. And in Kiriwina proper, the full moon of *milamala* falls in the second half of August or first half of September.[32]

When the time approaches, the *baloma*, taking advantage of any spell of fair wind that may occur, sail from Tuma to their native villages. It is not quite clear to the natives where the *baloma* live during the *milamala*. They probably stay in the houses of their *veiola*, that is their maternal relatives. Possibly they, or some of them, camp on the beach near their canoes, if the beach is not too far, exactly as a party of near kinsmen from another village or from another island would do.

At any rate, preparations for them are made in the village. Thus, in villages belonging to chiefs, special rather high, though small, platforms, called *tokaikaya*, are erected for the *baloma* of the *guya'u* (chiefs). The chief is always supposed to be in a physically higher position than the commoners. Why the platforms for the spirit *guya'u* are so very high (they measure some 5 to 7 meters in height) I could not ascertain.[33] Besides these platforms several other arrangements are made in connection with the display of valuables and of food, with the professed intention of pleasing the *baloma*.[34]

The display of valuables is called *ioiova*. The headman of each village, or the headmen, as there are at times more than one, have usually a smaller covered platform in the neighborhood of their houses. This is called *buneiova*, and here the man's valuables, such articles of wealth as fall under the native name of *vaigu'a*, are displayed. Large polished axe blades, strings of red shell discs, large arm shells made of the conus shell, circular pigs' teeth or their imitation, these, and these only, form the proper *vaigu'a*. They are all placed on the platform, the strings of *kaboma* (red shell discs) being hung under the roof of the *buneiova*, so as to be readily accessible to view. When there are no *buneiova*, I saw temporary roofed platforms erected in the village, on which the valuables were displayed. This display takes place during the last three days of the full moon, the articles being put up in the morning and removed at night. The proper thing, when visiting a village during the *ioiova*, is to look at the things, even handle them, ask their names (every individual piece of *vaigu'a* has a proper name), and, of course, express great admiration.

Besides the exhibition of valuables, there is a great display of food, and this gives a much more "showy" and festive aspect to the villages. For this, long scaffoldings of wood, called *lalogua*, are erected, consisting of vertical stakes, about 2 to 3 meters high, planted in the ground, with one or two rows of horizontals running along the verticals. To the horizontals are attached bunches of bananas, taro, yams of exceptional size, and coconuts. Such structures run round the central place (*baku*), which is the dancing ground and center of all ceremonial and festive life in every village. The year I was in Bwoiowa was an exceptionally poor one, and the *lalogua* did not reach more than 30 to 60 meters, encircling only one third or less of a *baku*. I was told by several informants, however, that in a good year they might extend not only all round the central place, but also round the circular street which runs concentrically with the *baku*, and even outside the village into the "high road," that is the path leading to another village. The *lalogua* are supposed to please the *baloma*, who get angry whenever there is little display of food.

All this is merely a show which must afford the *baloma* a purely aesthetic pleasure. But they receive also more substantial tokens of affection, in the form of direct offerings of food. The first repast which is given to them takes place at the *katukuala*, the opening feast of the *milamala*, with which the festive period really begins. The *katukuala* consists of a distribution of cooked food, which takes place on the *baku*, and for which the food is supplied by all the members of the village and redistributed among them.[35] This food is exposed to the spirits by being placed on the *baku*. They partake of the "spirit substance" of the food exactly in the same way as they take away to Tuma the *baloma* of the valuables with which men are adorned at death. From the moment of the *katukuala* (which is connected with the inauguration of the dancing) the festive period begins for the *baloma* as well. Their platform is, or ought to be, placed on the *baku,* and they are stated to admire the dance and enjoy it, though, in fact, mighty little notice is taken of their presence.

Food is cooked early every day, and exposed in big, fine wooden dishes (*kaboma*) in each man's house, for the *baloma.* After an hour or so the food is taken away and is presented to some friend or relative, who in turn will present the donor with an equivalent dish. The chiefs have the privilege of giving to the *tokay* (commoners) betel nut and pig, and of receiving in return fish and fruits.[36] Such food, offered to the *baloma,* and subsequently given away to a friend, is called *bubualu'a.* It is usually put on the bedstead in the house, and the man, laying down the *kaboma,* says: "*Balom' kam bubualua.*" It is a universal feature of all offerings and gifts in Kiriwina that they are accompanied by an oral declaration.

Silakutuva is the name for a dish of scraped coconut exposed to the *baloma* (with the words "*Balom' kam silakutuva*"), and then presented also to some man.

It is characteristic that this *baloma* food is never eaten by the man who offers it, but always presented after the *baloma* has finished with it.

Finally, in the afternoon before the departure of the *baloma,* some food is prepared, and some coconuts, bananas, taro, and yams are put handy, and the *vaigu'a* (valuables) are placed in a basket. When the man hears the characteristic beat of the drums, which constitutes the *ioba,* or chasing away of the spirits, he may put these things outside, the idea being that the spirit might take away their *baloma* as a parting present (*taloi*). This custom is called *katubukoni.* The putting of these things in front of the house (*okaukueda*) is not quite essential, because the *baloma* can take them out of the house equally well. This was the explanation given to me when I was looking for the *baloma* gifts in front of the houses, and saw only in one place (in front of the chief's house) a few stone tomahawks.

As said above, the presence of the *baloma* in the village is not a matter of great importance in the mind of the native, if compared with such all-absorbing and fascinating things as dancing and feasting and sexual licence, which go on with great intensity during the *milamala*. But their existence is not altogether ignored, nor is their role by any means purely passive—consisting in the mere admiring of what goes on, or in the satisfaction of eating the food they receive. The *baloma* show their presence in many ways. Thus, while they are in the village it is remarkable how many coconuts will fall down, not by themselves, but plucked by the *baloma*. Whilst the *milamala* was on in Omarakana, two enormous bunches of coconuts fell down quite close to my tent. And it is a very pleasant feature of this spirit activity that such nuts are considered public property, so that even I enjoyed a coconut drink, free of charge, thanks to the *baloma*.

Even the small unripe coconuts that fall down prematurely do it much more often during the *milamala*. And this is one form in which the *baloma* show their displeasure, which is invariably caused by scarcity of food. The *baloma* get hungry (*kasi molu*, their hunger), and they show it. Thunder, rain, bad weather during the *milamala*, interfering with the dancing and feasting, is another and more effective form in which the spirits show their temper. As a matter of fact, during my stay, the full moon, both in August and September, fell on wet, rainy and stormy days. And my informants were able to demonstrate to me by actual experience the connection between scarcity of food and a bad *milamala*, on the one hand, and the anger of the spirits and bad weather on the other. The spirits may even go further and cause drought, and thus spoil the next year's crops. This is the reason why very often several bad years follow each other, because a bad year and poor crops make it impossible for the men to arrange a good *milamala*, which again angers the *baloma,* who spoil next year's crops, and so on in a *circulus vitiosus.*

Again, at times, the *baloma* appear to men in dreams during the *milamala.* Very often people's relatives, especially such as are recently deceased, come in a dream. They usually ask for food, and their wish is satisfied by gifts of *bubualu'a* or *silakutuva.* At times they have some message to impart. In the village of Olivilevi, the main village of Luba, the district south of Kiriwina, the *milamala* (at which I was present) was very poor, there being hardly any food display at all. The chief, Vanoi Kiriwina, had a dream. He went to the beach (about half an hour from the village), and saw a big canoe with spirits, sailing towards the beach from Tuma. They were angry, and spoke to him: "What are you doing at Olivilevi? Why don't you give us food to eat, and coconut water to drink? We send this constant rain for we are angry. Tomorrow, prepare much food; we will eat it and there will be fine weather; then you will dance." This dream was quite true. Next day anybody could see a handful of white sand on the threshold (*okaukueda*), of Vanoi's *lisiga* (chief's house). How this sand was connected with the dream, whether it had been brought there by the spirits or by Vanoi in his dream existence and dream walk, none of these details was clear to my informants, among whom was Vanoi himself. But it was certain that the sand was a proof of the anger of the *baloma* and the reality of the dream. Unfortunately, the prophecy of the fine weather failed entirely, and there was no dancing that day, as the rain was pouring. Perhaps the spirits were not quite satisfied with the amount of food offered that morning!

But the *baloma* are not entirely materialistic. They not only resent scarcity of food and poor offerings, but they also keep strict watch over the maintenance of custom, and they punish with their displeasure any infraction of the traditional customary rules which ought to be observed during the *milamala.* Thus I was told that the spirits strongly disapproved of the general laxity and slowness with which the *milamala* was at present observed. Formerly, nobody would work in the fields or do any kind of labor during the festive period. Everybody had to be bound on pleasure, dancing and sexual licence, in order to please the *baloma*. Nowadays, people will go to their gardens and potter about, or go on preparing wood for house building or canoe making, and the spirits do not like it. Therefore their anger, which results in rain and storm, spoils the *milamala*. This was the case at Olivilevi, and later on at Omarakana. At Omarakana there was still another cause for their anger, connected with the ethnographer's presence in that place, and I had to hear several times reproachful allusions and remarks from the elders and from To'uluwa, the chief, himself. The fact was that I had bought from various villages some twenty dancing shields (*kaidebu*); I wanted to see what the *kaidebu* dances were like. Now, in Omarakana there was only one dance in progress, the *rogaiewo*, a dance performed with *bisila* (pandanus streamers). I distributed the *kaidebu* among the *jeunesse dorée* of Omarakana, and the charm of novelty being too strong (they had not had sufficient *kaidebu* to dance with properly for the last five years at least), they at once began to dance the *gumagabu*, a dance performed with the dancing shields. This was a serious breach of the customary rules (though I did not know it at the time), for every new form of dance has to be ceremonially inaugurated.[37] The omission was very much resented by the *baloma*, hence bad weather, falling coconuts, etc. This was brought up against me several times.

After the *baloma* have enjoyed their reception for two or four weeks (the *milamala* has a fixed end, the second day after the full moon, but it may begin any time between the previous full moon and the new moon), they have to leave their native village and return to Tuma.[38] This return is compulsory, and is induced by the *ioba*, or ceremonial hunting away of the spirits. The second night after the full moon, about one hour before sunrise, when the leatherhead (*saka'u*) sings out, and the morning star (*kubuana*) appears in the heavens, the dancing, which has been going on

the whole night, ceases, and the drums intone a peculiar
beat, that of the *ioba*.[39] The spirits know the beat, and
they prepare for their return journey. Such is the power of
this beat that if somebody struck it a couple of nights
earlier, all the *baloma* would leave the village, and go to
their home in the nether world. The *ioba* beat is therefore
strictly tabooed whilst spirits are in the village, and I could
not prevail upon the boys in Olivilevi to give me a sample of
this beat during the *milamala*, whereas, at a time when
there were no spirits in the village (a couple of months
before the *milamala*), I was able to obtain quite a performance of the *ioba* in Omarakana. Whilst the *ioba* beat
is sounded on the drums, the *baloma* are addressed, en-
treated to go, and bidden farewell:

> "*Baloma, O!*
> *Bukulousi, O!*
> *Bakalousi ga*
> *Yuhuhuhu . . . . . .*"

"O spirits, go away, we shall not go (we'll remain)." The
last sound seems to be just a kind of scream, to rouse up the
sluggish *baloma* and to spur them to go.

This *ioba*, which takes place as stated above, before sunrise on the night of Woulo, is the main one. It is meant to
drive away the strong spirits, those that can walk. The next
day, before noon, there is another *ioba*, called *pem ioba*, or
chasing away the lame. It purports to rid the village of the
spirits of women and children, the weak and the crippled.
It is performed in the same manner, by the same beat and
with the same words.

In both cases the cortège starts at the end of the village
farthest from where the road to Tuma strikes the village
grove (*weika*), so that no part of the village remains "un-
swept." They go through the village, stopping for a time on
the *baku* (central place) and then they walk up the place,
where the road to Tuma leaves the village. There they
finish the *ioba*, and always end up with a beat of a peculiar
form of dance, the *kasawaga*.[40]

This concludes the *milamala*.

This information, as it stands here, was collected and written down before I had an opportunity of witnessing the *ioba* in Olivilevi. It is correct in all points, it is complete and detailed. I was even told by my informants that the drums are beaten by the young boys only, and that the elder men do not take much part in the *ioba*. Yet, in no instance, perhaps, of my field work, have I had such a striking demonstration of the necessity of witnessing things myself, as I had when I made the sacrifice of getting up at three in the morning to see this ceremony. I was prepared to witness one of the most important and serious moments in the whole customary cycle of annual events, and I definitely anticipated the psychological attitude of the natives towards the spirits, their awe, piety, etc. I thought that such a crisis, associated with a well-defined belief, would, in one way or another, express itself in outward form, that there would be a "moment" passing over the village. When I arrived at the *baku* (central place), half an hour before sunrise, the drums were still going on and there were still a few of the dancers sleepily moving round the drummers, not in regular dance, but in the rhythmic walk of the *karibom*. When the *saka'u* was heard, everybody went quietly away —the young people in pairs, and there remained to farewell the *baloma* only five or six urchins with the drums, myself and my informant. We went to the *kadumalagala valu*— the point where the path for the next village leaves the settlement, and we started to chase the *baloma*. A more undignified performance I cannot imagine, bearing in mind that ancestral spirits were addressed! I kept at a distance so as not to influence the *ioba*—but there was little to be influenced or marred by an ethnographer's presence! The boys from six to twelve years of age sounded the beat, and then the smaller ones began to address the spirits in the words I had been previously given by my informants. They spoke with the same characteristic mixture of arrogance and shyness, with which they used to approach me, begging for tobacco, or making some facetious remark, in fact, with the typical demeanor of boys in the street, who perform some nuisance sanctioned by custom, like the proceedings on Guy Fawkes' day or similar occasions. And so they went through the village, and hardly any grown-up man was to be seen. The only other sign of the *ioba* was some wailing in a house where a death had recently occurred. I was told it was the right thing to wail at the *ioba* as the *baloma* of the kindred were just leaving the village. Next day, the *pem ioba* was a still more paltry affair: the boys doing their part with laughter and jokes, and the old men looking on with smiles, and making fun of the poor lame spirits, which have to hobble away. Yet there is no doubt that the *ioba*, as an event, as a critical point in tribal life, is a matter of importance. It would never on any account be omitted.[41] As already noted, it would not be performed except at the proper moment, and the *ioba* drum beat must not be trifled with. But in its performance it has no traces of sanctity or even seriousness.

There is one fact in connection with the *ioba* which must be mentioned in this place, as in a way it may seem to qualify the general statement made at the beginning of this article, that there is no connection between the mortuary ceremonies and the lot of the spirit that has departed. The fact in point is, that the final casting off of mourning (called "washing of the skin," *iwini wowoula*, literally "he or she washes her skin") always takes place after a *milamala* on the day following the *ioba*. The underlying idea would seem to be that the mourning is still kept during the *milamala*, as the spirit is there to see it, and as soon as this spirit departs, the "skin is washed." But strangely enough I never found the natives either volunteering this explanation or even endorsing it. Of course, when you ask the question, "Why do you perform washing of the skin just after the *ioba*?" you receive the invariable answer, "*Tokua bogwa bubunemasi*—[our old custom]." You then have to beat about the bush, and finally ask the leading question. And to this (as to all leading questions which contain an untrue or doubtful statement) the natives always answer in the negative, or else they consider your view as a new one, and throwing some light on the problem, but such consideration and acquiescence is at once distinguishable from a direct endorsement of a statement. There was never the slightest difficulty in deciding whether an opinion obtained was a customary, well-established, orthodox native view, or whether it was an idea new to the native mind.[42]

Some general remarks about the natives' attitude towards the *baloma* during *milamala* may follow this account of details. This attitude is characterized by the manner in which the natives speak about them, or behave during the ceremonial performances; it is less tangible than customary items, and more difficult to describe, but it is a fact, and as such must be stated.

The *baloma*, during their stay, never frighten the natives, and there is not the slightest uneasiness felt about them. The small tricks they play in showing their anger, etc. (see above), are done in broad daylight and there is nothing at all "uncanny" about them.

At night the natives are not in the least afraid to walk about alone from village to village, whereas they are distinctly afraid of doing so for some time after a man's death (see above). Indeed, this is the period of amorous intrigues, which entail lonely walks, and walks in couples. The most intense period of *milamala* coincides with full moon, where the superstitious fear of night is naturally reduced to its minimum. The whole country is gay with the light of the moon, with the loud beat of drums, and with the songs which resound all over the place. By the time a man is out of the radius of one village, he hears the music from the next. There is nothing of any oppressive atmosphere of ghosts, of any haunting presence, quite the reverse. The mood of the natives is gay and rather frivolous, the atmosphere in which they live pleasant and bright.

Again, it is to be noted that, though there is a certain amount of communion between the living and the spirits by dreams, etc., the latter are never supposed to influence in any serious way the course of tribal affairs. No trace of divination, taking counsel with the spirits, or any other form of customary communion in matters of any importance, is to be detected.

Apart from the lack of superstitious fear, there are no taboos connected with the behavior of the living towards the spirits. It can be even safely asserted that not too much respect is paid to them. There is no shyness whatever in speaking about the *baloma*, or mentioning the personal names of such as are presumably present in the village. As mentioned above, the natives make fun of the lame spirits, and in fact all kinds of jokes are passed about the *baloma* and their behavior.

Again, except in the cases of people recently dead, there is little personal feeling about the spirits. There are no provisions for singling out individual *baloma* and preparing a special reception for them, excepting perhaps the gifts of food solicited in dreams by individual *baloma*.

To sum up: the *baloma* return to their native village, like visitors from another place. They are left to a great extent to themselves. Valuables and food are displayed to them. Their presence is by no means a fact constantly in the native's mind, or foremost in his anticipations of, and views about, the *milamala*. There is not the slightest scepticism to be discovered in the mind of the most civilized natives as to the real presence of the *baloma* at the *milamala*. But there is little emotional reaction with reference to their presence.

So much about the annual visit of the *baloma* during the *milamala*. The other form in which they influence tribal life is through the part they take in magic.

v.

Magic plays an enormous part in the tribal life of the Kiriwinians (as it undoubtedly does with the majority of native peoples). All important economic activities are fringed with magic, especially such as imply pronounced elements of chance, venture, or danger. Gardening is completely wrapped up in magic; the little hunting that is done has its array of spells; fishing, especially when it is connected with risk and when the results depend upon luck and are not absolutely certain, is equipped with elaborate magical systems. Canoe building has a long list of spells, to be recited at various stages of the work, at the felling of the tree, at the scooping out of the dugout; and, towards the end, at painting, lashing together, and launching. But this magic is used only in the case of the larger sea-going canoes. The small canoes, used on the calm lagoon or near the shore, where there is no danger, are quite ignored by the magician. Weather—rain, sun and wind—have to obey a great number of spells, and they are especially amenable to the call of some eminent experts, or, rather, families of experts, who practice the art in hereditary succession. In times of war—when fighting still existed, before the white man's rule—the Kiriwinians availed themselves of the art of certain families of professionals, who had inherited war magic from their ancestors. And, of course, the welfare of the body—health—can be destroyed or restored by the magical craft of sorcerers, who are always healers at the same time. If a man's life be endangered by an attempt on the part of the above-mentioned *mulukuausi*, there are spells to counteract their influence, though the only safe way to escape the danger is to apply to a woman who is a *mulukuausi* herself—there is always some such woman in a distant village.

Magic is so widespread that, living among the natives, I used to come across magical performances, very often quite unexpectedly, apart from the cases where I arranged to be present at a ceremony. The hut of Bagido'u, the garden magician of Omarakana, was not fifty meters from my tent, and I remember hearing his chant on one of the very first days after my arrival, when I hardly knew of the existence of garden magic. Later on I was allowed to assist at his chanting over magical herbs; in fact, I could enjoy the privilege as often as I liked, and I used it several times. In many

garden ceremonies part of the ingredients are chanted over
in the village, in the magician's own house, and, again,
before being used in the garden. On the morning of such
a day the magician goes alone into the bush, sometimes
far away, to fetch the necessary herbs. In one charm as
many as ten varieties of ingredients, practically all herbs,
have to be brought. Some are to be found on the seabeach
only, some must be fetched from the *raiboag* (the stony
coral woodland), others are brought from the *odila,* the
low scrub. The magician has to set out before daybreak and
obtain all his material before the sun is up. The herbs
remain in the house, and somewhere about noon he proceeds to chant over them. A mat is spread on the bedstead,
and on this mat another is laid. The herbs are placed on one
half of the second mat, the other half being folded over
them. Into this opening the magician chants his spell. His
mouth is quite close to the edges of the mat, so that none
of his voice can go astray; all enters the yawning mat,
where the herbs are placed, awaiting to be imbued with
the spell. This catching up of the voice, which carries the
spell, is done in all magical recitations. When a small object
has to be charmed, a leaf is folded so as to form a tub and
at the narrow end of this the object is placed, while the
magician chants into the broad end. To return to Bagido'u
and his garden magic. He would chant his charm for about
half an hour, or even longer, repeating the spell over and
over again, repeating various phrases in it and various important words in a phrase. The spell is sung in a low voice,
there being a peculiar, half-melodic fashion of recital, which
slightly varies with the divers forms of magic. The repetition
of the words is a kind of rubbing in of the spell into the
substance to be medicated.

After the garden magician has finished his spell, he wraps
up the leaves in the mat and puts them aside, to be presently used in the field, usually the next morning. All actual
ceremonies of garden magic take place in the field, and
there are many spells which are chanted in the garden. There
is a whole system of garden magic consisting of a series of

complex and elaborate rites, each accompanied by a spell. Every gardening activity must be preceded by a proper rite. Thus there is a general inaugurative rite, previous to any work in the gardens whatever, and this rite is performed on each garden plot separately. The cutting down of the scrub is introduced by another rite. The burning of the cut and dried scrub is in itself a magical ceremony, and it brings in its wake minor magical rites performed for each plot, the whole perfomance extending over four days. Then, when the planting begins, a new series of magical acts takes place, which lasts for a few days. Again, the weeding and the preliminary digging are introduced by magical performances. All these rites, as it were, a frame, into which the garden work is fitted. The magician orders rest periods, which have to be observed, and his work regulates the work of the community, forcing all the villagers to perform certain labors simultaneously, and not to lag behind or be too far in advance of the others.

His share is very much appreciated by the community; indeed, it would be difficult to imagine any work done in the gardens without the co-operation of the *towosi* (garden magician).[43]

In the management of gardens the *towosi* has a great deal to say, and great respect is shown to his advice, a respect which is in reality purely formal, because there are very few controversial, or even doubtful, questions about gardening. Nevertheless, the natives appreciate such formal deference and acknowledgment of authority to a degree which is really astonishing. The garden magician receives also his payment, which consists of substantial gifts of fish offered him by the members of the village community. It must be added that the dignity of village magician is usually vested in the person of the village headman, though this is not invariably the case. But only a man who belongs by birth to a certain village, whose maternal ancestors have always been the lords of that village and of that soil, can "strike the soil" (*iwoie buiagu*).

In spite of its great importance, Kiriwinian garden magic

does not consist in any stately, sacred ceremonies, surrounded with strict taboos, performed with as much display as the natives can afford. On the contrary, any person uninitiated into the character of Kiriwinian magic might walk through the most important ceremony without being aware that anything of importance is going on. Such a person might come across a man scratching the soil with a stick, or making a small heap of dried branches and stalks, or planting a taro tuber, and perhaps muttering some words. Or else the imaginary spectator would walk through a Kiriwinian new garden field, with its soil freshly moved and cleared, with its diminutive forest of stems and sticks put into the ground to serve as supports for the *taitu*, a field which will presently look like a hop garden, and in such a walk he might meet a group of men, halting here and there and adjusting something in the corner of each garden plot. Only when loud spells are chanted over the fields would the visitor's attention be directly drawn to the magical reality of the performance. In such cases the whole act, otherwise insipid, assumes some dignity and impressiveness. A man may be seen standing alone, with a small group behind him, and addressing in a loud voice some unseen power, or, more correctly, from the Kiriwinian's point of view, casting this unseen power over the fields: a power which lies in the spell condensed there through the wisdom and piety of generations. Or voices may be heard all over the field chanting the same spell, as not seldom the *towosi* summons the help of his assistants, who consist always of his brothers or other matrilineal successors.

By way of illustration, let us go through one such ceremony—that consisting in the burning of the cut and dried scrub. Some herbs, previously chanted over, have to be wrapped, with a piece of banana leaf, round the tops of dried coconut leaflets. Leaves so prepared will serve as torches to set fire to the field. In the forenoon (the ceremony I witnessed in Omarakana took place about 11 a.m.), Bagido'u the *towosi* of that village, went to the gardens accompanied by To'uluwa, his maternal uncle and headman of the village, and by some other people, among whom was Bokuioba, one of the headman's wives. The day was hot, and there was a slight breeze; the field was dry, so setting fire to it was easy. Everyone present took a torch—even Bokuioba. The torches were lit quite without ceremony (by means of wax matches, produced by the ethnographer, not without a pang), and then everyone went along the field on the windward side, and the whole was soon ablaze. Some children looked on at the burning, and there was no question of any taboo. Nor was there much excitement in the village about the performance, for we left a number of boys and children behind, playing in the village and not at all interested or inclined to come and see the rite. I assisted at some other rites, where Bagido'u and I were alone, though there was no taboo to prevent anyone who wished from being present. Of course, if anyone was present, a certain minimum of decorum would be observed. The question of taboo, moreover, varies with the village, each having its own system of garden magic. I assisted at another garden burning ceremony (on the day following the wholesale burning when a small heap of rubbish, together with some herbs, was burnt on each plot) in a neighboring village, and there the *towosi* got very angry because some girls looked on at the performance from a fair distance, and I was told that the ceremonies were taboo to women in that village. Again, whereas some ceremonies are performed by the *towosi* alone, in others several people usually assist, while there are still others in which the whole village community has to take part. Such a ceremony will be described in detail below, as it bears more particularly on the question of the participation of the *baloma* in magic.

I have spoken here of garden magic only in order to illustrate the general nature of Kiriwinian magic. Garden magic is by far the most conspicuous of all magical activities, and the broad statements exemplified in this particular case hold good with reference to all other kinds of magic as well. All this is just intended to serve as a general picture, which must be kept in mind in order that my remarks about the part played by the *baloma* in magic may appear in the right perspective.[44]

The backbone of Kiriwinian magic is formed by its spells. It is in the spell that the main virtue of all magic resides. The rite is there only to launch the spell, to serve as an appropriate mechanism of transmission. This is the universal view of all Kiriwinians, of the competent as well as of the profane, and a minute study of the magical ritual well confirms this view. It is in the formulae, therefore, that the clue to the ideas concerning magic is to be found. And in the formulae we find frequent mention made of the ancestral names. Many formulae begin with long lists of such names, serving, in a way, as an invocation.

The question whether such lists are real prayers, in which an actual appeal is made to the ancestral *baloma*, who are supposed to come and act in the magic, or whether the ancestral names figure in the formulae as mere items of tradition—hallowed and full of magical virtue, just because of their traditional nature—does not seem to allow of any definite decision either way. In fact, both elements are undoubtedly present: the direct appeal to the *baloma* and the traditional value of the mere ancestral names. The data given below should allow of closer determination. As the traditional element is closely bound up with the mode of inheritance of the magical formulae, let us begin with the latter question.

The magical formulae are passed from generation to generation, inherited from father to son in the paternal line, or from *Kadala* (mat. uncle) to nephew in the maternal line, which, in native opinion, is the real line of kindred (*veiola*). The two forms of inheritance are not quite equivalent. There is a class of magic which may be termed local, because it is bound up with a given locality. To this class belong all the systems of garden magic,[45] as well as all such magical spells as are connected with certain spots endowed with magical properties. Such was the most powerful rain magic in the island, that of Kasana'i, which had to be performed in a certain waterhole in the *weika* (grove) of Kasana'i.

Such was the official war magic of Kiriwina, which had to be performed by men belonging to Kuaibuaga, and which was associated with a *kaboma* (a sacred grove) near that village. Again, the elaborate systems of magic which were essential to shark and *kalala* fishing had each to be carried out by a man belonging to the village of Kaibuola or Laba'i respectively. All such formulae were hereditary in the female line.[46]

The class of magic which is not bound up with locality, and which may be easily transmitted from father to son, or even from stranger to stranger, at a fair price, is much smaller. Here belong, in the first place, the formulae of native medicine, which always go in couples, a *silami*, a formula of evil magic, the object of which is to produce illness, being always coupled with *vivisa*, a formula for annihilating the respective *silami*, and so curing the disease. The magic which initiates a man into the craft of carving, the *tokabitam* (carver) magic, belongs to this class, as well as the canoe-making charms. And a series of formulae of minor importance, or at least of less esoteric character, such as love magic, magic against the bite of insects, magic against the *mulukuausi* (this latter rather important), magic for removing the bad effects of incest, etc. But even these formulae, though they are not necessarily performed by the people of one locality, are usually associated with a locality. There is very often a myth at the bottom of a certain system of magic, and a myth is always local.[47]

Thus the more numerous examples, and certainly the more important class of magic (the "matrilineal" magic), is local, both in its character and in its transmission, whereas only part of the other class is distinctly local in its character. Now locality is in the mind and tradition of the Kiriwinian most intimately associated with a given family or sub-clan.[48] In each locality the line of men who have succeeded each other as its rulers, and who in turn performed those acts of magic essential to its welfare (such as garden magic), would naturally loom large in the minds of the natives. This probably is confirmed by the facts, for, as mentioned above, the names of matrilineal ancestors play a great part in magic.

Some examples may be given to confirm this statement, though the full discussion of the question must be deferred to another occasion, because it would be necessary to compare this feature with the other elements recurring in magic, and to this end the full reproduction of all the formulae would be necessary. Let us begin with the garden magic. I have recorded two systems of this magic, that of the village of Omarakana called *kailuebila*, which is generally considered to be the most powerful; and the *momtilakaiva* system, associated with the four small villages, Kupuakopula, Tilakaiva, Iourawotu', and Wakailuva.

In the Omarakana system of garden magic there are ten magical spells, each associated with a special act: one said while striking the ground on which a new garden is to be made; another in the ceremony initiating the cutting down of the scrub; another during the ceremonial burning of the cut, dried scrub, and so on. Out of these ten spells there are three in which reference is made to *baloma* of ancestors. One of those three is by far the most important, and it is said during the performance of several rites, at the cutting down ceremony, at the planting ceremony, etc.

This is the beginning:

> "*Vatuvi, vatuvi;* (repeated many times)
> *Vitumaga, imaga;*
> *Vatuvi, vatuvi;* (many times)
> *Vitulola, ilola:*
> *Tubugu Polu, tubugu Koleko, tubugu Takikila,*
> *Tubugu Mulabuoita, tubugu Kuaiudila,*
> *Tubugu Katupuala, tubugu Buguabuaga, tubugu Nu-*
>   *makala;*
> *Bilumava'u bilumam;*
> *Tabugu Muakenwa, tamagu Iowana . . . .*"

After this follows the rest of the formula, which is very long, and which, in the main, describes the state of things which the formula is meant to produce, *i.e.*, it describes the growth of the garden, the ridding of the plants from all pests, blights, etc.

The correct translation of such magical formulae presents certain difficulties. There are in them archaic expressions which the natives only partially understand, and even then it is extremely difficult to make them translate the meaning correctly into modern Kiriwinian. The typical form of a spell consists of three parts: (1) The introduction (called *u'ula*=lowest part of a stem, used also to denote something akin to our conception of cause); (2) The body of the spell (called *tapuala*=the back, the flanks, the rump; (3) The final part (*dogina*=the tip, the end, the peak; etymologically connected with *doga*, a tusk, a sharp, long tooth). Usually the *tapuala* is much more easy to understand and to translate than the other parts. The invocation of ancestors, or, more correctly, perhaps, the list of their names, is always contained in the *u'ula*.

In the *u'ula* just quoted, the first word, *vatuvi*, was not understood by my informant, Bagido'u, the *towosi* (garden magician), of Omarakana, or at least, he was not able to translate it to me. On etymological grounds it can be translated, I think, by "cause" or "make." [49]

The words *vitumaga imaga* are composed of the prefixes *vitu* (to cause), and *i* (third person, singular, verbal prefix); and of the root *maga*, which is composed again of *ma*, the root of come, and *ga*, a suffix often used, which plays merely the role of giving emphasis. The words *vitulola*, *ilola* are quite symmetrical with the former, only the root *la*, "to go" (reduplicated into *lola*), figures instead of *ma*, to come.

In the list of ancestors, two points are to be noted: the first names are attached to the word *tubugu*, whereas the last but one is used with *tabugu*. *Tubugu* is a plural, and means "my grandfathers" (*gu* being the pronominal suffix of the first person); *tabugu* means "my grandfather" (in the singular). The use of the plural in the first group is connected with the fact that in each subclan there are certain names, which are the property of this subclan; and every member of this subclan must possess one of these ancestral names, though he may be called also by another non-hereditary name, by which he is known more generally. Thus, in the first part of the spell, not one ancestor of the name of Polu is addressed, but the magician invokes "all my ancestors of the name of Polu, all my ancestors of the name of Koleko," etc.

The second characteristic feature, which is also general in all such lists of ancestors, is that the last names are preceded by the words *"bilumava'u bilumam,"* which broadly mean (without entering into a linguistic analysis) "you new *baloma,*" and then the names of the few last ancestors are enumerated. Thus Bagido'u mentions his grandfather, Muakenuva, and his father, Iowana.[50] This is important, because it is a direct invocation of a *baloma,* "O thou *baloma*" (in *"bilumam'"* the *m'* being the suffix of the second person). In the light of this fact, the ancestor names appear to be more likely invocations of the ancestral *baloma* than a simple enumeration, even though the ancestral names have an intrinsic, active, magical power.

In a free translation, the fragment may be rendered thus:—

> "Cause! Make it! Be efficient!
> Cause to come!
> Cause to go!
> My grandfathers of the name Polu, etc. . . .
> And you, recent *baloma*, grandfather Muakenuva,
>   and father Iowana."

This free translation leaves still a great deal ambiguous, but it must be emphatically stated that this ambiguity does exist in the mind of the man who is best acquainted with the formula. Asked, what had to go and what to come, Bagido'u expressed his opinion in guesses. Once he told me that the reference was to the plants which have to enter the soil; on another occasion he thought that the garden pests are to go. Whether "come" and "go" are meant to be antithetical or not, was not clear either. The correct interpretation must, I think, insist on the very vague meaning of the *u'ula*, which is merely a kind of invocation. The words are believed to embody some hidden virtue, and that is their main function. The *tapuala*, which presents no ambiguities, explains the exact purpose of the spell.

It is also noteworthy that *u'ula* contains rhythmical elements in the symmetry in which the four groups of words are placed. Again, though the number of times the word *vatuvi* is repeated varies (I have heard the formula actually chanted several times), it is repeated the same number of times in both periods. The alliteration in this formula is undoubtedly also not accidental, as it is to be found in many other spells.

I have dwelt somewhat at length on this formula, treating it as representative of the others, which will be adduced without detailed analysis.

The second formula in which ancestor names are mentioned is spoken at the very first of the series of successive ceremonies at the *iowota*, when the *towosi* strikes the ground on which the gardens are going to be made. This formula begins:

"*Tudava, Tu-Tudava,
Malita, Ma-Malita,*" etc.,

mentioning here the names of two ancestral heroes, about whom there exists a mythological cycle. Tudava is claimed to be in a way an ancestor of the *tabalu* (the most aristocratic subclan, who rule Omarakana), though there is no doubt that he belonged to the Lukuba clan (whereas the *tabalu* belong to the Malasi clan).

The same two names are invoked in another formula, which is spoken over certain herbs, used in garden-planting magic, and over some structures of wood, made for magical purposes only, called *kamkokola*. This formula begins:

"*Kailola, lola; Kailola, lola;
Kaigulugulu; kaigulugulu;
Kailalola Tudava,*

Kaigulugulu Malita,
Bisipela Tudava; bisila'i otokaikaya," etc.

In free translation this means—

Go down [O you roots]; bore [into the ground, O you
roots]; [help them] to go down, O Tudava; [help
them] to bore [into the ground] O Malita; Tudava
climbs up [lit. changes]; [Tudava] settles down on
the *tokaikaia* (*i.e.*, the platform for the *baloma*).

In the Omarakana system of garden magic there are no
special references to any sacred places near the village.[51]
The only ritual action performed in connection with the
baloma during the ceremony is of a very trifling character.
After reciting the appropriate spell over the first taro planted
in a *baleko* (a garden plot, the economic and magical unit
in gardening), the magician constructs a miniature hut and
fence of dry branches, called *si buala baloma* ("the *baloma,*
their house"). No spells are said over it, nor could I discover
any tradition, or obtain any further explanation in connection with this quaint act.

Another reference to the *baloma,* and a much more important one, though it does not take place during a ceremony, is the exposition or offering to the spirits of the
ula'ula, the fee paid for the magic. The *ula'ula* is brought
to the *towosi* (garden magician) by the members of the
community, and consists usually of fish, but there may be
betel nuts or coconuts, or, nowadays, tobacco. This is exposed in the house; the fish only in the form of a small
portion of the whole gift, and, as far as I know, in a cooked
condition. While the magician chants over the magical
leaves and implements in his house, previous to taking them
out into the garden, the *ula'ula,* offered to the *baloma,*
ought to be exposed somewhere near the medicated substance. This offering of the *ula'ula* to the *baloma* is not
a feature particular to the Omarakana garden magic, but it
obtains in all the other systems.

The other system (*momtilakaiva*), to which reference

has been made, contains only one formula, in which there is a list of *baloma*. As this resembles that quoted above, the proper names only being different, I omit it here. In this system of magic, however, the role played by the *baloma* is much more pronounced, for in one of the main ceremonies, that of the *Kamkokola*, there is an offering made to the *baloma*. The *kamkokola* are large, bulky erections, consisting of vertical poles some 3 to 6 meters high, and of slanting poles of the same length, leaning against the vertical poles. The two side poles of the *kamkokola* are propped against a lateral bifurcation of the erect pole, formed by the stump of a protruding branch. Seen from above, the constructions present a right angle, or the shape of the letter L, with the vertical pole at the angle. From the side they look somewhat the shape of the Greek letter λ. These structures have no practical importance whatever, their only function being a magical one. They form the magical prototype, so to speak, of the poles put in the ground as supports for the *taitu* vine. The *kamkokola*, though they represent a merely magical item, require, nevertheless, a considerable amount of labor to erect. The heavy poles have to be brought very often from a great distance, as few are found near the villages in the low scrub, which is cut down every four or five years. For weeks men are busy searching for, felling, and bringing into their gardens the material for the *kamkokola*, and disputes about stealing the poles are frequent.

The *kamkokola* ritual occupies a couple of days in all the systems; four or more days are further taken up by the obligatory rest from all field work, which precedes the magical performance. The first day of the magic proper is devoted, in the *momtilakaiva* system, to the chanting over the fields. The magician, attended perhaps by one or two men, walks across the whole garden site—it was about three-quarters of a mile across country in the case which I witnessed—and on each garden plot he chants the spell, leaning on one of the slanting poles of the *kamkokola*. He faces the plot, and chants in a loud voice, which carries well over the whole plot. He has some thirty or forty such recitations to make.

It is the second day which is really of interest in this connection, for then a ceremony is performed in the gardens in which all the villages take part, and in which the *baloma* also are said to participate. The object of this ceremony is to charm some leaves which will be put into the ground at the foot of the *kamkokola* and also at the junction of the vertical and the slanting poles. In the morning of this day the whole village is busy with preparations. The large earthenware pots used for boiling food on festive occasions are put on the stones which support them, and they bubble and steam while women move round and watch the cooking. Some women bake their *taitu* in the ground between two layers of red-hot stones. All the boiled and baked *taitu* will be brought out into the field, and there it will be ceremonially distributed.

In the meantime some men have gone into the bush, some have gone right down to the seashore, others to the *raiboag* (the rocky wooded ridge), in order to get the herbs necessary for the magic. Large bunches have to be brought, as after the ceremony the medicated herbs are distributed among all the men, each taking his share and using it on his own plot.

At about ten o'clock in the morning I went into the field, accompanied by Nasibowa'i, the *towosi* of Tilakaiva. He had a large ceremonial stone axe hanging over his shoulder which, indeed, he uses in several ceremonies, whereas Bagido'u of Omarakana never makes use of this instrument. Soon after we had arrived and seated ourselves on the ground, waiting till all were present, the women began to troop in one after the other. Each was carrying a wooden dish with *taitu* on her head, often leading a child by the hand and carrying another astride on her flank. The spot where the ceremony had to be performed was at a point where the road from Omarakana entered the garden of Tilakaiva. On this side of the fence there was dense low scrub of a couple of years' growth; on the other the garden lay bare, the ground naked, the wooded ridge of the *raiboag* and several groves in the distance showing through the fairly dense agglomeration of poles planted as supports for the *taitu* vine. Two rows of specially fine ones ran along the path, forming a nice espalier in front of me. They terminated on this side with two specially fine *kamkokola*, at the foot of which the ceremony was to be performed, and which were to be supplied with herbs by the magician himself.

The women seated themselves all along the alley and on both sides in the fields. It took them about half an hour to collect, after which the food they brought was made into heaps, one heap for each man present, and each contribution was divided among the heaps. By this time all the men, boys, girls, and small children had arrived, and, the whole village being present, the proceedings began. The normal *sagali* (distribution) started the ceremony; a man walked past the heaps of food, and at each heap called out the name of one of those present, after which this portion (which had been placed on a wooden dish) was taken by a woman (a connection of the man called) and carried into the village. The women thus departed to the village, taking with them the babies and children. This part of the ceremony was said to be for the benefit of the *baloma*. The food thus distributed is called *baloma kasi* (food of the *baloma*), and the spirits are said to take some part in the proceedings, to be present there, and to be pleased with the food. Beyond these generalities, however, it was absolutely impossible to obtain a more definite or detailed statement from any of the natives, including Nasibowa'i himself.

After the women had departed, such of the small boys as remained behind were hunted away, as the ceremony proper was to begin. Even I and my "boys" had to step on the other side of the fence. The ceremony consisted simply of the recital of a spell over the leaves. Large bunches of these were put upon the ground on a mat, and Nasibowa'i squatted down in front of them and recited his spell right into the herbs. As soon as he had finished, the men pounced upon the leaves, each taking a handful, and running to his garden plot to put them under and on the *kamkokola*. This ended the ceremony, which with the waiting had lasted well over one hour.

Again, in the *momtilakaiva* magic, one of the spells refers to a "sacred grove" (*kaboma*), called Ovavavile. This place (a large clump of trees obviously not cut for many generations) is situated quite close to the villages of Omarakana and Tilakaiva. It is tabooed, swelling of the sexual organs (elephantiasis?) being the penalty for not observing the prohibition. I never explored its interior, for fear, not so much of the taboo, as of the small red ticks (scrub itch), which are a veritable pest. To perform one of the magical rites, the *towosi* of Tilakaiva goes into this sacred wood and puts a large tuber of a species of yam called *kasi-iena* on a stone, this being an offering made to the *baloma*.

The spell runs:—

U'ula: *"Avaita'u ikavakavala Ovavavala?*
Iaegula'i Nasibowa'i,
Akavakavala Ovavavala!"
Tapuala: *"Bala baise akavakavala, Ovavavala Iaegula'i*
Nasbowa'i akavakavala Ovavavala; bala
baise,
Agubitamuana, olopoulo Ovavavala; bala
baise
Akabinaiguadi olopoulo Ovavavala."

There is no *dogina* (final piece) in this formula. The translation runs as follows:—

"Who bends down in Ovavavile? [52] I, Nasibowa'i (personal name of the present *towosi*) am bending down in Ovavavile! I shall go there and bend down in Ovavavile; I, Nasibowa'i, shall bend down in Ovavavile; I shall go there and bear the burden [here the magician identifies himself with the stone on which the *kasi-iena* is put] within the *kaboma* of Ovavavile. I shall go there and bulge out [here he speaks in the name of the planted tuber] within the grove of Ovavavile."

In this ceremony the association between the *baloma* and the magic is very slight, but it exists, and the connection with the locality affords another link between ancestral tradition and magic. So much concerning garden magic.

In the two most important systems of fish magic of Kiriwina—*i.e.*, the shark magic of the village of Kaibuola and the *kalala* (mullet?) magic of the village of Laba'i—the spirits also play some part. Thus in both systems one of the ceremonies consists of an offering to the *baloma*, which is also subtracted from the *ula'ula* payment given to the magician by the people of his village. In the shark magic one of the rites takes place in the magician's house. The performer puts small parcels of the cooked fish (which he had received as *ula'ula*) and some betel nut on one of the three stones (*kailagila*), which are placed round a fireplace and serve to support the large cooking pots. There he utters the following formula:

U'ula: "*Kamkuamsi kami Ula'ula kubukuabuia, Inene'i, Ibuaigana I'iovalu, Vi'iamoulo, Ulopoulo, Bowasa'i, Bomuagueda.*"

Tapuala and Dogina: "*Kukuavilasi poulo, kuminum kuaidasi poulo; okawala Vilaita'u; okawala Obuwabu; Kulousi kuvapuagise wadola kua'u obuarita, kulousi kuluvabouodasi kua'u obuarita kuiaioiuvasi kukapuagegasi kumaise kuluvabodasi matami pualalala okotalela Vinaki.*"

The *U'ula* may be translated:—

"Eat your *ula'ula* (gift, payment for magic), O unmarried women, Inene'i," etc. (all these are personal names of female *baloma*).

In the *tapuala* there are certain words I was unable to translate, but the general meaning is clear: "Spoil our fishing, bring bad luck to our fishing" (so far the spell is negative; it suggests in imperative form that which it is desired to prevent); ——(?); ——(?); "Go, open the mouth of the shark in the sea; go, make the shark to be met in the sea; remain open (yawning); come; make them meet the shark; your eyes are (?); on the beach of Vinaki."

This fragmentary translation shows, at any rate, that the *bili baloma* (a plural form of *baloma*, used when they are treated as a kind of effective agent in magic) of the unmarried females are directly invoked to lend a hand in making the fishing lucky.

My informant was as puzzled as myself by the question why female and not male *baloma* are supposed to be effective in this magic. But it was a fact known, not only to the magician, but to everybody, that the female *baloma* are the *tolipoula*, the "masters of the fishing." The magician and some other men in council tentatively suggested that the male *baloma* go out to the fishing with the men, and the female *baloma* remain behind and have to be fed by the magician, lest they should be angry. Another man pointed out that in the myth which explains the existence of the shark fishing in Kaibuola, a woman plays an important part. But it was clear that to all my informants the fact of women being *tolipoula* was so natural that it had never occurred to them to question it previously.

The *kalala* fishing in the village of Laba'i is connected with the mythical hero Tudava, who is specially associated with that village, and who is, in a way, reputed to be an ancestor of the present rulers of Laba'i. The magic which accompanies this fishing is essentially bound up with the mythological doings of Tudava. Thus, he lived on the beach where the fishing takes place and where the most important magical formulae are spoken. Again, Tudava used to walk on the road leading from the beach to the village, and there are some traditional spots connected with his doings on that road. The "traditional presence," if such an expression may be coined, of the hero is felt in all the fishing places. The whole neighborhood is also enveloped in taboos, which are especially stringent when the fishing is going on. This is periodical, and lasts for about six days each moon, beginning on the *yapila* (the day of the full moon), when the fish are coming in shoals into the shallow water between the barrier reef and the beach. The native tradition says that Tudava ordered the *kalala* fish to live in "big rivers" on the d'Entrecasteaux Archipelago, and once a month to come up to the beach of Laba'i. But the magic spells, also ordered by Tudava, are essential, for if these were omitted the fish would not come. Tudava's name, coupled with those of other ancestors, figures in a long spell said at the beginning of the fishing period on the beach near a large tabooed stone called Bomlikuliku.[53] The spell begins:—

"*Tudava kulu Tudava;*
Ibu'a kulu, Wa'ibua;
Kuluvidaga, Kulubaiwoie, Kulubetoto,
Muaga'i, Karibuiuwa," etc.

Tudava and Wa'ibua are mythical ancestors who both belonged to the village of Laba'i, the first being, as we know already, the great "culture hero" of the island. Noteworthy is the play on the name Wa'ibua, evidently for the purposes of rhythm. Again, the word *kulu* inserted between the two first names (that of Tudava and of Ibu'a and prefixed to the three following names) could not be translated by my informants, nor do I see any etymological solution of the difficulty. After the personal names enumerated above follow eight names without a kinship term and sixteen with the kinship term *tubugu* ("my grandfathers") preceding each. Then comes the name of the immediate predecessor of the present magician. My informant was unable to explain why some of the names were furnished with the kinship determination, whilst the others were not. But he was very positive that those two classes were not equivalent or interchangeable.

An offering is made daily to the *baloma* during the six days the fishing lasts. Small bits of cooked fish (about the size of walnuts) and bits of betel nut (now also tobacco) are put by the magician on the Bomlikuliku stone with the following words:—

"Kamkuamsi kami ulá ula, nunumuaia:
Ilikilaluva, Ilibualita;
Kulisasisama,"[54]

which mean—

"Eat your *ulá'ula* (present for performing magic), O old women: Ilikilaluva (personal name), Ilibualita (personal name); open it."

This shark spell or invocation is repeated daily with each offering. Another charm, called *guvagava*, is chanted daily for the six days over some leaves; it has the power of attracting the *kalala* fish. The spell begins with a list of ancestors, all of them styled "ancestor" or "grandfather."

There is a spell performed once only, at the beginning of the fishing period, on the road leading from the village of Laba'i to the beach. It is chanted over a plant (*libu*) uprooted from the soil and put across the path. In this spell there is the following phrase:—

"Iamuana iaegulo, Umnalibu
Tai'ioko, Kubugu, Taigala, Likiba," [55]

which is also an enumeration of names, all of which are said to have belonged to the present magician's ancestors.

Another formula in which names of ancestors occur is that recited while the magician sweeps his house at the beginning of the fishing period. This spell begins:—

"Boki'u, Kalu Boki'u; Tamala, Kuri Tamala;
Tageulo, Kuritageulo."

All these are names of ancestors of the magician's subclan. Characteristic is the repetition of the names with a superadded prefix, *"Boki'u Kalu Boki'u,"* etc. Whether the man's real name is represented by the first word and the second one is an embellished replica, or whether the first is only a curtailed second syllable of the real name, was not quite clear to my informants.

In the system of *kalala*-fishing magic just discussed the

number of formulae in which ancestral names figure is five out of a total of seven, which makes a large proportion.

It would take up too much space to discuss in detail all the remaining magical formulae which have been recorded. A synoptic table (see next page) will be sufficient as a basis for a short discussion.[56]

As mentioned above, there are the two classes of magic, the "matrilineal" and "patrilineal," the former bound up with a locality, the latter often handed over from one place to another. It is also necessary in Kiriwinian magic to distinguish between magic which forms a system, and that which naturally consists of unconnected formulae. The term "system" may be taken to denote that magic in which a number of formulae form an organic consecutive whole. This whole is usually connected with activities which are also part of a large organic total—activities all of which are directed towards the same end. Thus it is quite clear that garden magic forms a system. Every formula is connected with some activity, and all together form a consecutive series tending towards one end. The same applies to magic performed at different stages of a fishing period or to magical formulae said during the successive phases of a trading expedition. No single formula of such a system would be of any use. They must all be recited successively; they must all belong to the same system, and each must mark off some phase of the given activity. On the other hand, love magic consists of a number of spells (and they are innumerable in Kiriwina), every one of which forms an independent unit.

Description of magic.	Total number of formulae recorded.	Number of formulae in which ancestral names are mentioned.	Number of formulae in which no ancestral names are mentioned.
1. Weather charms .	12	6	6
2. War magic	5	—	5
3. Kaitubutabu (coconut)	2	1	1
4. Thunder	2	1	1
5. Sorcery and medicine	19	4	15
6. Canoe	8	—	8
7. Muasila (trading, exchange of wealth)	11	—	11
8. Love	7	—	7
9. Kaiga'u (mulukuausi magic) .	3	—	3
10. Kabitam' (carving charms)	1	—	1
11. Fishing magic ...	3	2	1
12. Sting ray fishing .	1	—	1
13. Wageva (beauty magic)	2	—	2
14. Areca nut	1	—	1
15. Saikeulo (child magic)	1	—	1

War magic (No. 2) again forms a system. All spells have to be recited, one after the other, in connection with consecutive magical activities. This system is connected with a certain locality, and references to this locality (and other places, too) are made, but no ancestor names are mentioned.

Weather magic (No. 1), chiefly rain magic and, less important, fine weather magic, is local and connected with a myth. The twelve spells all belong to one locality, and they are the most powerful rain magic in the island. They are the monopoly of the rulers of the village of Kasana'i (a small village, which forms practically one unit with the village of Omarakana), a monopoly which in times of drought brings an enormous income in gifts to the magician.

Again, in *kaitubutabu* magic (No. 3) the two formulae are part of a system; they must both be said at two different stages of a period, during which coconuts are tabooed, and the object of the whole series of observances and rites is to foster the growth of coconuts.

Thunder magic (No. 4) is connected with a tradition, in which there figures a mythical ancestor, and this is mentioned in the spell.

Canoe-making magic (No. 6) and *muasila* magic (No. 7), connected with a remarkabe system of trading and exchange of valuables (called *kula*), form each an extremely important system of magic. No ancestral names are mentioned in the formulae recorded. Unfortunately, I have not recorded any complete system of *muasila*, and though one system of canoe magic has been recorded, it could not be properly translated. In both forms of magic there are references to localities, but none to ancestors.

The three spells of fishing magic (No. 11) belong to one system.

The other spells (Nos. 12–15) do not form systems. In the love spells there is naturally no mention of ancestral names. The only formulae where such names appear are those designed to bring a disease upon a man or to exorcise it. Some of these charms are associated with myths.

The data here given concerning the role of ancestors in magic must speak for themselves. It has not been possible to obtain much additional information from natives upon this subject. The references to the *baloma* form an intrinsic and essentially important part of the spells in which they occur. It would be no good asking the natives "What would happen if you omitted to invoke the *baloma?*" (a type of question which sometimes reveals the ideas of the native as to the sanction or reason for a certain practice), because a magical formula is an inviolable, integral item of tradition. It must be known thoroughly and repeated exactly as it was learnt. A spell or magical practice, if tampered with in any detail, would entirely lose its efficacy. Thus the enumeration of ancestral names cannot conceivably be omitted. Again, the direct question, "Why do you mention those names?" is answered in the time-honored manner, "*Tokunabogu bubunemasi* [our (excl.) old custom]." And in this matter I did not profit much from discussing matters with even the most intelligent natives.

That the names of the ancestors are more than a mere enumeration is clear from the fact that the *ula'ula* is offered in all the most important systems, which have been thoroughly examined, and also from the offerings and *sagali* described above. But even these presents and the partaking of the *sagali*, though undoubtedly they imply the presence of the *baloma*, do not express the idea of the spirits' actual participation in fostering the aim of the magic; of their being the agents through whom the magician works, to whom he appeals or whom he masters in the spell, and who perform subsequently the task imposed on them.

The natives at times express meekly the idea that a benevolent attitude of the spirit is very favorable to the fishing or gardening, and that if the spirits were angry they would do harm. This latter negative view was undoubtedly more pronounced. The *baloma* participate in some vague manner in such ceremonies as are performed for their benefit, and it is better to keep on the right side of them, but this view by no means implies the idea that they are the main agents, or even the subsidiary agents, of any activity.[57] The magical virtue lies in the spell itself.

The native attitude of mind towards the *baloma* in magic may become more clear when compared with that obtaining during the *milamala*. There the *baloma* are participants and onlookers, whose favor ought to be gained, whose wishes are naturally respected, who, further, are not slow in showing their disapproval, and who can make a nuisance of themselves if not properly treated, though their anger is not nearly so terrible as that of the normal type of supernatural beings, savage or civilized. In the *milamala* the *baloma* are not real agents in anything that goes on. Their role is purely passive. And out of this passivity they can be roused only by being put into bad humor, when they begin to show their existence in a negative manner, so to speak.

There is another side to the lists of ancestral names in magic, which must be remembered here. In all Kiriwinian magic a great role is played by myths, underlying a certain system of magic, and by tradition in general. How far this tradition is local and how far it thus becomes focussed on the family tradition of a certain subclan has been discussed above. The ancestral names mentioned in the several formulae form therefore one of the traditional elements so conspicuous in general. The mere sanctity of those names, being often a chain linking the performer with a mythical ancestor and originator, is in the eyes of the natives a quite sufficient *prima facie* reason for their recital. Indeed, I am certain that any native would regard them thus in the first place, and that he would never see in them any appeal to the spirits, any invitation to the *baloma* to come and act; the spells uttered whilst giving the *ula'ula* being, perhaps, an exception. But even this exception does not loom first and foremost in his mind and does not color his general attitude towards magic.[58]

VI.

All these data bearing upon the relations between the *baloma* and the living, are, in a way, a digression from the story of the afterlife of the *baloma* in Tuma, and to this let us now return.

We left the *baloma* settled to his new life in the nether world, more or less comforted concerning those left behind; having, very likely, married again and formed new ties and connections. If the man died young, his *baloma* is also young, but with time he will age, and finally his life in Tuma will also come to an end. If the man was old at his death, his *baloma* is old, and after a period his life in Tuma will also cease.[59] In all cases the end of the life of the *baloma* in Tuma brings with it a very important crisis in the cycle of his existence. This is the reason why I have avoided the use of the term death in describing the end of the *baloma*.

I shall give a simple version of these events and discuss the details subsequently. When the *baloma* has grown old, his teeth fall out, his skin gets loose and wrinkled; he goes to the beach and bathes in the salt water; then he throws off his skin just as a snake would do, and becomes a young child again; really an embryo, a *waiwaia*—a term applied to children *in utero* and immediately after birth. A *baloma* woman sees this *waiwaia*; she takes it up, and puts it in a basket or a plaited and folded coconut leaf (*puatai*). She carries the small being to Kiriwina, and places it in the womb of some woman, inserting it *per vaginam*. Then that woman becomes pregnant (*nasusuma*).[60]

This is the story as I obtained it from the first informant who mentioned the subject to me. It implies two important psychological facts: the belief in reincarnation, and the ignorance of the physiological causes of pregnancy. I shall now discuss both these subjects in the light of the details obtained on further inquiry.

First of all, everybody in Kiriwina knows, and has not the slightest doubt about, the following propositions. The real cause of pregnancy is always a *baloma*, who is inserted into or enters the body of a woman, and without whose existence a woman could not become pregnant; all babies are made or come into existence (*ibubulisi*) in Tuma. These tenets form the main stratum of what can be termed popular or universal belief. If you question any man, woman, or even an intelligent child, you will obtain from him or her this information. But any further details are much less universally known; one obtains a fact here and a detail there, and some of them contradict the others, and none of them seems to loom particularly clear in the native mind, though here and there it is obvious that some of these beliefs influence behavior, and are connected with some customs.

First, as to the nature of these "spirit children," *waiwaia*.[61] It must be kept in mind that, as is usual in dogmatic assertions, the natives take very much for granted, do not trouble to give clear definitions or to imagine details very concretely and vividly. The most natural assumption—namely, that, of the "spirit child" being a small undeveloped child, an embryo—is the most frequently met with. The term *waiwaia*, which means embryo, child in the womb, and also infant immediately after birth, is also applied to the non-incarnated spirit children. Again, in a discussion on this subject, in which several men took part, some asserted that the man, after his transformation in Tuma, becomes just some sort of "blood," *buia'i*. In what manner he could be subsequently transported in such liquid form was not certain. But the term *buia'i* seems to have a slightly wider connotation than fluid blood merely, and it may mean something like flesh in this case.

Another cycle of beliefs and ideas about reincarnation implies a pronounced association between the sea and the spirit children. Thus I was told by several informants that after his transformation into a *waiwaia*, the spirit goes into the sea. The first version obtained (quoted above) implied that the spirit, after having washed on the seabeach and become rejuvenated, is taken up immediately by a female *baloma* and carried to Kiriwina. Other accounts state that the spirit, after being transformed, goes into the sea and dwells there for a time. There are several corollaries to this version. Thus in all the coastal villages on the western shore (where this information was collected) mature unmarried girls observe certain precautions when bathing. The spirit children are supposed to be concealed in the *popewo*, the floating sea scum; also in some stones called *dukupi*. They come along on large tree trunks (*kaibilabala*), and they may be attached to dead leaves (*libulibu*) floating on the surface. Thus when at certain times the wind and tide blow plenty of this stuff towards the shore, the girls are afraid of bathing in the sea, especially at high tide. Again, if a married woman wants to conceive, she may hit the *dukupi* stones in order to induce a concealed *waiwaia* to enter her womb. But this is not a ceremonial action.[62]

In the inland villages the association between conception and bathing is also known. To receive the *waiwaia* whilst in the water seems to be the most usual way of becoming pregnant. Often whilst bathing a woman will feel that something has touched her, or even hurt her. She will say, "A fish has bitten me." In fact, it was the *waiwaia* entering or being inserted into her.

Another rather important connection between the belief of the *waiwaia* dwelling in the sea and conception is expressed in the only important ceremony connected with pregnancy. About four to five months after the first symptoms of pregnancy the woman begins to observe certain taboos, and at the same time a large and long *dobe* (grass petticoat) is made (called *saikeulo*), which she will wear after the birth of the child. This is made by certain female relatives, who also perform magic over it, in order to benefit the child. On the same day the woman is taken to the sea, where relatives of the same class as those that made the *saikeulo* bathe her in the salt water. A *sagali* (ceremonial distribution of food) follows the proceedings.

The usual explanation of the *u'ula* (reason) for this ceremony is that it makes the "skin of the woman white," and that it makes the birth of the baby easier.[63] But in the coastal village of Kavataria a very definite statement was volunteered, to the effect that the *kokuwa* ceremony is connected with incarnation of the spirit children. The view taken by one of my informants was that during the first stage of pregnancy the *waiwaia* has not really entered the woman's body, but that there is merely a kind of preparation made for its reception. Then, during the ceremonial bathing, the spirit child enters the body of the woman. Whether this volunteered interpretation was only his opinion or whether it is a universal belief in the coastal villages, is not known to me, but I am inclined to believe that it does represent an aspect of the coastal natives' belief. But it must be emphatically stated that this interpretation was absolutely pooh-poohed by my informants of the inland villages, who also pointed out the contradiction that this ceremony is performed later on, during pregnancy, and that the *waiwaia* has been established long ago in the mother's womb. It is characteristic that any inconsistency is noted in a view which is not the informant's own standpoint, while similar contradictions are most blandly overlooked in his own theories. The natives are, remarkably enough, not a whit more consistent on this point or intellectually honest than civilized people.

Besides the belief in reincarnation by action of the sea, the view that the *waiwaia* is inserted by a *baloma* is prevalent. These two ideas blend in the version that the *baloma* who inserts the *waiwaia* does it under water. The *baloma* often appears in a dream to the prospective mother, who will tell her husband: "I dreamed that my mother (or maternal aunt, or my elder sister or grandmother) inserted a child into me; my breasts are swelling." As a rule, it is a female *baloma* that appears in the dream and brings the *waiwaia*, though it may be a man, but the *baloma* must always be of the *veiola* (maternal kindred) of the woman. Many know who brought them to their mother. Thus To'uluwa, the chief of Omarakana, was given to his mother (Bomakata) by Buguabuaga, one of her *tabula* ("grandfathers"—in this case her mother's mother's brother).[64] Again, Bwoilagesi, the woman mentioned on page 162, who goes to Tuma, had her son, Tukulubakiki, given her by Tomnavabu, her *kadala* (mother's brother). Tukulubakiki's wife, Kuwo'igu, knows that her mother came to her, and gave her the baby, a girl now about twelve months old. Such knowledge is possible only in the cases when the *baloma* actually appears in a dream to the woman and tells her that he will insert a *waiwaia* into her. Of course, such annunciations are not absolutely in the program; indeed, the majority of people do not know who it is to whom they owe their existence.

There is one extremely important feature of the beliefs about reincarnation, and however opinions differ about the other details, this feature is stated and affirmed by all the informants; namely, that the social division, the clan and subclan of the individual, is preserved through all his transformations. The *baloma*, in the nether world, belongs to the same subclan as the man before death; and the reincarnation moves also strictly within the boundaries of the subclan. The *waiwaia* is conveyed by a *baloma* belonging to the same subclan as the woman, as just stated, the carrier is even as a rule some near *veiola*. And it was considered absolutely impossible that any exception to this rule could happen, or that an individual could change his or her subclan in the cycle of reincarnation.[65]

So much about the belief in reincarnation. Though it is a universal and popular belief, *i.e.*, though it is known to everybody, it does not play an important role in social life. The last mentioned detail only about the persistence of kinship ties throughout the cycle is decidedly a belief illustrating the strength of the social division, the finality of belonging to a social group. Conversely, this belief must strengthen those ties.

VII.

It might seem quite safe to say that the belief in reincarnation, and the views about a spirit child being inserted into, or entering the womb of the mother, exclude any knowledge of the physiological process of impregnation. But any drawing of conclusions, or arguing by the law of logical contradiction, is absolutely futile in the realm of belief, whether savage or civilized. Two beliefs, quite contradictory to each other on logical grounds, may coexist, while a perfectly obvious inference from a very firm tenet may be simply ignored. Thus the only safe way for an ethnological inquirer is to investigate every detail of native belief, and to mistrust any conclusion obtained through inference only.

The broad assertion that the natives are entirely ignorant of the existence of physiological impregnation may be laid down quite safely and correctly. But though the subject is undoubtedly difficult, it is absolutely necessary to go into details in order to avoid serious mistakes.

One distinction must be made at the outset: the distinction between impregnation, that is the idea of the father having a share in building up the body of the child on the one hand, and the purely physical action of sexual intercourse on the other. Concerning the latter, the view held by the natives may be formulated thus: it is necessary for the woman to have gone through sexual life before she can bear a child.

I was forced to make the above distinction under the stress of the information I was gathering, in order to explain certain contradictions which cropped up in the course of inquiries. And it must be therefore accepted as a "natural" distinction, as one which corresponds to and expresses the native point of view. In fact, it was impossible to foresee how the natives would look upon these matters, and from which side they would approach the correct knowledge of facts. Nevertheless, the distinction once made, its theoretical importance is obvious. It is clear that only the knowledge of the first fact (that of the father's share in impregnation) would have any influence in shaping native ideas about kinship. As long as the father does nothing to form the body of the child (in the ideas of a people), there can be no question of consanguinity in the agnatic line. A mere mechanical share in opening up the child's way into the womb, and out of it, is of no fundamental importance. The state of knowledge in Kiriwina is just at the point where there is a vague idea as to some *nexus* between sexual connection and pregnancy, whereas there is no idea whatever concerning the man's contribution towards the new life which is being formed in the mother's body.

I shall sum up the data which led me to make this statement. Beginning with ignorance of the father's share, to direct questions as to the cause (*u'ula*) of a child being created, or a woman becoming pregnant, I received the invariable answer, *"Baloma boge isaika* [the *baloma* gave it]."[66]

Of course, like all questions about the *u'ula,* this one has to be put with patience and discrimination, and it may at times remain unanswered. But in the many cases when I put this question bluntly and directly, and when it was comprehended, I received this answer, though I must add here at once that it was at times complicated in an extremely puzzling manner by some hints about copulation. As I was puzzled by that, and as I was very keen on getting this point clear, I discussed it whenever it could be approached as a side issue, I put it *in abstracto,* and I discussed it very often in concrete instances wherever any special case of pregnancy, past or present, was the subject of conversation.

Specially interesting and crucial were the cases where the pregnant woman was not married.[67]

When I asked who was the father of an illegitimate child, there was only one answer, that there was no father, as the girl was not married. If, then, I asked, in quite plain terms, who is the physiological father, the question was not understood, and when the subject was discussed still further, and the question put in this form: "There are plenty of unmarried girls, why did this one get with child, and the others not," the answer would be: "It is a *baloma* who gave her this child." And here again I was often puzzled by some remarks, pointing to the view that an unmarried girl is especially exposed to the danger of being approached by a *baloma,* if she is very unchaste. Yet the girls deem it much better precaution to avoid directly any exposure to the *baloma* by not bathing at high tide, etc., than indirectly to escape the danger by being too scrupulously chaste.

Illegitimate, or according to the Kiriwinian ideas, fatherless children, and their mothers are, however, regarded with scant favor. I remember several instances in which girls were pointed out to me as being undesirable, "no good," because they had children out of wedlock. If you ask why

IN THE TROBRIAND ISLANDS

such a case is bad, there is the stereotyped answer, "Because there is no father, there is no man to take it in his arms" (*Gala taitala Cikopo'i*). Thus Gomaia, my interpreter, had had an intrigue, such as is usual before marriage, with Ilamueria, a girl of a neighboring village. He had previously wanted to marry her. She had a child subsequently, and Gomaia married another woman. Asked why he did not marry his former sweetheart, he replied, "She had a child, this is very bad." Yet he was sure that she had never been unfaithful to him during the period of their "betrothal" (Kiriwinian youths are much the prey of such illusions). He had not the slightest idea about there being any question of fatherhood of the child. If he had he would have acknowledged the child as his own, because he believed in his sexual exclusiveness with regard to the mother. But the fact that it came at an improper time was enough to influence him. This by no means implies that a girl who has been a mother, finds any serious difficulty in marrying afterwards. During my stay in Omarakana, two such girls were married, without any comment. There are no unmarried women in what might be termed the "marriage age" (25–45 years), and when I asked whether a girl might remain a spinster because she had a child, the answer was an emphatic negative. All that has been said above about the *baloma* bringing a child, and the concrete cases adduced, must also be borne in mind in this connection.

When, instead of merely asking about the *u'ula* of pregnancy, I directly advanced the embryological view of the matter, I found the natives absolutely ignorant of the process suggested. To the simile of a seed being planted in the soil and the plant growing out of the seed, they remained quite irresponsive. They were curious, indeed, and asked whether this was "the white man's manner of doing it," but they were quite certain that this was not the "custom" of Kiriwina. The spermatic fluid (*momona*) serves merely the purposes of pleasure and lubrication, and it is characteristic that the word *momona* denotes both the male and female discharge. Of any other properties of the same they have not the slightest idea. Thus, any view of paternal consanguinity or kinship, conceived as a bodily relation between father and child, is completely foreign to the native mind.

The above-mentioned case of a native not being able to understand the question, Who is the father of an unmarried woman's child? can be supplemented by two other instances concerning married women. When I asked my informants what would happen if a woman became pregnant in her husband's absence, they calmly agreed that such cases might occur, and that there would be no trouble at all. One of them (I have not noted his name, and I do not remember it), volunteered his own case as an instance in point. He went to Samarai [68] with his white master, and stayed there for a year, as he said, during which time his wife became pregnant and gave birth to a child. He returned from Samarai, found the child, and it was all right. On further questioning, I came to the conclusion that the man was absent for about 8–10 months, so there is no urgent necessity to doubt the virtue of his wife, but it is characteristic that the husband had not the slightest tendency to count the moons of his absence, and that he stated the broad approximate period of one year without the slightest concern. And the native in question was an intelligent man; he had been a long time with white men, as a "signed-on" boy, and he seemed to be by no means of a timorous or henpecked disposition.

Again, when I once mentioned this matter in the presence of a few white men, resident in the Trobriands, Mr. Cameron, a planter of Kitava, told me a case which had struck him at that time, though he had not the slightest idea of the native ignorance of impregnation. A native of Kitava had been away for two years, signed on to a white man on Woodlark Island. After he came back, he found a baby born a couple of months before his return. He cheerfully accepted it as his own, and did not understand any taunts or allusions made by some white men, who asked him whether he had not better repudiate, or, at least, thoroughly thrash his wife. He found it not in the slightest degree suspicious or suggestive that his wife became pregnant about a year after his departure. These are two striking examples which I find in my notes; but I had before me a considerable amount of corroborating evidence derived from less telling facts, and from imaginary instances, discussed with independent informants.

Finally, the ideas concerning the relationship between father and child, as it is conceived by the natives, bear upon this subject. They have only one generic term for kinship, and this is *veiola*. Now this term means kinship in the maternal line, and does not embrace the relationship between a father and his children, nor between any agnatically related people. Very often, when inquiring into customs and their social basis, I received the answer, "Oh, the father does not do it; because he is not *veiola* to the children." The idea underlying maternal relationship is the community of body. In all social matters (legal, economic, ceremonial) the relationship between brothers is the very closest, "because they are built up of the same body, the same woman gave birth to them." Thus the line of demarcation between paternal and agnatic relationship (which as a generic conception and term does not exist for the natives), and maternal kinship, *veiola*, corresponds to the division between those people who are of the same body (strictly analogous, no doubt, to our consanguinity), and those who are not of the same body.

But in spite of this, as far as all the minute details of daily life are concerned, and further, in various rights and privileges, the father stands in an extremely close relation to the child. Thus the children enjoy membership of the father's village community, though their real village is that of their mother. Again, in questions of inheritance they have various privileges granted them by the father. The most important of these is connected with the inheritance of that most valuable of all goods, magic. Thus very often, especially in such cases as those mentioned above (in Section v), when the father is able to do it legally, he leaves his magic to his son instead of to his brother or nephew. It is remarkable that the father is, sentimentally, always inclined to leave as much as possible to his children, and he does so whenever he can.

Now, such inheritance of magic from father to son shows one peculiarity: it is given, and not sold. Magic has to be handed over during the man's lifetime, of course, as both the formulae and the practices have to be taught. When the man gives it to any of his *veiola*, to his younger brother, or his maternal nephew, he receives a payment, called in this case *pokala*, and a very considerable payment it has to be. When magic is taught to the son, no payment whatever is levied. This, like many features of native custom, is extremely puzzling, because the maternal relatives have the right to the magic, and the son has really no right whatever, and he may be, under certain circumstances, deprived of the privilege by those entitled to it; yet he receives it free of charge, and they have to pay for it heavily.

Forbearing other explanations, I simply state the native answer to this puzzling question (my informants saw the contradiction quite clearly, and perfectly well understood why I was puzzled). They said: "The man gives it to the children of his wife. He cohabits with her, he possesses her, she does for him all that a wife must do for a man. Whatever he does for a child is a payment (*mapula*) for what he has received from her." And this answer is by no means the opinion of one informant only. It sums up the stereotyped answers given to me whenever I discussed this matter. Thus, in the native mind, the intimate relationship between husband and wife, and not any idea, however slight or remote, of physical fatherhood, is the reason for all that the father does for his children. It must be clearly understood that social and psychological fatherhood (the sum of all the ties, emotional, legal, economic) is the result of the man's obligations towards his wife, and physiological fatherhood does not exist in the mind of the natives.

Let us now proceed to the discussion of the second point in the previously made distinction: the vague ideas about some connection existing between sexual intercourse and pregnancy. I mentioned above, that in the answers given about the cause of pregnancy, I was puzzled by the assertion that cohabitation is also the cause of the advent of children, an assertion which ran parallel, so to speak, with a fundamental view that the *baloma,* or reincarnating *waiwaia,* are the real cause.

The said assertion was very much less conspicuous, in fact it was so much overshadowed by the main view, that at first I noticed only the latter, and was persuaded that I had obtained this information quite smoothly and that there were no more difficulties to be cleared up. And when I was quite satisfied that I had finally settled the matter, and inquired into it, prompted merely by the instinct of pure pedantry, I received a severe shock, in finding that there was a flaw in the very foundations of my construction, which latter seemed threatened with complete collapse. I remember being told about a very fickle young lady of Kasanai, known by the name of Iakalusa, "*Sene nakakaita, Coge ivalulu guadi* [very wanton, she had a child]." On inquiring further into this very perplexing sentence, I found that, undoubtedly, a girl of very loose conduct would be more likely to have a child, and that if a girl could be found who had never had intercourse, she certainly could have no child. The knowledge seemed to be as complete here as the ignorance was previously, and the very same men seemed to take, in turn, two contradictory points of view. I discussed the matter as thoroughly as I could, and it seemed to me as if the natives would say *yes* or *no,* according to whether the subject was approached from the side of knowledge or of ignorance. They were puzzled at my persistence, and (I admit with shame) impatience, and I was unable to explain to them my difficulty, though I pointed, as it seemed to me, straight to the contradiction.

I tried to make them compare animals with men, asking whether there is also anything like a *baloma* bringing the small pigs to their mother. I was told of the pigs: "*Ikaitasi ikaitasi makateki bivalulu minana* [they copulate, copulate, presently the female will give birth]." Thus here copulation appeared to be the *u'ula* of pregnancy. For a time, the contradictions and obscurities in the information appeared to me quite hopeless; I was in one of the desperate blind alleys, so often encountered in ethnographical field work, when one comes to suspect that the natives are untrustworthy, that they tell tales on purpose; or that one has to do with two sets of information, one of them distorted by white man's influence. As a matter of fact, in this case as in most cases, nothing of the sort was the cause of my difficulties.

The final shock my confidently constructed views about "native ignorance" received brought also order into the chaos. In my mythological cyclus about the hero Tudava, the story opens with his birth. His mother, Mitigis or Bulutukua, was the only woman of all the inhabitants of the village, Laba'i, who remained on the island. All the others fled in fear of an ogre, Dokonikan, who used to eat men, and had in fact almost finished off the whole population of Kiriwina. Bulutukua, left behind by her brothers, lived alone in a grotto, in the *raiboag* of Laba'i. One day she fell asleep in the grotto, and the water dripping from the stalactites fell on her vulva and opened the passage. After she became pregnant, and gave birth in succession to a fish, called *bologu*; to a pig; to a shrub, called *kuebila* (having aromatic leaves and much appreciated by the natives as ornament); to another fish (the *kalala*, of which mention has been made above in Section v); to the cockatoo (*katakela*); the parrot (*karaga*); to the bird *sikuaikua*; to a dog (*ka'ukua*); and finally to Tudava. In this story the motive of "artificial impregnation" was most surprising. How was it possible to find, what appeared to be survival of a previous ignorance, among people with whom this ignorance seemed to be still complete? And again, how was it that the woman in the myth had several children in succession, but had been only once under the dripping stalactite? All these were puzzling questions for me, and I put them to the natives on the chance of getting some light, but with little hope of success.

I was, however, rewarded and received a clear and final solution of my difficulties, a solution which has withstood a series of most pedantic subsequent tests. I tried my best informants one after the other, and this is their view of the matter: a woman who is a virgin (*nakapatu; na,* female prefix; *kapatu,* closed, shut up) cannot give birth to a child, nor can she conceive, because nothing can enter or come out of her vulva. She must be opened up, or pierced through (*ibasi,* this word is used to describe the action of the water drops on Bulutukua). Thus the vagina of a woman who has much intercourse will be more open and easier for a spirit child to enter. One that keeps fairly virtuous will have much poorer chances of becoming pregnant. But copulation is quite unnecessary except for its mechanical action. In default, any other means of widening the passage may be used, and if the *baloma* chooses to insert the *waiwaia,* or if one chooses to enter, the woman will become pregnant.

That this is so is proved, beyond any doubt, to my informants by the case of Tilapo'i, a woman living in Kabululo, a village close to Omarakana. She is half blind, almost an idiot, and so plain that no one would think of approaching her sexually. In fact, she is the favorite theme of a certain class of jokes all turning on the assumption of someone having had connection with her: jokes which are always relished and repeated, so that *"Kuoi Tilapo'i!* [Have connection with Tilapo'i]" has become a form of jocular abuse. In spite, however, of the fact that it is supposed that she never had connection, she once gave birth to a child, which died subsequently. A similar example, though even more striking, is afforded by another woman in Sinaketa, who, I was told, is so plain that any man would commit suicide, if he were even seriously suspected of having had anything to do with her sexually. Yet this woman has had no less than five children. In both these cases, it is explained that pregnancy was made possible by dilation of the vulva, due to digital manipulation. My informants dwelt on this subject with much relish, graphically and diagramatically explaining to me all the details of the process. Their account did not leave the slightest doubt about their sincere belief in the possibility of women becoming pregnant without intercourse.

Thus I was taught to make the essential distinction between the idea of the mechanical action of intercourse, which covers all the natives know about the natural conditions of pregnancy, and the knowledge of impregnation, of the man's share in creating the new life in the mother's womb, a fact of which the natives have not even the slightest glimpse. This distinction accounts for the puzzle in the Bulutukua myth, where the woman had to be opened up, but this once done, she could bear the whole set of children successively, without any new physiological incident being necessary. It accounts also for the "knowledge" about animal impregnation. In the case of the animals—and the domestic animals such as the pig and the dog would loom most conspicuously in the native's picture of the universe—the natives know nothing about afterlife or spiritual existence. If asked directly, a man might answer "yes" or "no" with regard to the existence of animal *baloma*, but this would be his extemporized opinion and not folklore. Thus, in the case of animals, the whole problem about reincarnation and about the formation of new life is simply ignored. The physiological aspect, on the other hand, is well-known. Thus when you ask about the animals, you get the answer that it is necessary that the physiological conditions should exist, but the other side, the real problem of how life is created in the womb, is simply ignored. And it is no good to fret over it, because the native never troubles about consistently carrying over his beliefs into domains where they do not naturally belong. He does not trouble about questions referring to animal afterlife, and he has no views about their coming into the world. Those problems are settled with reference to man, but that is their proper domain, and beyond that they ought not to be extended. Even in non-savage theologies such questions (*e.g.*, that of animal soul and animal immortality) are very puzzling, and answers to them often are not much more consistent than those of a Papuan.

In conclusion, it may be repeated that such knowledge as the natives have in this matter has no sociological importance, does not influence the native ideas of kinship, nor their behavior in matters of sex.

It seems necessary to make a somewhat more general digression on this subject after having dealt with Kiriwinian material. As is well known, the ignorance of physical fatherhood was first discovered by Sir Baldwin Spencer and Mr. F. Gillen among the Arunta tribe of Central Australia. Subsequently the same state of things was found among a large number of other Australian tribes, by the original discoverers and by some other investigators, the area covered being practically the whole central and northeastern portion of the Australian continent, as far as it was still open to ethnological investigation.

The main controversial questions raised as to this discovery were: Firstly, is this ignorance a specific feature of the Australian culture, or even the Arunta culture, or is it a universal fact existing among many or all of the lower race? Secondly: is this state of ignorance primitive, is it simply the absence of knowledge, due to insufficient observation and inference, or is it a secondary phenomenon, due to an obscuring of the primitive knowledge by superimposed animistic ideas? [69]

I would not join in this controversy at all, if it were not that I desire to state some additional facts, partly derived from work done outside Kiriwina, partly consisting of some general observations made in the field and bearing directly upon these problems. Therefore, I hope I shall be excused for this digression, on the plea that it is not so much speculation upon controversial points, as additional material bearing upon these questions.

First of all I want to state some non-Kiriwinian observations which seem to show that a state of ignorance similar to that found in the Trobriands obtains among a wide

range of the Papuo-Melanesians of New Guinea. Prof.
Seligman writes about the Koita: "It is stated that a single
sexual act is not sufficient to produce pregnancy, to ensure
which cohabitation should be continued steadily for a
month." [70] I have found a similar state of things among
the Mailu on the south coast of New Guinea: ". . . The
connection between cohabitation and conception seems to
be known among the Mailu, but to direct inquiries as to
the cause of pregnancy I did not obtain emphatic and
positive answers. The natives—of this I am positive—do
not clearly grasp the idea of the connection between the
two facts. . . . Like Prof. Seligman among the Koita, I
found the firm belief that it is only continuous intercourse
for a month or more that leads to pregnancy, and that one
single act is not sufficient to produce the result." [71]

Neither of these statements is very emphatic, and in fact
they do not seem to imply a complete ignorance of physical
fatherhood. Yet as neither of the investigators seems to
have gone into detail, one may *a priori* suspect that the
statements allow of some further qualification. As a matter
of fact, I was able to inquire into the matter on my second
visit to New Guinea, and I know that my statement about
the Mailu is incomplete. At the time of my visit to Mailu
I was puzzled in the same manner as in Kiriwina. I had
with me in Kiriwina two boys from a district adjacent to
that of the Mailu, who gave me exactly the same information as that gathered in Kiriwina, *i.e.*, they affirmed the
necessity of sexual intercourse before pregnancy, but were
absolutely ignorant as to impregnation. Again looking
through my notes taken in the summer of 1914 at
Mailu and through some notes taken among the Sina-
ugholo, a tribe closely allied to the Koita, I see that the
native statements really imply only the knowledge of the
fact that a woman must have experienced some sexual life
before conceiving. And that to all direct questions, whether
there is anything in intercourse that induces pregnancy, I
received negative answers. Unfortunately, in neither place
did I directly inquire whether there are any beliefs about

the "supernatural cause of pregnancy." The boys from Gadogado'a (from the district near Mailu) told me there were no such beliefs among them. Their statement cannot, however, be considered final, as they have spent much of their time in white man's service and might not have known much of the traditional knowledge of their tribe. There can be no doubt, however, that both Prof. Seligman's statement and my information obtained in Mailu would, if developed with the help of native informants, yield similar results to the Kiriwinian data with regard to the ignorance of impregnation.

All these natives, the Koita, the Southern Massim of Gadogado'a, and the Northern Massim of Kiriwina[72] are representative of the Papuo-Melanesian stock of natives, the Kiriwinians being a very advanced branch of that stock; in fact, as far as our present knowledge goes, the most advanced.[73]

The existence of complete ignorance, of the type discovered by Spencer and Gillen, among the most advanced Papuo-Melanesians, and its probable existence among all the Papuo-Melanesians, seems to indicate a much wider range of distribution and a much greater permanence through the higher stages of development than could be assumed hitherto. But it must be emphatically repeated that unless the inquiry be detailed, and especially unless the above-made distinction be observed, there is always the possibility of failure and of erroneous statement.[74]

Passing to the second controversial point named above, whether the ignorance in question may not be the secondary result of some obscuring, superimposed, animistic ideas. The general character of the Kiriwinian mental attitude certainly would answer this question with an emphatic negation. The above-detailed account, if read from this point of view, is perhaps convincing enough, but some further remarks may add additional weight to the statement. The native mind is absolutely blank on this subject, and it is not as if one found very pronounced ideas about reincarnation running parallel with some obscure knowledge. The ideas and beliefs about reincarnation, though undoubtedly there, are of no eminent social importance, and are not at all to the fore in the native's store of dogmatic ideas. Moreover, the physiological process and the part played by the *baloma* could perfectly well be known to exist side by side, exactly as there exist side by side ideas about the necessity of the mechanical dilation of the vulva and the action of the spirit, or as in innumerable matters the native considers the natural and rational (in our sense) sequence of events and knows its causal nexus, though these run parallel with a magical sequence and nexus.

The problem of the ignorance of impregnation is not concerned with the psychology of belief, but with the psychology of knowledge based on observation. Only a belief can be obscured or overshadowed by another belief. Once a physical observation is made, once the natives have got hold of a causal nexus, no belief or "superstition" can obscure this knowledge, though it may run parallel with it. The garden magic does not by any means "obscure" the natives' causal knowledge of the nexus between proper clearing of the scrub, manuring the ground with ashes, watering, etc. The two sets of facts run parallel in his mind, and the one in no way "obscures" the other.

In the ignorance of physiological fatherhood we do not deal with a positive state of mind, with a dogma leading to practices, rites, or customs, but merely with a negative item, the absence of knowledge. Such an absence could not possibly be brought about by a positive belief. Any widespread gap in knowledge, any universal absence of information, any general imperfection in observation found among native races, must, pending contrary evidence, be considered as primitive. We might as well argue that humanity once had a primitive knowledge of wax vestas, but that this was obscured subsequently by the more complex and picturesque use of the fire drill and other friction methods.

Again, to explain this ignorance by assuming that the natives "make believe that they do not know it" seems rather a brilliant *jeu de mots* than a serious attempt to get at the bottom of things. And yet things are as simple as they can be for anyone who for a moment stops to realize the absolutely unsurmountable difficulties which a native "natural philosopher" would have to overcome if he had to arrive at anything approaching our embryological knowledge. If one realizes how complex this knowledge is, and how lately we arrived at it, it would seem preposterous to suppose even the slightest glimmer of it among the natives. All this might appear plausible, even to someone who approached the subject from a merely speculative standpoint, arguing from what probably must be the natives' point of view in this matter. And here we have authors who, after this state of mind has been found positively among natives, receive the news with scepticism, and try to account for the native state of mind in the most devious manner. The way from the absolute ignorance to the exact knowledge is far, and must be passed gradually. There is no doubt that the Kiriwinians have made a step on the way by acknowledging the necessity of sexual intercourse as a preliminary condition of pregnancy, as, indeed, this recognition, though perhaps in a less clear form, has been made by the Arunta in Central Australia, among whom Spencer and Gillen have found the idea that sexual intercourse prepares the woman for the reception of a spirit child.

Another consideration which has been put forward by some authors previously, seems to me to be very much to the point, and, what is more, has seemed so to several of my native informants. I mean the fact that in the majority of savage races sexual life begins very early and is carried on very intensely, so that sexual intercourse is for them not an outstanding rare fact, which would strike them from its singularity, and therefore compel them to look for consequences; on the contrary, sexual life is for them a normal state. In Kiriwina the unmarried girls from six (sic) upwards are generally supposed to practice licence well-nigh every night. It is immaterial whether this is so or not; it matters only that for the native of Kiriwina sexual inter-

course is almost as common an occurrence as eating, drinking, or sleeping. What is there to guide the native
observation, to draw his attention to the nexus between a
perfectly normal, everyday occurrence, on the one hand,
and an exceptional, singular event on the other? How is
he to realize that the very act which a woman performs
almost as often as eating or drinking, will, once, twice, or
three times in her life, cause her to become pregnant?

It is certain that only two outstanding, singular events
easily reveal a nexus. To find out that something extraordinary is the result of an entirely ordinary event requires,
besides a scientific mind and method, the power of investi-
gating, of isolating facts, of excluding the non-essential, and
experimenting with circumstances. Given such conditions,
the natives would probably have discovered the causal connection, because the native mind works according to the
same rules as ours: his powers of observation are keen,
whenever he is interested, and the concept of cause and
effect is not unknown to him.[75] But although cause and
effect in the developed form of these conceptions are of
the category of the regular, lawful, and ordinary, in their
psychological origin they are undoubtedly of the category
of the lawless, irregular, extraordinary, and singular.

Some of my native informants very clearly pointed out to
me the lack of consistency in my argument when I bluntly
stated that it is not the *baloma* that produce pregnancy,
but that it is caused by something like a seed being thrown
on soil. I remember that I was almost directly challenged
to account for the discrepancy why the cause which was
repeated daily, or almost so, produced effects so rarely.

To sum up, there seems to be no doubt that if we are at
all justified in speaking of certain "primitive" conditions of
mind, the ignorance in question is such a primitive condition, and its prevalence among the Melanesians of New
Guinea seems to indicate that it is a condition lasting right
into much higher stages of development than it would have
seemed possible to assume on the basis of Australian material only. Some knowledge of the mental mechanism of the

native, and of the circumstances under which he has to
carry out his observations on this subject, ought to per-
suade anyone that no other state of things could exist,
and that no far-fetched explanations or theories are necessary to account for it.

VIII.

Besides the concrete data about native beliefs which have
been given above, there is another set of facts of no less
importance which must be discussed before the present
subject can be considered exhausted. I mean the general
sociological laws that have to be grasped and framed in the
field, in order that the material, which observation brings
in a chaotic and unintelligible form, may be understood by
the observer and recorded in a scientifically useful form.
I have found the lack of philosophical clearness on matters
connected with ethnographical and sociological field work
a great setback in my first attempts to observe and describe
native institutions, and I consider it quite essential to state
the difficulties I encountered in my work and the manner
in which I tried to cope with them.

Thus one of the main rules with which I set out on my
field work was "to gather pure facts, to keep the facts and
interpretations apart." This rule is quite correct if under
"interpretations" be understood all hypothetical speculations about origins, etc., and all hasty generalizations. But
there is a form of interpretation of facts without which no
scientific observation can possibly be carried on—I mean
the interpretation which sees in the endless diversity of
facts general laws; which severs the essential from the irrelevant; which classifies and orders phenomena, and puts
them into mutual relationship. Without such interpretation all scientific work in the field must degenerate into
pure "collectioneering" of data; at its best it may give odds
and ends without inner connection. But it never will be
able to lay bare the sociological structure of a people, or to

give an organic account of their beliefs, or to render the picture of the world from the native perspective. The often fragmentary, incoherent, non-organic nature of much of the present ethnological material is due to the cult of "pure fact." As if it were possible to wrap up in a blanket a certain number of "facts as you find them" and bring them all back for the home student to generalize upon and to build up his theoretical constructions upon.

But the fact is that such a proceeding is quite impossible. Even if you spoil a district of all its material objects, and bring them home without much bothering about a careful description of their use—a method which has been carried out systematically in certain non-British possessions in the Pacific—such a museum collection will have little scientific value, simply because the ordering, the classifying, and interpreting should be done in the field with reference to the organic whole of native social life. What is impossible with the most "crystallized" phenomena—the material objects—is still less possible with those which float on the surface of native behavior, or lie in the depths of the native mind, or are only partially consolidated into native institutions and ceremonies. In the field one has to face a chaos of facts, some of which are so small that they seem insignificant; others loom so large that they are hard to encompass with one synthetic glance. But in this crude form they are not scientific facts at all; they are absolutely elusive, and can be fixed only by interpretation, by seeing them *sub specie aeternitatis,* by grasping what is essential in them and fixing this. *Only laws and generalizations are scientific facts,* and field work consists only and exclusively in the interpretation of the chaotic social reality, in subordinating it to general rules.

All statistics, every plan of a village or of grounds, every genealogy, every description of a ceremony—in fact, every ethnological document—is in itself a generalization, at times quite a difficult one, because in every case one has first to discover and formulate the rules: what to count and how to count; every plan must be drawn to express certain economic or sociological arrangements; every genealogy has to express kinship connections between people, and it is only valuable if all the relevant data about the people are collected as well. In every ceremony the accidental has to be sifted from the essential, the minor elements from the essential features, those that vary with every performance from those that are customary. All this may appear almost a truism, yet the unfortunate stress on keeping to "pure fact only" is constantly being used as the guiding principle in all instructions for field work.

Returning from this digression to the main subject, I want to adduce some general sociological rules which I had to formulate in order to deal with certain difficulties and discrepancies in the information, and in order to do justice to the complexity of facts, at the same time simplifying them in order to present a clear outline. What will be said in this place applies to Kiriwina, but not necessarily to any other or wider area. And, again, only those sociological generalizations will be discussed here which bear directly on belief, or even, more specially, on the beliefs described in this article.

The most important general principle concerning belief that I have been forced to respect and consider in the course of my field studies is this: Any belief or any item of folklore is not a simple piece of information to be picked up from any haphazard source, from any chance informant, and to be laid down as an axiom to be drawn with one single contour. On the contrary, every belief is reflected in all the minds of a given society, and it is expressed in many social phenomena. It is therefore complex, and, in fact, it is present in the social reality in overwhelming variety, very often puzzling, chaotic and elusive. In other words, there is a "social dimension" to a belief, and this must be carefully studied; the belief must be studied as it moves along this social dimension; it must be examined in the light of diverse types of minds and of the diverse institutions in which it can be traced. To ignore this social dimension, to pass over the variety in which any given item of folklore is

found in a social group, is unscientific. It is equally unscientific to acknowledge this difficulty and to solve it by
simply assuming the variations as non-essential, because
that only is non-essential in science which cannot be formulated into general laws.

The manner in which ethnological information about beliefs is usually formulated is somewhat like this: "The natives believe in the existence of seven souls"; or else, "In
this tribe we find that the evil spirit kills people in the
bush," etc. Yet such statements are undoubtedly false, or
at the best incomplete, because no "natives" (in the
plural) have ever any belief or any idea; each one has his
own ideas and his own beliefs. Moreover, the beliefs and
ideas exist not only in the conscious and formulated opinions of the members of a community. They are embodied
in social institutions and expressed by native behavior, from
both of which they must be, so to speak, extricated. At
any rate, it appears clearly that the matter is not as simple
as the ethnological usage of "one-dimensional" accounts
would imply. The ethnographer gets hold of an informant,
and from conversation with him is able to formulate the
native's opinion, say, about afterlife. This opinion is written down, the grammatical subject of the sentence put into
the plural, and we learn about the "natives believing so-
and-so." This is what I call a "one-dimensional" account, as
it ignores the social dimensions, along which belief must
be studied, just as it ignores its essential complexity and
multiplicity.[76]

Of course, very often, though by no means always, this
multiplicity may be ignored, and the variations in detail
overlooked as unessential, in view of the uniformity which
obtains in all essential and main features of a belief. But
the matter must be studied, and methodical rules applied
to the simplification of the variety, and unification of the
multiplicity of facts. Any haphazard proceeding must, obviously, be discarded as unscientific. Yet, as far as I am
aware, no attempt has been made by any inquirer in the
field, even the most illustrious, to discover and lay down

such methodical rules. The following remarks ought, therefore, to be treated indulgently, being only an unaided attempt to suggest certain important connections. They deserve indulgence also on account of being the result of actual experiences and difficulties encountered in the field. If, in the account of beliefs given above, there is a certain lack of uniformity and smoothness; if, further, the observer's own difficulties are somewhat brought into relief, this must be excused on the same account. I attempted to show as plainly as possible the "social dimension" in the domain of belief, not to conceal the difficulties which result from the variety of native opinions, and also from the necessity of constantly holding in view both social institutions and native interpretation, as well as the behavior of the natives; of checking social fact by psychological data, and *vice versa*.

Now let us proceed to lay down the rules which allow us to reduce the multiplicity of the manifestations of a belief to simpler data. Let us start with the statement made several times, namely, that the crude data present almost a chaos of diversity and multiplicity. Examples may be easily found among the material presented in this article, and they will allow the argument to be clear and concrete. Thus, let us take the beliefs corresponding to the question, "How do the natives imagine the return of the *baloma*?" I have actually put this question, adequately formulated, to a series of informants. The answers were, in the first place, always fragmentary—a native will just tell you one aspect, very often an irrelevant one, according to what your question has suggested in his mind at the moment. Nor would an untrained "civilized man" do anything else. Besides being fragmentary, which could be partially remedied by repeating the question and using each informant to fill up the gaps, the answers were at times hopelessly inadequate and contradictory. Inadequate because some informants were unable even to grasp the question, at any rate unable to describe such a complex fact as their own mental attitude, though others were astonishingly clever, and almost able to understand what the ethnological inquirer was driving at.

What was I to do? To concoct a kind of "average" opinion? The degree of arbitrariness seemed much too great. Moreover, it was obvious that the opinions were only a small part of the information available. All the people, even those who were unable to state what they thought about the returning *baloma* and how they felt towards them, none the less behaved in a certain manner towards those *baloma*, conforming to certain customary rules and obeying certain canons of emotional reaction.

Thus, in searching for an answer to the above question —or to any other question of belief and behavior—I was moved to look for the answer in the corresponding customs. The distinction between private opinion, information gathered by asking the informants, and public ceremonial practices, had to be laid down as a first principle. As the reader will remember, a number of dogmatic tenets have been enumerated above, which I have found expressed in customary traditional acts. Thus the general belief that the *baloma* return is embodied in the broad fact of the *milamala* itself. Again, the display of valuables (*ioiova*), the erection of special platforms (*tokaikaya*), the display of food on the *lalogua*—all this expresses the presence of the *baloma* in the village, the efforts to please them, to do something for them. The food presents (*silakutuva* and *bubualu'a*) show an even more intimate participation in village life by the *baloma*.

The dreams, which often preceded such offerings, are also customary features, just because they are associated with, and sanctioned by, such customary offerings. They make the communion between the *baloma* and the living, in a way, personal, and certainly more distinct. The reader will be able easily to multiply these examples (connection between belief in Topileta and his fee, and the valuables laid round the body before burial; beliefs embodied in the *ioba*, etc.)

Besides the beliefs expressed in the traditional ceremonies, there are those embodied in magical formulae. These formulae are as definitely fixed by tradition as the customs. If anything, they are more precise as documents than the customs can be, since they do not allow of any variations. Only small fragments of magical formulae have been given above, yet even these serve to exemplify the fact that beliefs can be unmistakably expressed by spells, in which they are embedded. Any formula accompanied by a rite expresses certain concrete, detailed, particular beliefs. Thus, when, in one of the above-named garden rites, the magician puts a tuber on the stone in order to promote the growth of the crops, and the formula which he recites comments on this action and describes it, there are certain beliefs unmistakably documented by it: the belief in the sacredness of the particular grove (here our information is corroborated by the taboos surrounding that grove); the belief in the connection between the tuber put on the sacred stone and the tubers in the garden, etc. There are other, more general, beliefs embodied and expressed in some of the above-mentioned formulae. Thus the general belief in the assistance of ancestral *baloma* is standardized, so to speak, by the spells by which those *baloma* are invoked, and the accompanying rites in which they receive their *ula'ula*.

As mentioned above, some magical spells are based upon certain myths, details of which appear in the formulae. Such myths, and myth in general, must be put side by side with the magical spells as traditional, fixed expressions of belief. As an empirical definition of a myth (again only claiming a validity for the Kiriwinian material) the following criteria can be accepted: it is a tradition explaining essential sociological features (*e.g.*, myths about the division in clans and subclans), referring to persons who performed notable feats, and whose past existence is implicitly believed in. Traces of such existence in various memorial spots are still shown: a dog petrified, some food transformed into stone, a grotto with bones, where the ogre Dokonikan lived, etc. The reality of mythical persons and

mythical occurrences stands in vivid contrast to the un-
reality of ordinary fables, many of which are told.

All beliefs embodied in mythological tradition can be
assumed to be almost as invariable as those embodied in
magical formulae. In fact, the mythical tradition is extremely well fixed, and accounts given by natives of different places in Kiriwina—natives of Luba and natives of
Sinaketa—agreed in all details. Moreover, I obtained an
account of certain myths of the Tudava cycle during a short
visit to Woodlark Island, which lies some sixty miles to the
east of the Trobriands but belongs to the same ethnological
group, called by Prof. Seligman the Northern Massim,
which agrees in all essential features with the facts obtained
in Kiriwina.

Summing up all these considerations, we may say that
all beliefs as implied in native customs and tradition must
be treated as invariably fixed items. They are believed and
acted upon by all, and, as customary actions do not allow
of any individual varieties, this class of belief is standardized by its social embodiments. They may be called the
dogmas of native belief, or the social ideas of a community,
as opposed to individual ideas.[77] One important addition
has to be made, however, to complete this statement: only
such items of belief can be considered as "social ideas" as
are not only embodied in native institutions, but are also
explicitly formulated by the natives and acknowledged to
exist therein. Thus all the natives will acknowledge the
presence of the *baloma* during the *milamala*, their expul-
sion at the *ioba*, etc. And all the competent ones will give
unanimous answers in the interpretation of magical rites,
etc. On the other hand, the observer can never safely venture to read his own interpretations into the native customs.
Thus, for instance, in the above-mentioned fact, that
mourning is always finally discarded immediately after an
ioba, there seems to be unmistakably expressed the belief
that the person waits till the *baloma* of the deceased has
gone before giving up the mourning. But the natives do not
endorse this interpretation, and therefore it cannot possibly

be considered as a social idea, as a standardized belief. The question whether this belief was not originally the reason for the practice belongs to quite a different class of problem, but it is obvious that the two cases must not be confounded; one, where a belief is formulated in a society universally, besides being embodied in institutions; the other, where the belief is ignored, though apparently expressed in an institution.

This allows us to formulate a definition of a "social idea": *It is a tenet of belief embodied in institutions or traditional texts, and formulated by the unanimous opinion of all competent informants.* The word "competent" simply excludes small children and hopelessly unintelligent individuals. Such social ideas can be treated as the "invariants" of native belief.

Besides the social institutions and traditions, both of which embody and standardize belief, there is another important factor, which stands in a somewhat similar relation to belief—I mean the general behavior of the natives towards the object of a belief. Such behavior has been described above as illuminating important aspects of native belief about the *baloma*, the *kosi*, the *mulukuausi*, and as expressing the natives' emotional attitude towards them. This aspect of the question is beyond doubt of extreme importance. To describe the ideas of the natives concerning a ghost or spirit is absolutely insufficient. Such objects of belief arouse pronounced emotional reactions, and one ought to look, in the first place, for the objective facts corresponding to these emotional reactions. The above data concerning this aspect of native belief, insufficient as they are, show clearly that with more experience in method a systematic inquiry could be carried out into the emotional side of belief on lines as strict as ethnological observations admit.

The behavior can be described by putting the natives to certain tests concerning their fear of ghosts, or their respect for spirits, etc. I have to admit that, though realizing the importance of the subject, I did not quite see, whilst in the field, the proper manner to deal with this difficult and new subject. But I now clearly see that, had I been better on the look out for relevant data in this line, I should have been able to present much more convincing and objectively valid data. Thus in the problem of fear my tests were not sufficiently elaborate, and even as they were made, not sufficiently minutely recorded in my notes. Again, though I will remember the tone in which I heard them speaking —rather irreverently—about the *baloma*, I also remember that a few characteristic expressions struck me at the time, which I ought to have noted at once, and did not. Again, watching the behavior of the performers and spectators in a magical ceremony, certain small facts characterizing the general "tone" of the natives' attitude are to be found. Such facts I have observed partly, though, I think, insufficiently (they were only just mentioned in this article when speaking about the *kamkokola* ceremony, as they really do not bear on the subject of spirits or afterlife). The fact is, however, that until this aspect is more generally taken under observation and some comparative material exists, the full development of the method of observation is very difficult.

The emotional attitude expressed in behavior, and characterizing a belief, is not an invariable element: it varies with individuals, and it has no objective "seat" (such as the beliefs embodied in institutions have). Nevertheless, it is expressed by objective facts, which can be almost quantitatively stated, as in measuring the amount of inducement needed and the length of an expedition on which a native will venture alone under fear-inspiring conditions. Now, in each society there are braver and more cowardly individuals, emotional people and callous ones, etc. But divers types of behavior are characteristic for different societies, and it seems enough to state the type, since the variations are well-nigh the same in all societies. Of course, if it be possible to state the variations, so much the better.

To illustrate the matter concretely, by the simplest example, that of fear, I have experimented with this element in another district in Papua—in Mailu, on the south coast—and found that no normal inducement, no offering of even an excessive payment in tobacco, would prevail upon any native to cover at night and alone any distance out of sight and earshot of the village. Even here, however, there were variations, some men and boys being unwilling to run the risk even at dusk, others being ready to go out at night to some inconsiderable distance for a payment of a stick of tobacco. In Kiriwina, as described above, the type of behavior is absolutely different. But here again some people are much more timorous than others. Perhaps these variations could be expressed more exactly, but I am not in the position to do it, and at any rate the type of behavior characterizes the corresponding beliefs, when compared with the Mailu type, for instance.

It seems feasible, therefore, as the first approach to exactness, to treat elements of belief expressed by behavior as types; that is, not to trouble about the individual variation. In fact, the types of behavior seem to vary considerably with the society, whereas the individual differences seem to cover the same range. This does not mean that they ought to be ignored, but that, in the first approach, they may be ignored without making the information incorrect through incompleteness.

Let us pass now to the last class of material which must be studied in order to grasp the beliefs of a certain community—the individual opinions or interpretations of facts. These cannot be considered as invariable, nor are they sufficiently described by indicating their "type." Behavior, referring to the emotional aspect of belief, can be described by showing its type, because the variations move within certain well-described limits, the emotional and instinctive nature of man being as far as one can judge, very uniform, and the individual variations remaining practically the same in any human society. In the domain of the purely intellectual aspect of belief, in the ideas and opinions explaining belief, there is room for the greatest range of variations. Belief, of course, does not obey the laws of logic, and the contradictions, divergencies, and all the general chaos pertaining to belief must be acknowledged as a fundamental fact.

One important simplification in this chaos is obtained by referring the variety of individual opinions to the social structure. In almost every domain of belief there is a class of men whose social position entitles them to a special knowledge of the beliefs in question. In a given community they are generally and officially considered to be the possessors of the orthodox version, and their opinion is considered the correct one. Their opinion, moreover, is to a considerable extent based on a traditional view which they have received from their ancestors.

This state of things is, in Kiriwina, very well exemplified in the tradition of magic and of the connected myths. Although there is as little esoteric lore and tradition, and as little taboo and secrecy, as in any native society which I know from experience or literature, nevertheless there is complete respect for a man's right to his own domain. If you ask in any village any question referring to more detailed magical proceedings in the gardening department, your interlocutor will immediately refer you to the *towosi* (garden magician). And then on further inquiry you learn, as often as not, that your first informant knew all the facts absolutely well and was perhaps able to explain them better than the specialist himself. None the less, native etiquette, and the feeling of what is right, compelled him to refer you to the "proper person." If this proper person be present, you will not be able to induce anyone else to talk on the matter, even if you announce that you do not want to hear the specialist's opinion. And, again, I have several times obtained information from one of my usual instructors and subsequently the "specialist" has told me that it is not correct. When, later, I referred this correction to my original informant, he would, as a rule, withdraw his opinion saying, "Well, if he says so, it must be correct." Special caution ought of course to be exercised when the specialist is naturally inclined to lie, as is often the case with the sorcerers (those who possess the power to kill people by magic).

Again, if the magic and corresponding tradition belong to another village, the same discretion and reserve is observed. You are advised to go to that village for information. When pressed, your native friends may perhaps tell you what they know about the matter, but they will always wind up the report by saying: "You must go there and gather the right knowledge at the right source." In the case of magic formulae, this is absolutely necessary. Thus I had to go to Laba'i in order to get the *kalala*-fishing magic, and to Kuaibola to record the shark-fishing charms. I obtained the canoe-building magic from men of Lu'ebila, and I went to Buaitalu to get the tradition and spell of the *toginivaiu*, the most powerful form of sorcery, though I was unable to procure the *silami* or evil spell and was only partially successful in getting the *vivisa* or healing spell. Even if the knowledge to be obtained is not spells, but mere traditional lore, one is often sorely disappointed. Thus, for instance, the proper seat of the Tudava myth is Laba'i. Before I went there I had gathered all that my informants in Omarakana could tell me and expected to reap an enormous harvest of additional information, but as a matter of fact, it was I who impressed the natives of Laba'i, by quoting details which were hailed by them as quite true, but which had escaped their memory. In fact, no one there was half as good on the Tudava cyclus as my friend Bagido'u of Omarakana. Again, the village of Ialaka is the historic spot where once a tree was erected up to heaven. And this was the origin of thunder. If you ask about the nature of thunder, everybody will tell you straight off: "Go to Ialaka and ask the *tolivalu* (the headman)," although practically everybody is able to tell you all about the origin and nature of thunder, and your pilgrimage to Ialaka, if you undertake it, will prove a great disappointment.

Nevertheless, these facts show that the idea of specialization in traditional lore is strongly developed; that in many items of belief, and in many opinions about belief, the natives recognize a class of specialist. Some of these are associated with a certain locality; in such cases it is always the headman of the village who represents the orthodox doctrine, or else the most intelligent of his *veiola* (maternal kinsmen). In other cases the specialization goes within the village community. In this place we are not concerned with this specialization, in so far as it determines the right to obtain magical formulae, or the correct reciting of certain myths, but only in so far as it refers to the interpretation of all beliefs connected with such formulae or myths. Because, besides the traditional text, the "specialists" are always in possession of the traditional interpretations or commentaries. It is characteristic that, when talking with such specialists, you always get clearer answers and opinions. You clearly see that the man does not speculate or give you his own views, but that he is fully aware of being asked about the orthodox view, about the traditional interpretation. Thus when I asked certain informants about the meaning of the *"si buala baloma,"* the miniature hut made of dry twigs during one of the garden rites (see above, v), they tried to give me a kind of explanation, which I saw at once, was their own private view of the matter. When I asked Bagido'u, the *towosi* (garden magician) himself, he simply waved away all explanations and said, "This is merely an old traditional thing, no one knows its meaning."

Thus in the diversity of opinions there is one important line of demarcation to be drawn: that between the opinions of competent specialists and the views of the profane public. The opinions of the specialists have a traditional basis: they are clearly and categorically formulated and, in the eyes of the native, they represent the orthodox version of the belief. And, since on each subject there is a small group of people, in the last instance one man, to be considered, it is easy to see that the most important interpretation of belief does not present any great difficulties in handling.

But in the first place, this most important interpretation does not represent all the views, it cannot be taken even as typical, at times. Thus for instance, in sorcery (evil, homicidal magic), it is of absolute importance to distinguish between the views of the specialist and those of the outsider, because both represent equally important and naturally different aspects of the same problem. Again, there are certain classes of belief where one would in vain look for departmental specialists. Thus about the nature of the *baloma* and their relation to the *kosi*, there were some statements more trustworthy and detailed than others, but there was no one who would be a naturally and generally acknowledged authority.

In all matters where there are no specialists, and again in matters in which the opinion of non-specialists is of intrinsic interest, it is necessary to have certain rules for fixing the fluctuating opinion of the community. Here I see only one clear and important distinction: namely, between what can be called public opinion, or more correctly —since public opinion has a specific meaning—the general opinion of a given community on the one hand, and the private speculations of individuals on the other. This distinction is, as far as I can see, sufficient.

If you examine the "broad masses" of the community, the women and children included (a proceeding which is easy enough when you speak the language well and have lived for months in the same village, but which otherwise is impossible), you will find that, whenever they grasp your question, their answers will not vary: they will never venture into private speculations. I have had most valuable information on several points from boys and even girls of seven to twelve years of age. Very often, on my long afternoon walks, I was accompanied by the children of the village and then, without the constraint of being obliged to sit and be attentive, they would talk and explain things with a surprising lucidity and knowledge of tribal matters. In fact, I was often able to unravel sociological difficulties with the help of children, which old men could not explain to me. The mental volubility, lack of the slightest suspicion and sophistication, and, possibly a certain amount of training received in the Mission School, made of them incomparable informants in many matters. As to the danger of their views being modified by missionary teaching, well, I can only say that I was amazed at the absolute impermeability of the native mind to those things. The very small amount of our creed and ideas they acquire remains in a watertight compartment of their mind. Thus the general tribal opinion in which practically no variety is to be found can be ascertained even from the humblest informants.

When dealing with intelligent grown-up informants, things are quite different. And as they are the class with whom an ethnographer has to do most of his work, the variety of their opinion comes very much to the fore, unless the inquirer is satisfied in taking one version of each subject and sticking to it through thick and thin. Such opinions of intelligent, mentally enterprising informants, as far as I can see, cannot be reduced or simplified according to any principles: they are important documents, illustrating the mental faculties of a community. Further on, they very often represent certain typical ways of conceiving a belief, or of solving a difficulty. But it must be clearly borne in mind that such opinions are sociologically quite different from what we called above dogmas or social ideas. They are also different from generally accepted or popular ideas. They form a class of interpretation of belief, which closely corresponds to our free speculation on belief. They are characterized by their variety, by not being expressed in customary or traditional formulae, by being neither the orthodox expert opinion, nor the popular view.

These theoretical considerations about the sociology of belief may be summarized in the following table, in which the various groups of belief are classified in a manner which seems to express their natural affinities and distinctions, as far, at least, as the Kiriwinian material requires:—

1. *Social ideas or dogmas.*—Beliefs embodied in institutions, in customs, in magico-religious formulae and rites and in myths. Essentially connected with and

characterized by emotional elements, expressed in behavior.

2. *Theology or interpretation of the dogmas.—*
   (*a*) Orthodox explanations, consisting of opinions of specialists.
   (*b*) Popular, general views, formulated by the majority of the members of a community.
   (*c*) Individual speculations.

Examples for each group can be easily found in this article, where the degree and quality of social depth, the "social dimension" of every item of belief, has been given, at least approximately. It must be remembered that this theoretical scheme, though dimly recognized at the beginning, has been only imperfectly applied, because the technique of its applicability in field work had to be elaborated bit by bit, through actual experience. It is, therefore, with reference to my Kiriwinian material, rather a conclusion *ex post facto* than a basis of method adopted at the outset and systematically carried out throughout the work.

Examples of dogma or social ideas are to be found in all the beliefs, which have been described as embodied in the customs of the *milamala* and in the magical rites and formulae. Also in corresponding myths, as well as in the mythological tradition, referring to afterlife. The emotional aspect has been treated, as far as my knowledge allows, in describing the behavior of the natives towards magical performances during the *milamala*, their behavior towards the *baloma*, the *kosi*, and the *mulukuausi*.

Of the theological views, several orthodox interpretations have been given in the explanations by a magician of his magic. As popular views (barring such as are dogmas at the same time) I may note the belief concerning spiritism: everybody, even the children, knew well that certain people went to Tuma and brought back songs and messages to the living. This, however, was in no way a dogma, since it was even open to scepticism on the part of some exceptionally sophisticated informants, and since it was connected with no customary institution.

The speculations about the nature of the *baloma* are the best example illustrating the purely individual class of theology, consisting of private opinions.

I wish to remind the reader that local differences, that is the variation of belief according to district, have not been considered at all in this theoretical section. Such differences belong to the domain of anthropogeography rather than sociology. Moreover, they affect only to a very small extent the data presented in this paper, as practically all of my material has been collected within a small district, where local variations hardly exist at all. Only as regards the reincarnation, local differences may account for some divergencies in belief (see above, vi).

From such district variations the above-mentioned localized specialization in certain departments (thunder in Ialaka, shark in Kuaibuola, etc.) must be carefully distinguished, because this is a factor connected with the structure of society and not merely an example of the broad anthropological fact, that everything changes as we move over the surface of the earth.

All these theoretical remarks, it is plain, are the outcome of experience in the field, and it was considered well to print them here in connection with the data already given, because they are also ethnological facts, only of a much more general nature. This, however, makes them, if anything, more important than the details of custom and belief. Only the two aspects, the general law and the detailed documentation, make information really complete, as far as it goes.

Notes

BALOMA; THE SPIRITS OF THE DEAD IN THE TROBRIAND
ISLANDS

[1] This article contains part of the results of ethnographical work in British New Guinea carried on in connection
with the Robert Mond Travelling Studentship (University
of London), and the Constance Hutchinson Scholarship of
the London School of Economics (University of London),
with assistance from the Commonwealth Department of
External Affairs, Melbourne.

The writer spent some ten months, May, 1915–March,
1916, at Omarakana and the neighboring villages of
Kiriwina (Trobriand Islands), where he lived among the
natives in a tent. By October, 1915, he had acquired
sufficient knowledge of the Kiriwinian language to be able
to dispense with the services of an interpreter.

The writer desires to acknowledge the assistance he has
received from Mr. Atlee Hunt, Secretary to the Commonwealth Department of External Affairs, and from Dr. C. G.
Seligman, Professor of Ethnology in the University of London. The unfailing kindness and encouragement of Dr.
Seligman have been of the greatest assistance throughout,

and his work, *The Melanesians of British New Guinea,* provided a solid foundation on which to base the present investigations. Sir Baldwin Spencer, K.C.M.G., has been kind enough to read parts of the MS. and to give the writer his valuable advice on several important points.

[2] For an account of Kiriwina sociology, *cf.* Seligman's work, *The Melanesians of British New Guinea,* chaps. xlix–lii, pp. 660–707, and chap. lix for a description of the mortuary practices. Prof. Seligman gives also an outline of the native beliefs concerning an afterlife (chap. lv), and his data, which were collected in a different locality of the district, will be quoted hereafter.

[3] Seligman, *op. cit.,* p. 733.

[4] *Cf.* below, where the various versions are discussed. The nature of the *baloma* and *kosi,* and the material of which they are built, so to speak—whether shadow or reflection or body—will also be dealt with there. It may suffice here to say that the *baloma* are certainly considered to retain exactly the likeness of the living individual.

[5] I have been struck by the enormous difference in this respect obtaining between the Northern Massim and the Mailu, a tribe on the south coast of New Guinea, which I visited during a six months stay in Papua in 1914–15. The Mailu people are conspicuously afraid of darkness. When, towards the end of my stay, I visited Woodlark Island, the natives there, who belong to the same group as the Kiriwinians (a group called by Seligman the Northern Massim), differed so obviously in that respect from the Mailu that I was struck with this the first evening, which I spent in the village of Dikoias. *Cf.* "The Natives of Mailu: Preliminary Results of the Robert Mond Research Work in British New Guinea," *Trans. Roy. Soc. South Australia,* vol. xxxix, 1915.

[6] *Cf.* C. G. Seligman, *op. cit.*, chap. xlvii, where similar maleficent women from another district (Southern Massim) are described. I do not dwell here in detail on the beliefs about the *mulukuausi*, but I am under the impression that the natives are not quite sure whether it is a kind of "sending" or "double" that leaves the body of the witch or whether she goes out herself on her errand in an invisible form. *Cf.* also "The Natives of Mailu," p. 653, and footnote on p. 648.

[7] The preliminary burial, as well as burying in the middle of the village, has recently been suppressed by Government.

[8] It must be noted that the grave was in olden days situated right in the middle of the village, and that a close vigil was kept over it, having, among other motives, that of protecting the corpse from these female ghouls. Now that the grave is outside the village the vigil has had to be abandoned, and the *mulukuausi* can prey on the corpse as they like. There seems to be an association between the *mulukuausi* and the high trees on which they like to perch, so that the present site of burial, placed as it is right among the high trees of the grove (*weika*) surrounding each village, is specially odious to the natives.

[9] This well is situated not far from the shore, in the *raiboag*, the elevated, stony, wooded coral ridge, which runs in a ring round almost all the smaller islands of the archipelago and the greater part of the large island Boiowa. All the stones and the well here mentioned are real and can be seen by mortals.

[10] This effect of the Gilala water was explained by one of my informants only; the others did not know the object of this ablution, though all affirmed its existence.

[11] This is a contradiction of the statement that the

baloma assemble round the new arrival and help him in wailing. See below, VIII, the remarks about such inherent inconsistencies.

[12] The natives strictly distinguish between the *vaigu'a* (valuable possessions) and *gugu'a* (the other less valuable ornaments and objects of use). The main objects classified as *vaigu'a* will be enumerated in this article later on.

[13] In practice the corpse is most carefully stripped of all valuables just before burial, and I saw even small shell earrings being extracted from the ear lobes, articles which the natives would not hesitate to sell for half a stick of tobacco (three farthings). On one occasion, when a small boy had been buried in my presence, and a very small and poor belt of *kaloma* (shell discs) was left on the body by mistake, there was great consternation and a serious discussion whether the body ought to be unearthed.

[14] During my stay one young man committed suicide in the *lo'u* manner in a neighboring village. Though I saw the corpse a few hours after death, and was present at the wailing and burial and all the mortuary ceremonies, it was only after a few months that I learned he had committed suicide, and I never could learn his motive. The Rev. E. S. Johns, the head of the Methodist Mission in the Trobriands, informs me that he used at times to register as many as two suicides a week (through poison) in Kavataria, a group of large villages situated in the immediate neighborhood of the Mission station. Mr. Johns tells me that suicides occur in epidemics, and that they have been fostered by the discovery by the natives of the white man's power to counteract the poison. The aim of the suicide is to punish the survivors, or some of them.

[15] This poison is prepared from the roots of a cultivated vine; its action is not very rapid, and if emetics be properly administered in time life is usually saved.

¹⁶ There seems to be some possibility of death by old age, especially in the case of very insignificant old men and women. Several times, when I was asking of what a man had died, I received the answer, "He was very old and weak and he just died." But when I asked about M'tabalu, a very old and decrepit man, the chief of Kasana'i, whether he was going to die soon, I was told that, if no *silami* (evil spell) were thrown on him, there was no reason why he should not go on living. Again, it must be remembered that a *silami* is a private thing, not to be talked about except with intimate friends. It must be emphasized that the "ignorance of natural death" is the general typical attitude expressed in custom and reflected in such legal and moral institutions as exist, rather than some kind of absolute apodictic statement, excluding any contradictions or uncertainties.

¹⁷ Seligman, *op. cit.*, p. 733.

¹⁸ The distinction between rank and authority is important in Kiriwinian sociology. The members of the Tabalu section of the Malasi clan have the highest rank. The head of this clan wields authority over the village of Omarakana and, in a way, over a great portion of the main island and some adjacent islands. Whether he will retain this authority after death in Tuma seemed doubtful to To'uluwa, the present chief of Omarakana. But there was not the slightest doubt that he and all the other Tabalu, as well as everyone else, would retain their respective rank and their membership in clan and subclan. To understand this, *cf.* the excellent account of the Trobriand social system, in Seligman, *op. cit.*, chaps. xlix-liii.

¹⁹ In order to understand this statement the reader must be acquainted with the social system of the Kiriwinians (*see* Seligman, *loc. cit.*). There is a very close connection between every village and a certain section of a clan. Usually, but not always, this section is descended from an

ancestor, who came out of the ground in that locality. In any case, the head of this section is always said to be the master or owner of the land (*tolipuaipucaia*, from *toli*, a prefix denoting mastership, ownership, and *puaipuaia*, ground, soil, land).

[20] This wooing in Tuma, as described to me by my informants, corresponds to the manner in which people mate on certain occasions called *katuyausi*. The *katuyausi* are expeditions of amorous adventure, in which the unmarried girls of a village go *en bloc* to another village and there sleep with the youths of that village. Any single male who fancies one of the girl guests gives her (through an intermediary) some small present (a comb, some shell discs or turtle shell rings), which is handed over with the words "*kam paku*." If accepted, the two belong to each other for the night. Such expeditions, though well established and sanctioned by custom, are strongly resented by the young men of the village from which the *katuyausi* starts, and they end as a rule in a sound thrashing administered by the male to the female youth of the village.

[21] A "lifetime" is undoubtedly a much less definite period to the natives than it is to ourselves.

[22] Another center is the Island of Kaileula.

[23] Seligman, *op. cit.*, p. 734.

[24] Similar songs have also been brought by other people from Tuma.

[25] To judge leniently such "inconsistencies" of native belief, it is sufficient to remember that we meet the same difficulties in our own ideas about ghosts and spirits. No one who believes in ghosts or spirits ever doubts that they can speak, and even act; they can rap on tables or with table legs, lift objects, etc.

26 *Op. cit.*, p. 733.

27 *Op. cit.*, p. 679.

28 "Ceremonial in the narrower sense," as opposed to the mere uttering of the spell over a certain object.

29 For instance, the Mailu on the south coast. See *Trans. Roy. Soc. South Australia*, vol. xxxix, p. 696.

30 In this short, purely descriptive account of harvesting, I have purposely avoided sociological technicalities. The complex system of mutual gardening duties is an extremely interesting feature of Kiriwinian social economics. It will be described in another place.

31 In this and other instances I do not dwell upon such sociological details as do not bear directly upon the subject of this article.

32 The calendar arrangements in the Trobriand Islands are complicated by the fact that there are four districts, each of which places the beginning of the year, *i.e.*, the end of the *milamala* moon—at a different time. Thus in Kitava, an island to the east of the main island of the group, the *milamala* is celebrated some time in June or July. Then follow in July and August the southern and western districts of Bwoiowa, the main island, and some islands to the west (Kaileula and others). After which the *milamala* takes place in August or September in the central and eastern districts of the main island, in what is called by the natives Kiriwina, and last there follows Vakuta, the island to the south of Bwoiowa, where the *milamala* takes place in September or October. Thus the feast, and with it the whole calendar, is shifted over the space of four moons in one district. It seems that the dates of the garden activities also vary, keeping time with the calendar. This was stated by the natives with emphasis, but I found dur-

ing the year I was in Bwoiowa that the gardens were more advanced in Kiriwina than in the western district, though the latter is one moon in advance of the former.

The dates of the moons are fixed by the position of the stars, in which astronomical art the natives of Wawela, a village lying on the beach in the southern half of the main island, excel. The Rev. M. K. Gilmour told me that the appearance of the *palolo,* the marine annelid *Eunice viridis,* which takes place on the reef near Vakuta, is a very important factor in regulating the native calendar, in fact, in doubtful cases it decides the question. This worm appears on certain days towards the full moon, falling early in November or late in October, and this is the *milamala* time of Vakuta. In Kiriwina the natives told me, however, that they thoroughly rely on the astronomical knowledge of the Wawela men.

[33] No *tokaikaya* were made in Omarakana or Olivilevi during the *milamala* I saw in those villages. The custom is on the decline, and the erection of a *tokaikaya* necessitates a considerable amount of labor and trouble. I saw one in the village of Gumilababa, where there lives a chief of the highest rank (Mitakata, a *guya'u* of the *tabalu* rank).

[34] How far, besides and behind this professed aim, vanity and the aesthetic motive are at work in prompting such displays, cannot be discussed here.

[35] This is one of the innumerable food distributions (generic name *sagali*) which are connected with almost every feature of social life in the Trobriands. It is usually one clan (or two clans) that arranges the *sagali,* and other clans receive the food. Thus in the *katukuala* the Malasi clan first distribute the food and the *lukulabuta,* the *lukuasisiga* and the *lukuba* receive it. After a few days another *katukuala* is held, with the inverse social grouping. The dual arrangements of the clans varies according to

the district. In Omarakana the Malasi are so preponderant that they form one moiety for themselves, the three remaining clans forming the other. It is impossible to enter here into the detailed examination of the social mechanism and of the other features of the *sagali*.

³⁶ Of course, the chiefs have as much pig as they require before giving any to the *tokay*. But it is characteristic that the privileges of the chief have much more to do with the liberty to give than with the liberty to consume. Vanity is a stronger passion than greed—though perhaps this reflection does not express the whole truth of the matter!

³⁷ Thus dancing in general is inaugurated by the initiation of the drums (*katuvivisa kasausa'u*), which is connected with the *katukuala*. The *kaidebu* have to be initiated separately by a *katuvivisa kaidebu*.

³⁸ There are names for each day about full moon. Thus the day (and night) of the full moon are called *Yapila* or *Kaitaulo*. One day before, *Yamkevila*; two days, *Ulakaiwa*. The day after full moon, *Valaila*; the following one, *Woulo*. The *ioba* takes place on the night of *Woulo*.

³⁹ The drums of the Kiriwinians consist of: (1) the large drum (normal size of New Guinea drum) called *kasausa'u* or *kupi* (this latter word being an obscene synonym for the *glans penis*): and (2) the small drum, about one third the size of the larger, called *katunenia*. All their drumbeats are a combination of the two drums, the *kupi* and the *katunenia* leading each its separate voice.

⁴⁰ There are two main types of dance in Boiowa. The circular dances, where the orchestra (the drums and the singers) stands in the middle, and the performers go round them in a circle, always in the opposite direction to the hands of a watch. These dances are again subdivided into: (1) *bisila* (pandanus streamer) dances with slow move-

ment (2) *kitatuva* (two bunches of leaves), with a quick movement; and (3) *kaidebu* (wooden painted shield), dances with the same quick movement. In the *bisila* dances women can take part (very exceptionally), and all the performers wear women's petticoats. The second group of dances are the *kasawaga*, where only three men dance, always in imitation of animal movements, though these are very conventionalized and unrealistic. These dances are not circular, there are no songs (as a rule) to accompany them; the orchestra consists of five *kupi* drums and one *katunenia*.

41 When a village is in mourning (*bola*), and drums are taboo, the *ioba* is performed by means of a conch shell (*ta'uio*)—but it must not be omitted even under such circumstances.

42 The dread of "leading questions," as expressed over and over again in all instructions for ethnographical field work is, according to my experience, one of the most misleading prejudices. "Leading questions" are dangerous with a new informant, for the first half hour or couple of hours, at the outside, of your work with him. But any work done with a new, and consequently bewildered, informant is not worth being recorded. The informant must know that you want from him exact and detailed statements of fact. A good informant, after a few days, will contradict and correct you even if you make a *lapsus linguae*, and to think of any danger from leading questions in such a case is absolutely groundless. Again, real ethnographical work moves much more in statement of actual details, details which, as a rule, can be checked by observation—where again there is in no case any danger from leading questions. The only case where direct questioning is necessary, where it is the only instrument of the ethnographist, is when he wants to know what is the interpretation of a ceremony, what is his informant's opinion about some state of things; then leading questions are absolutely necessary. You might ask a native, "What is your interpretation of such and such a ceremony?"

and wait for years before getting your answer (even if you know how to word it in native language). You would more or less solicit the native to take up your attitude, and look at things in ethnographical perspective. Again, when dealing with facts that are just out of range of immediate observation, like customs of war, and some of the obsolete technological objects, it is absolutely impossible to work without leading questions, if many important features are not to be omitted, and as there is no earthly reason to avoid this type of questioning, it is directly erroneous to brand the leading questions. Ethnological inquiry and judicial examination are essentially different, in that in the latter the witness has usually to express his personal, individual opinion, or to relate his impressions, both of which can be easily modified by suggestion: whereas in ethnological inquiry the informant is expected to give such eminently crystallized and solidified items of knowledge as an outline of certain customary activities, or a belief or a statement of traditional opinion. In such cases a leading question is dangerous only when dealing with a lazy, ignorant, or unscrupulous informant—in which case the best thing is to discard him altogether.

⁴³ A characteristic fact to illustrate this statement is furnished by a Scotchman, who has been living for years among the natives as trader and pearl buyer. He has in no way lost the "caste" and dignity of the white man, in fact, he is an extremely kind, hospitable gentleman; nevertheless, he has assumed certain native peculiarities and habits such as the chewing of areca nut, a habit seldom adopted by white men. He is also married to a Kiriwinian. In order to make his garden thrive, he uses the help of a native *towosi* (garden wizard) from the next village, and that is the reason, my informants told me, that his garden is always considerably better than that of any other white man.

⁴⁴ The broad generalities given about Kiriwinian garden magic are, of course, not to be taken even as an outline of

this magic, which, it is hoped, will be described in another paper.

⁴⁵ It should be remembered that each village has its own system of garden magic, intimately connected with that village, and transmitted in the maternal line. The membership in a village community is also transmitted in the female line.

⁴⁶ I cannot deal here in detail with this rule, to which there are many apparent exceptions. This will be done in another place. The statement in the text ought to be amended: "hereditary in the female line in the long run." For instance, very often a father gives the magic to his son, who practices it during his lifetime, but this son cannot pass it on to his son unless he has married a girl of his father's clan, so that his son belongs to the original clan again. Cross-cousin marriage, prompted by this and similar motives, is fairly frequent, and is considered distinctly desirable.

⁴⁷ Thus, for instance, the *kainagola*, one of the most powerful *silami* (evil spells), is associated with a myth localized in the villages of Ba'u and Buoitalu. Again, certain canoe-building magic, called *wa'iugo*, contains references to a myth, the scene of which is the island of Kitava. Many other examples could be adduced.

⁴⁸ The native name for a subclan is *dala*, cf. Seligman, *op. cit.*, p. 678, where the form *dalela* is *dala*, with the pronominal suffix of the third person, "his family." The author gives there the names of *dala* belonging to the four clans. They include the most important *dala*, but there are many others. As Professor Seligman says, the members of each *dala* trace their origin to a common ancestor. Such an ancestor emerged originally out of a hole in the earth in a given locality. And, as a rule, the *dala* lives in, or near, that locality—very often the "hole" is in the grove sur-

rounding the village, or even right in the village. These holes, called "houses" (*buala*), are, at present, either waterholes or stone heaps, or small shallow cavities. The hole mentioned by Professor Seligman on p. 679 is the one out of which emerged several of the most aristocratic *dala*. But this is an exception, the rule being one *buala*, one *dala*.

49 I am almost certain that it is an archaic form, connected with *vitu*, a prefix expressing causation. Thus, "to show the way," "to explain," *vitu loki*, is composed of *vitu*, to "cause," and *loki*, to "go there." There are a number of such causative prefixes in Kiriwinian, each possessing a different shade of meaning. In this place, of course, they cannot be discussed.

50 This is an example of the above-mentioned exceptions to the matrilineal descent of certain magical formulae. Iowana, father of Bagido'u, was the son of a *tabalu* (*i.e.*, of one of the family who "own" Omarakana). His father, Puraiasi, gave him the magic, and as Iowana married Kadu Bulami, his cousin, a *tabalu* woman, he could transmit the magic to his son, Bagido'u, and the office of *towosi* (garden magician) thus returned to the *tabalu* subclan.

51 As a matter of fact, this system is imported from another village, Luebila, situated on the northern coast. Hence its name, *kailuebila*. It contains only one or two references to some places near that village, but it was not known in Omarakana whether those places were sacred or not.

52 *Ovavavala* is an archaic form of the name Ovavavile.

53 *Bom'* is abbreviated from *boma*, which means taboo. *Likuliku* is an expression for earthquake, which is an important item in the magical vocabulary.

54 *Kamkuam*, eat; *kami*, the personal prefix of the second

person plural, used with food; *nunumuaia*, plural of *numuaia*, old woman. The two personal names of the *baloma* old women are remarkable for beginning with *ili*, very likely derived from *ilia*—fish. *Bualita* means sea. It seems thus possible that they are some mythical persons, associated with fishing, concerning whom the tradition has been lost. But such guesses have little charm, and still less value, in the opinion of the present writer.

55 The first name is that of a woman; *iaegulo* means "I"; Iamuana is said to have been the mother of Umnalibu. Here also the name is suggestive of some connection with the spell, which is said over the *libu* plant. The last name but one, Taigala, means, literally, his ear, but here it was said to stand for a *bili baloma* name.

56 It must be stated that several of these formulae have not been translated in a satisfactory manner. It was often impossible to secure the help of the man who recited the spell. Several spells were collected during short visits to outlying villages. In several cases the man was too old or too stupid to help in the, from the native point of view, extremely difficult and puzzling task of translating the archaic and condensed formula, and of commenting upon all its obscurities. And, as a rule, it is no use asking anyone but the original owner to translate or comment upon any formula. I have been able, however, from my knowledge of the "colloquial" language to grasp the general meaning of almost all the formulae.

57 The full discussion of this subject must be deferred to another place. It is interesting that in a certain class of *silami* (evil spells) there is a direct invocation to a being, *tokuay* (a wood spirit living in trees), to come and perform the evil. And everybody agrees that it is the *tokuay* who is the *u'ula* (basis, reason, cause) of the *silami*, that he enters the body and produces disastrous internal disorders.

⁵⁸ All these general statements must be regarded as preliminary, they will be supported by proper documents in the proper place.

⁵⁹ Compare those data with the above-discussed "ignorance of natural death." In this ignorance there ought to be distinguished: (1) the ignorance of the necessity of death, of the life coming to an end; (2) ignorance of the natural causes of sickness as we conceive it. Only the second ignorance seems to be quite prevalent, the action of evil sorcerers being always assumed, except, perhaps, in the above-mentioned cases of very old and insignificant folk.

⁶⁰ *Suma* is the root for pregnancy; *nasusuma,* a pregnant woman; *isume,* she becomes pregnant. There is no term denoting conception, as distinguished from pregnancy. The general meaning of *suma* is "take," "take possession of."

⁶¹ I am using here the expression "spirit child" as a *terminus technicus.* This is the term used by Spencer and Gillen to denote analogous beings in Australia, where this type of reincarnation was first discovered. How far the Kiriwinian facts are ethnographically or psychologically connected with those described by Spencer and Gillen will not be discussed in this place.

⁶² This information was obtained from a woman on the west coast. I think the woman belonged to the village of Kavataria. Mr. G. Auerbach, a pearl buyer, who resides in Sinaketa, a coastal village on the southern half of the island, told me that there are some stones there, to which a woman who wants to become enceinte may have recourse. My informant was unable to tell me whether this was ceremonial or not.

⁶³ There is a remarkable rule which compels the woman to perform all sorts of practices in order to have her skin quite light after childbirth; she keeps in the house, she has

to wear the *saikeulo* over her shoulders, she washes with hot water, and frequently puts coconut cream on her skin. The degree of lightness of skin thus achieved is remarkable. The above described ceremony is a kind of magical inauguration of the period when she will have to keep her skin light.

[64] A genealogy shows the relationship in an instant—

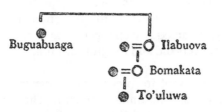

The black discs represent males, the rings, females.

[65] The majority of my informants were equally positive about the rule that a *baloma* of the *veiola* must convey the child. But I have come across one or two dissenting opinions, affirming that the father's mother may bring the child. It was said by one man that if the child resembles the mother it has been brought by some of her *veiola*; if it resembles the father it has been brought by his mother. But this opinion may be my informant's private speculation.

[66] In which, *nota bene,* by the *baloma* who "gave" the child, the natives mean either the original *baloma*, who has become the child, or the *baloma* who brought the *waiwaia*.

[67] The sexual freedom of unmarried girls is complete. They begin intercourse with the other sex very early, at the age of six to eight years. They change their lovers as often as they please, until they feel inclined to marry. Then a girl settles down to a protracted and, more or less, exclusive intrigue with one man, who, after a time, usually becomes her husband. Illegitimate children are by no means rare,

cf. the excellent description of sexual life and marriage among the Southern Massim, who, in this respect, resemble the Kiriwinians to a great extent, in Seligman, *op. cit.*, xxxviii, p. 499, and the short but correct account there given of the same subject among the Northern Massim (including the Trobriand Islanders), chap. liii, p. 708.

[68] A white settlement in the east end of New Guinea.

[69] As I do not want to criticize particular views, so much as to add some data bearing on this problem, I shall not note any statements, especially from those authors whose opinions appear to me to be untenable. The probability of a "non-recognition in early times of the physical relation between father and child" was first suggested by Mr. E. S. Hartland (*The Legend of Perseus*, 1894–96), and the discoveries of Spencer and Gillen brilliantly confirmed his views. Mr. Hartland has subsequently devoted the most exhaustive inquiry extant to this problem (*Primitive Paternity*). Sir J. G. Frazer has also given the support of his illustrious opinion to the view that ignorance of physical fatherhood was universal among early mankind (*Totemism and Exogamy*).

[70] *The Melanesians of British New Guinea*, p. 84.

[71] *Trans. of Roy. Soc. South Australia*, vol. xxxix, 1915, p. 562.

[72] I use Professor Seligman's terminology, based on his classification of the Papuasians, *op. cit.*, pp. 1–8.

[73] *Cf.* Seligman, *op. cit.*, *passim*; also chap. xlix.

[74] My own notes taken among the Mailu, and the conclusion I drew from them, are typical of such a failure. As other instances, may be quoted the denial by Strehlow and von Leonhardi of the discoveries of Spencer and Gillen; a

denial which, if the argument of von Leonhardi be carefully read, and the data given by Strehlow examined, turns out to be only a futile controversy based upon inadequate premises, and, in fact, completely confirms the original discoveries of Spencer and Gillen. Here the explanation lies in the insufficient mental training of the observer (Strehlow). You can no more expect good all-round ethnographical work from an untrained observer than you can expect a good geological statement from a miner, or hydrodynamic theory from a diver. It is not enough to have the facts right in front of one, the faculty to deal with them must be there. But lack of training and mental capacity is not the only cause of failure. In the excellent book about the natives of New Guinea (Goodenough Bay on the N.E. coast), written by the Rev. H. Newton, now Bishop of Carpentaria, than whom none could be better equipped to understand the native mind and to grasp native customs, we read the following statement: "There may be races as ignorant [of the causal relation between connection and pregnancy] as is implied [in Spencer and Gillen's statement]; it is difficult to imagine such, when marital infidelity appears to be so severely punished everywhere, and when the responsibility of the father for the child is recognized, if only to a small extent." (*In Far New Guinea*, p. 194.) Thus, an excellent observer (such as the present Bishop of Carpentaria undoubtedly is), living for years among the natives, knowing their language, has to imagine a state of things which exists fully and completely all round him. And his arguments for denying this state (everywhere, not only among his tribe) is that marital jealousy and recognition of fatherhood both exist (a recognition, which again is not known in the tribe in question, on the physical side)! As if there were the slightest logical nexus between jealousy (a pure instinct) and ideas about conception; or, again, between these latter and the social ties of the family! I have taken this statement for criticism, just because it is found in one of the very best ethnographical books which we have about South Sea natives. But I wish to add that my criticism is in a way unfair, because Mr. Newton, as a missionary, could scarcely discuss with the natives all the details of the question, and also because Mr. Newton gives the reader fully to understand that he has not inquired into the question directly, and candidly states the reasons for his doubts. I have quoted the statement, nevertheless, in order to show the many technical difficulties which are connected with the obtaining of accurate information on this subject, and the many gaps through which errors can leak into our knowledge.

[75] My experience in the field has persuaded me of the complete futility of the theories which attribute to the savage a different type of mind and different logical faculties. The native is not "prelogical" in his beliefs, he is alogical, for belief or dogmatic thinking does not obey the law of logic among savages any more than among ourselves.

[76] To test this sociological principle on civilized instances; when we say that the "Roman Catholics believe in the infallibility of the Pope," we are correct only in so far as we mean that this is the orthodox belief, enjoined on all members of that church. The Roman Catholic Polish peasant knows as much about this dogma as about the Infinitesimal Calculus. And if it were proposed to study the Christian religion, not as a doctrine, but as a sociological reality (a study which, as far as I am aware, has never yet been attempted), all the remarks in this paragraph would apply, *mutatis mutandis,* to any civilized community with the same strength as to the "savages" of Kiriwina.

[77] I am purposely not using the term "collective ideas," introduced by Professor Durkheim and his school, to denote a conception, which in their hands, more especially in the writings of Hubert and Mauss, has proved extremely fertile. In the first place, I am not able to judge whether the above analysis would really cover what that school denotes by "collective ideas." Remarkably enough, there does not seem

to be anywhere a clear, candid statement of what they mean by "collective idea," nothing approaching a definition. It is obvious that in this discussion, and in general, I am under a great obligation to these writers. But I am afraid that I am entirely out of touch with Professor Durkheim's philosophical basis of sociology. It seems to me that this philosophy involves the metaphysical postulate of a "collective soul," which, for me, is untenable. Moreover, whatever discussion might be carried on as to the theoretical value of the conception of a "collective soul," in all practical sociological investigations one would be left hopelessly in the lurch by it. In the field, when studying a native or civilized community, one has to do with the whole aggregate of individual souls, and the methods and theoretical conceptions have to be framed exclusively with this multiplex material in view. The postulate of a collective consciousness is barren and absolutely useless for an ethnographical observer.

ISBN 0-88133-657-2

90000